THE
LOST SCRIPTURES
OF GIZA

Enoch and the Origin
of the World's Oldest Texts

Jason M. Breshears

THE BOOK TREE
San Diego, California

ISBN 978-1-58509-144-7

Cover layout by
Paul Tice

Published by
The Book Tree
P O Box 16476
San Diego, CA 92176
www.thebooktree.com

We provide fascinating and educational products to help awaken the public to new ideas and
information that would not be available otherwise.
Call 1 (800) 700-8733 for our FREE BOOK TREE CATALOG.

Contents

Foreword

This work was originally published in 2006. The Second Edition has become necessary because research on these fascinating topics did not cease with the release of the book. The study of Enoch and the monuments he left to posterity has been continued in this author's other works.

When The Sun Darkens was published in 2009. The work reveals that Enoch was a chronologist and prophet who was aware of the orbital secrets of a fragmented planetary body that visits the inner solar system every 138 years, anciently known as the Phoenix. This amazing orbital history is laid out for all to see and the research reveals the true chronology of Earth's past and *future*, the dating of the Apocalypse, the Sixth Seal disaster in 2040 AD and the return of the Chief Cornerstone. Also shown is a prophetic countdown encoded within the Great Pyramid's exterior architectural features.

The third book released was *Anunnaki Homeworld* in late 2011. In this heavily researched work Enoch's ministry of *prophetic engineering* is laid out for all to see. As architect of Newgrange and Stonehenge we find these monuments decoded into a linear timeline by a simple three-dimensional analysis. The Anunnaki planet NIBIRU, popularized by Zechariah Sitchin, is shown to be returning to the inner system. It will arrive and pass close by the Earth in 2046 AD, pushing our planet into a tighter orbit around the sun, which will end every terrestrial calendrical system – an event described in the Seven Trumpets of Revelation.

Released a year before 2012, *Anunnaki Homeworld* demonstrates that the cherished dating of 2012 AD for the end of the Mayan Long-Count calendar is fundamentally wrong. The error is revealed and through charts and irrefutable evidence, it is shown that the 13th Mayan baktun actually ends with the "collapse of time" in 2046.

Soon to be published is *Descent of the Seven Kings*, a book having more about Enoch and the pre-flood world he lived in than the first three books combined. This tome is packed with chronological data and shows the history of the world through the window of 600-year epochs. In studying the two approaching global cataclysms of 2040 and 2046 AD, the book reveals a tremendous amount of information on the two ancient planetary destructions in 4309 BC and 2239 BC – the end of the Pre-Adamic and Pre-Flood Worlds. Further revealed in this book are the extensive Zodiac Codes, which are prophetic messages concealed within the concepts and star-patterns of the twelve constellations.

The theme of *Descent of the Seven Kings* concerns how the future is the continuation and unfolding of events that have already occurred is distant antiquity. The Seven Kings of the Old World brought the pre-flood apocalypse and ruination of the world, just as they will again in the near future. They are destined to return to Earth in 2052 AD. Just as they ruled the world in the old Sumerian histories they will rule it once more, for the Seven Kings are a major theme of the Book of Revelation.

Though these are the works in print this series is by no means complete. Three more books are being prepared for publication.

Chronicon: Timelines of the Ancient Future is a vast chronology of world history from 5239 BC to 2106 AD in the future. The timeline synchronizes over 40 ancient and more contemporary calendars and timekeeping systems into one comprehensive chronology of date indexes. This monumental research reveals the incredible patterns and geometrical relationships of events past and present.

Nostradamus and the Planets of Apocalypse proves beyond any doubt that the French prophet of Jewish ancestry not only accurately knew the future of the Last Days, *he dated the events*. The prophet Nostradamus knew of the existence of planet Phoenix, its return in 2040 AD, the return of NIBIRU in 2046 AD, the Great War of Islam and the West from 2016-2022 AD and many other events of the Last Days. The science of Calendrical Isometrics is explained with over a hundred examples provided from the annals of history.

The author considers his greatest work to be *Chronotecture: Lost Science of Prophetic Engineering*. This book is filled with precise architectural charts showing how the internal arrangements of the Great Pyramid serve us as an exact rectilinear timeline of world history. Many authors have attempted to show this, but all have failed and in *Chronotecture* we will see how and why this came to be. Without an accurate chronology, previous authors were forced to manipulate architectural measurements that were scientifically made, opening themselves to censure and ridicule.

Having completed all of these works it has become necessary to update *Lost Scriptures of Giza* and supplement it with new additions. That the research is complete is not a claim one can honestly make. When writing about figures, projects, chronologies and concepts thousands of years old, we are forced to play the textual archeologist, ever building pictures out of pieces. And it is the inclusion of these new pieces that made this Second Edition necessary.

Author

Prologue

Mystery of the Pyramid Shape

In the mists of distance millennia was built a colossal monument covered in millions of tiny writings. This structure was the epicenter of global pilgrimage, an architectural legacy of arcane knowledge rooted in a world that no longer exists. This massive corpus of secrets from the archaic past, the present of their world and the distant future was originally protected by keepers but they violated their position as guardians of mankind, oppressing humanity until their sovereignty was fractured by an epic cataclysm that entombed the Old World.

At variance with the Creator these beings waged a terrible war against Him and the rest of Creation. These Guardians were among the first created, their intelligence ancient and matched only by the seething hatred they felt for humanity. This animosity toward mankind was pronounced in the Court of Heaven by the Word as blasphemy, for these newly created beings designed to tend and keep His garden were made in His *image*.

The leaders of this angelic insurrection were imprisoned below the Earth they were appointed to watch over and God led mankind to construct a monument directly over the entrance to their prison – one that would not be opened again until the Apocalypse. A stone guardian was sculpted out of the Earth to keep watch over this holy monument and the △ became the universal symbol embodying the sacred secrets of this magnificent building. It is the icon of the arcanum of mysteries that the Great Pyramid was designed to protect.

Though its origin lies in an obscure past, the Great Pyramid's foundation was laid exactly 666 years before a terrifying catastrophe fragmented the Earth, burying hundreds of millions of people and their cities deep below the surface in a series of meteoric impacts, tremendous earthquakes, volcanic explosions and resurfacing of entire buried landmasses, lakes and seas slipping from their basins, geologic upheavals and the bathing of the planet in billions of tons of cosmic dust that rained as mud over land and sea. The marine mesosphere was emptied and collapsed to the ground, this dense atmospheric layer of water raining for weeks and plunging the world into a barren waste of oceans and ice caps. The ancients relate that the Great Pyramid was specifically designed to survive this disaster, which had been foretold.

Though its presence in the Old World presaged death and ruin, it contains within it the beginning of the greatest gift from the Creator. It was sealed in the beginning because its purpose is in the end.

This monument is a mine of enigmas, an artifact from a dead world concealing an extinct knowledge we can barely penetrate. It was made marvelously to be an enduring shadow of things to come; an arcane theology in stone that typifies eternal truths in *images* for the earthly comprehension of men. The secrets of a thousand scriptures are unveiled within its manifold faces, corners and corridors. A depthless mine of revelations. By intense scrutiny of the mysteries of the Great Pyramid do we approach the arcanum of truth known simply as the Word of God.

Long ago this Arcanum walked among men teaching hidden wisdom and deep knowledge in the form of parables, for parables are *images* of truth masked in earthly symbols. And the greatest symbol of Him on earth is the Great Pyramid. A parable of rock.

Even centuries after the Great Deluge pilgrims travelled from afar to gaze upon the highly polished white surfaces of the Great Pyramid. The learned from scores of cultures visited Egypt to study the ancient antediluvian writings found upon its base casing blocks, copying down abbreviated versions of the histories of heaven and Earth they deemed most important. Few realized at the time that hidden within these fragments of divine truth spread across the world in cosmological texts was concealed a body of teaching that would remain buried within the oldest writings in the world.

Abraham was one of these pilgrims, a man of immense learning acquainted with the holy inscriptions of his ancestor Enoch. Almost four thousand years ago this patriarch visited Egypt in search of the arcanum, to unearth the past that he might glimpse the future. He is venerated by the adherents of Judaism, Christianity and Islam and is the central figure to many amazing legends and traditions.

Abraham at Giza discerned the truths of the Old World, penetrated myth and lore, saw the invisible, uncovered the hidden and divulged to men the long-buried secrets of his most distant pre-flood predecessors. It was he who discovered that the △ concealed the greatest of all mysteries, a secret for humanity so incredibly wonderful that its existence caused a rift in the Creation as forces beyond our senses fiercely contend over our right to enter into this inheritance.

In essence, the *Lost Scriptures of Giza* were never really lost. They exist today and can be found in any well-funded university library, found in the oldest writings in the world.

Archive One

The Pillar of Enoch

Memories of Enoch

A casual search through translations of the world's oldest writings uncovers a universal belief throughout antiquity that in a remote period during the world's infancy a holy man by virtue of his faith was taken physically from Earth by the creator to rule with Him in heaven. In the Genesis account this man is named Enoch [Henoch], the seventh descendant from Adam. References to him in Scripture are vague and scant but there exists a wealth of data about Enoch and his writings in the extracanonical, pseudopigraphical and apocryphal texts.

Traditions and records of this strange man, a chronicler, prophet, architect and king later made emperor are abundant and many are detailed in *Descent of the Seven Kings*. Much of our knowledge about him derived solely from writings passed down from earlier writers, most having passed through the halls of Alexandria, until in the last one hundred and forty years the wastes of Iraq, Syria and Lebanon have yielded forth hundreds of thousands of cuneiform tablets. These ancient writings mention Enoch and many other biblical figures and events and many of them claim to be copies of older Sumerian texts. In fact, much of the wisdom of the Psalms, Proverbs, Lamentations and other wisdom literature of the Old Testament find their precedents in the Sumerian writings. (1)

The Sumerians held that long before a ruinous flood destroyed their cities and killed off the population lived a powerful king named Etana who ascended into the heavens. Historians speculate that he ruled about 3100 BC. (2) Enoch was indeed alive at this time. As a chronologist-prophet it cannot be coincidence that the most ancient as well as sophisticated calendrical systems the world has ever known all began about this time.

The Mayan Long-Count system of 13 baktuns counting 144,000 days each for a total of 1,872,000 days until the "collapse of time" began in 3113 BC [13 year variance]. The Kali Yuga system, or Vedic Chronology of ancient

India began a 3100-year timeline to the appearance of the Savior. Scholars calculate the beginning of the Kali Yuga to be 3102 BC [2 year variance]. Amazingly, this corresponds perfectly to the 2 BC birth of Christ.

The Sumerian King-Lists record that Etana ruled for 1560 years (3), which is 96 years short of the entire duration of the pre-flood world's 1656 years which is obtained by calculating the references provided in the Genesis genealogical lists for the ten patriarchs before the Flood. The Sumerian texts also relate that the world prior to the Deluge was ruled by a lineage of ten men who were later usurped by the Seven Kings 600 years before the cataclysm. The King-Lists refer to them as kings while the Genesis narrative calls them patriarchs. There are old Hebraic writings that convey that Enoch was not merely a prophet, but an emperor who ruled over many kings and princes. This will be shown herein.

The decline of Sumer and later Akkad brought about the emergence of Assyrio-Babylonian cultures located along the Tigris and Euphrates rivers of Iraq. The dominant became the Babylonians who kept records concerning one called Utuabzu. He was the *seventh* sage who had an unusual ministry that involved the divine residents of the Abyss, a spiritual prison realm wherein languished particularly ancient beings that had rebelled against the Creator and were confined under the Earth until an appointed time. For this reason they named him Utuabzu, or Brother of the Deep. His ministry over, he was taken up into heaven and never seen again. (4)

Remarkably, this was the exact ministry appointed to Enoch in the *Book of the Watchers*, more commonly known as the first 36 chapters of the *Book of Enoch*. Enoch was God's earthly voice and messenger. So perfect was his testimony among the inhabitants of the Earth and to those beneath it that the Creator entrusted him with the divine knowledge of the past, the present and the future, with intimate knowledge of the Apocalypse that would one day afflict all men and the treacherous angels.

Many are the fragmented traditions and historical annals that mention this figure, his incredible life and accomplishments. Unfortunately, these are passed off as relics of myth and fable having moral rather than historical foundation. Most of the writings mentioning Enoch are outside the fold of accepted Scripture. In the biblical records there are but three passages that refer to him yet he is more popularly remembered by the nations of old than Adam, Noah or even Moses. Only Abraham and Nimrod can boast of greater remembrance. Interestingly, Adam, Noah, Enoch, Abraham and Nimrod are found by various titles and names many times in the stories of the Old World, but Moses is unknown outside Hebraic writings. This is not to infer that he is a fiction. His history only involved the Egyptians and Israelites and 80 years of his life was spent in the wilderness.

Enoch is found in the memories of cultures from the Far East to the distant shores of ancient America, from the snow-enshrouded north to sub-Saharan Africa. Enoch left a psychic imprint upon the imagination of mankind and with the approach of the Last Days his writings have become popular again, just as they prophesied they would be.

An unknown scribe over two thousand years ago happened upon a very old book known to us today as the *Book of Sirach*. In his preface to the translation that he composed after discovering the text among the aged records of his people, Sirach wrote, "I found a book of no small learning: therefore I thought it most necessary for me to bestow some diligence and travail to interpret it." In describing the text he wrote, ". . .it containeth therefore wise sayings, dark sentences, and parables, and certain particular ancient godly stories of men that pleased God." The *Book of Sirach* is an extensive text found today in most apocryphal collections. The book details the lives of many biblical people like Adam, Noah, Abraham, Isaac and David. But Sirach reads, "But upon the earth was no man created like Enoch: for he was taken from the Earth." (5)

And it is within these cryptic words in the Sirach text that the latent mysteries of apocalypse and resurrection begin to unfold.

The early Hebrews and later Jews passed down many books such as this one that are not included among the books of the Scriptures and hardly known outside academia. It is within the pages of these texts that we learn so much concerning this enigmatic patriarchal prophet.

The *Book of Jubilees* was a popular work of rabbinical literature that outlines the history of the Earth chronologically by depicting events as they related to the patriarchs. In this is written, "He [Enoch] was the first one from among the children of men that are born on the earth to learn writing, and knowledge and wisdom, and he wrote the signs of heaven according to the order of the months in a book [Book of Enoch]. . . he was the first to write a *testimony*, and he testified to the children of men concerning the *future* generations of the world. . . and what was and what will be *he saw in a vision* of the night in a dream as it will happen to the children of men in their generations until the Day of Judgment; he saw and learned everything and wrote it as a testimony and *laid the testimony on the earth* over all the children of men and their generations." (6)

Enoch's ministry was apocalyptic, one concerning judgment. Though it will require substantiation through other sources it can be assumed that this testimony that would be accessible to *future* generations laid upon the earth by the prophet before the Flood was a monument of some kind. By the end of this book you will have no doubt.

Even older than the Sirach and Jubilees writings is an historical tome from extreme antiquity so old that even in the days of the renowned Jewish historian Flavius Josephus two thousand years ago the book was largely unknown and forgotten outside of the Temple in Jerusalem. This book is more extensive than any of the biblical writings and is itself mentioned by name in the biblical books of Joshua and 2 Samuel, both references reading—". . .is this not written in the Book of Jasher?"

Josephus wrote ". . .that by this book are to be understood certain records kept in some place on purpose, giving an account of what happened among the Hebrews from year to year, and called Jasher, or the Upright, on account of the fidelity of the annals." (7) A copy of this book was found in rabbinical Hebrew, discovered in Jerusalem when the Roman General Titus, son of Emperor Vespasian, destroyed the city and looted the Temple before destroying it as well. The *Book of Jasher* is said to be one of the few manuscripts secreted out of the Alexandrian Library in Egypt just prior to its ruin by Islamic armies. In 800 AD the book was rediscovered by the Anglo-Saxon scholar Albinus Alcuin who translated it from the Hebrew into Latin. Another copy survived the centuries of book burnings brought on by the Inquisition and was printed in Venice in 1613. (8) A very damaging forgery of the *Book of Jasher* was published in 1751 in England. (9) It was republished in Bristol in 1829, a poorly written work of 62 pages that makes Jasher to be one of the Judges of the Old Testament. Had this plagiarist known that Jasher literally means *upright* and was a description of the text's historical integrity, he would not have committed so blatant an error as to claim that Jasher was some hitherto unknown man in biblical history.

But the damage was done. To the 19th century critics and scholars the forgery provided the prejudice enough to shun academia away for good. In the face of higher criticism the real *Book of Jasher* was fated to live on in obscurity, suppressed by those would have greatly benefited the world by studying it. Though the Royal Asiatic Society discovered yet another copy of the *Book of Jasher* in Calcutta, this fascinating chronological record of the pre-flood world and ancient history thereafter is only now beginning in the 21st century to gain prominence among serious researchers. (10)

Though the forgeries of *Jasher* were many there were some 19th century historians who recognized the importance of these records, writers who contributed to our understanding of the accomplishments of Enoch and the world he lived in. In 1875 the authors Hodder M. Westropp and C. Staniland Wake both referred to the *Book of Jasher* as a credible source of historical information in their own book *Ancient Symbol Worship*, a work that extensively expounds upon the religions of antiquity. (11) The translation of *Jasher* they cited in their research was by Dr. Donaldson which was in its second edition.

In 1883 Gerald Massey cited the *Jasher* writings in his huge work entitled *The Natural Genesis*. (12) Because of the amazing facts and formerly forgotten information found within these two books, *Ancient Symbol Worship* and *The Natural Genesis*, as well as other works by Massey, these books will be cited over and over again in our journey to understand Enoch and his times.

The Alcuin translation of 800 AD reads, "And the soul of Enoch was wrapped up in the instruction of the Lord, in knowledge and in understanding; and he wisely retired from the sons of men, and secreted himself from them for many days . . . and all the kings of the sons of men, both first and last, together with their princes and judges, came to Enoch when they heard of his fame, and they bowed down to him, and they also required of Enoch to reign over them, to which he consented. And they assembled all, *one hundred and thirty kings and princes*, and they were all under his power and command. And Enoch taught them wisdom and knowledge, and the ways of the Lord; and he made peace amongst them, and peace was throughout the earth during the life of Enoch. And Enoch reigned over the sons of men *two hundred and forty-three years*, and he did righteousness and justice with all his people." (13)

The identify of Enoch as having ruled over 130 kings and rulers who established an empire that endured 243 years, a regent spiritually attuned to the Creator who also left upon the earth an enduring *testimony* designed to last until the last generations could not possibly have been forgotten. As we will see, there remains astonishing confirmation concerning this antediluvian king and the legacy he left behind still standing silently upon the Giza plateau.

The geographical location of this testimony left on earth by Enoch and the fact that his reign endured 243 years links us to another body of ancient literature that provides us with a better understanding of the prophet's ministry concerning future generations. When Adam was 687 years old Enoch was made king. In the *Book of Adam and Eve II*, another text once housed in the famous Alexandrian Library, Adam said to Seth before he died in the year 930 Hebrew Reckoning—"Hereafter a flood shall come and overwhelm all creatures, and leave out only eight souls. But O my son, let those who it will leave out from among your people at that time, take my body with them out of this cave; and when they have taken it with them, let the oldest among them command his children to take my body and lay it in the *middle of the earth*, shortly after they have been saved from the waters of the flood. For the place where my body shall be laid is the *middle of the earth*; God shall come from thence and save all our kindred." (14)

Adam concluded by telling Seth, "Behold, I have revealed unto you the hidden mysteries, which God had revealed to me." (15) Enoch was an initiate through the Spirit to these hidden mysteries and was aware that the *middle of the earth* held a particularly special significance to his own apocalyptic ministry concerning the future epochs of humanity.

In a vision preserved in the *Book of Enoch* we read, ". . .And I went thence to the *middle of the earth*, and I saw a blessed place in which there were trees with branches abiding and blooming of a *dismembered tree*. And I saw a holy mountain, and underneath the mountain to the east there was a stream and it flowed to the south." Enoch looked and to the east there stood another large mountain and to the west was a smaller mountain of *lower elevation*. Enoch asked an angel with him about this blessed land with its three mountains and he was informed it was an accursed valley and the angel Uriel told him that it was at that place that the cursed ". . .be gathered together," in that place of judgment in the Last Days. (16) In Enoch's vision is introduced the symbol of the *pillar* [dismembered tree], an image of vital significance throughout this work. The pillar, represented by three mountains, stood at the center of the earth. This anciently universal concept is the focus of Archive Two.

After disobeying God and eating of the Tree of Knowledge, Adam erected an altar to Him in an act of penance for the forgiveness of his trespass. In this passage in the *Book of Adam and Eve I* the Word of God appeared and said to Adam, ". . .and as thou didst build an altar, so also will I make for thee an *altar upon the earth*." (17) The *Book of Jasher* conveys that Adam died at 930 years of age, in the ". . .two hundred and forty-third year of the reign of Enoch." (18) This was the year that saw Enoch's final year. *Jasher* reads that ". . .Adam died because he ate of the Tree of Knowledge, he and his children after him, as the Lord God has spoken." (19)

ENOCH'S VISION OF THE

BLESSED LAND

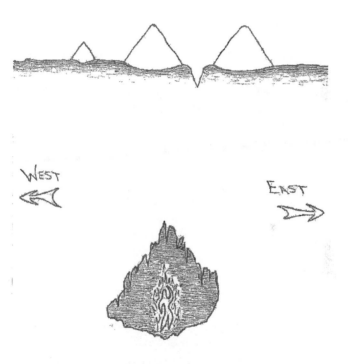

WEST

EAST

Another formerly lost book integral to our study from Alexandria is the *Book of the Secrets of Enoch*, a writing last edited by a Greek in Egypt during the early Church period. Attributed to Enoch, this writing was lost for over 1200 years and has only resurfaced from manuscripts from Russia and Serbia, a fact that has earned it the title of *Slavonic Enoch*. (20) It was rediscovered in 1886 by Prof. Solokov in the archives of the Belgrade Public Library having remarkably survived the Church burnings. The popularity of *Secrets* was largely due to the renewal of interest in Enochian writings after the publication of Richard Lawrence's translation of the *Book of Enoch* in 1821, forty-eight years after the Scottish explorer James Bruce discovered copies of the formerly lost *Book of Enoch* in Ethiopia in 1773. (21)

In this writing Adam was commanded by God to preserve the sacred books and writings of Adam and Seth, that they ". . .perish not in the deluge which I shall bring upon thy race." (22) These books contained many of the secrets of God and the Creation learned by early men and it was Enoch's duty to ensure that these writings and mysteries would not be lost in the cataclysm known as the Flood. These divine instructions were given to Enoch who passed them down to his sons at the death of Adam, the 243rd and final year of the prophet-king's reign. Two old manuscripts, both having survived millennia at separate locations, mention this 243rd year of Enoch.

It was at that exact time according to the *Book of Jasher* that the prophet learned that he was to ascend into heaven and not return. The text reads—"Enoch assembled all the inhabitants of the earth, and taught them wisdom and knowledge and gave them *divine instructions*, and he said unto them, I have been required to ascend unto heaven. I therefore do not know the day of my going." (23) We gather that the "divine instructions' that he gave his people, the Sethites before the Flood, concerned the preservation of knowledge imparted by God to humanity from the days of Adam, king Enos, the priest Jared, Enoch's father and Seth.

The charge given to Enoch by Adam concerned records of great importance. It would make little sense to go through heroic efforts to save mere books which could be easily protected from the elements by those surviving the Deluge. This must have been a truly colossal collection of knowledge. As we will find herein, these divine instructions concerned a massive construction project designed to preserve the writings of the Old World in such a way that humanity would gain access to them once again at a future date long after their own world was gone. Such a method of preservation would require a monument sufficiently large enough to survive the waters of the Flood.

In the sight of all men Enoch ascended into heaven on a cloud and according to the *Secrets of Enoch* the Sethite descendants immediately went to work—". . .Methuselah [son of Enoch] and his brethren, all the sons of Enoch, made, and erected an *altar* at the place called Achuzan, whence and where Enoch had been taken to heaven." (24) This was the altar of God promised to Adam and it was built at the *middle of the Earth* where the Sethites were to bury their forefather Adam, the same location Enoch vanished from.

As found in the *Book of Enoch* sometime in his prophetic career he had a vision of the Great Pyramid and its relation to the Tree of Life. He called it a Mountain of Fire at the *middle of the earth*, a description that we shall learn that was employed by the ancients when referring to the monument.

Enoch describes its stones as brilliant and beautiful, splendid to behold. An angel tells Enoch "That mountain thou beholdest, the extent of who's head resembled the Seat of the Lord, will be the seat on which shall sit the holy and great Lord of Glory [Chief Cornerstone], the Everlasting King, when He shall come and *descend* to visit the earth with goodness." See Enoch 24:1-2, 8; 25:1.

That Enoch fully understood the mystery of the coming of the Son of Man, the Christ, is clearly seen in Enoch 46:1-3, where we find that Enoch at the court of heaven beheld the Ancient of Days [Creator] and another figure named the Son of Man who would come to earth and break the power of the mighty and lay low the kings of the world. It was revealed to Enoch that the Son of Man was ancient, His name invoked in heaven before the sun and stars were created. He [Christ] would be a support [pillar] for the righteous and shall ". . .be the Light of the nations."

The Mountain of Fire at the middle of the earth is imagery of high antiquity, found in the earliest cosmologies and traditions from around the world. In the *Herder Dictionary of Symbols* we find clearly that it is associated with the concept of the altar. The altar is a very old universal image, considered long ago to mark the *center of the world*. In Latin altar is altus, meaning *high*. The connection between the Savior and the form of the pyramid concerns *light*. He is the Light of the World, and pyramid is the Grecianized word describing the older Semitic words Urim-middim, or *Light in the Middle*. The proofs linking the pyramid with the altar and center of the earth motif is the focus of the next Archive.

It is here that we can detect a pattern that runs consistently through the body of Scripture. Enoch received divine instructions that he, in turn, passed down to others that carried them out. This was the construction project known as the Mountain of Fire, or Mountain of God, the altar of Adam at Achuzan where Enoch disappeared. Over thirteen centuries after the completion of the Great Pyramid, Moses, also from Egypt, departed in the Exodus and received divine instructions from God that he passed to others who carried them out, building the Tabernacle and Ark of the Covenant. He also received the Tables of the Law which he passed down to the people, which were spiritually instructive patterns for righteous living. About eighteen centuries after the Great Pyramid was finished, King David received divine instructions from the Lord that he passed down to his son Solomon who set out and had the Temple built in Jerusalem. All of these things were to be shadows of things to come. Even the candlesticks were patterned from these holy instructions. (25) (26) (27).

Men are the means by which the Creator builds great things on earth. It has been the habit of men since time immemorial to erect colossal stone monuments in commemoration of important historical events and the Great Pyramid was no different. It cannot be argued that the geographical location where a mighty king-turned-emperor who was a prophet that vanished into the sky would not have been marked as a sacred spot by those who witnessed the event, a holy site to be remembered and protected.

This altar constructed by the Sethites was the Mountain of God, it was the testimony of Enoch laid upon the earth that contained the ancestral records from God that He passed down to Adam and Seth. By its placement at the center of the world's geographical landmasses it represents the pillar [dismembered tree], called the Axis Mundi [World Axis] where stand the three mountains holy to God that serve to remind both men and angels of the secrets of judgment, redemption and resurrection. Built to be protected from water the structure also served to remind the people that survived that the next flood would be of *fire*.

Concerning these Sethite architects before the Flood, Josephus almost two thousand years ago wrote:

> They also were the inventors of a peculiar
> sort of wisdom which is concerned with
> the heavenly bodies, and their order. And
> that their inventions might not be lost
> before they were sufficiently known, upon
> Adam's prediction that the world was to be
> destroyed at one time by the force of fire, at
> another time by the violence and quantity
> of water, they made two pillars; the one
> of brick, the other of stone; they inscribed
> their discoveries upon them both, that in
> case the pillar of brick should be destroyed
> by the Flood, the pillar of stone would
> remain, and exhibit these discoveries to
> mankind; and also inform them that there
> was another pillar of brick erected by them.
> Now this remains in the land of Siriad
> [Seiris] to this day." (28)

GIZA COMPLEX

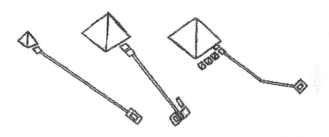

Much of the contents of the Enochian writings are astronomical. This knowledge, though known to have been recorded upon pillars, must have been inscribed upon unusually large monuments. True pillars were not made of bricks and knowledge can be preserved in scrolls or tablet collections so we can see here that the *volume* of information they sought to preserve must have been immense.

The use of pillars to describe stone monuments of importance is an occultic method designed to conceal the true nature of the information conveyed in the text. The pillar is a truly archaic symbol employed by arcane scribes that will be examined thoroughly in this work, an image even found in the Scriptures in the description of an *altar* located in the land of Egypt. This passage is in Isaiah's writings and reads—

> In that day shall there be an *altar* to the
> Lord in the midst of the land of Egypt,
> and a *pillar* at the border thereof to the
> Lord. And it shall be for a *sign* and *witness*
> [testimony] unto the Lord of Hosts in the
> land of Egypt.

This esoteric passage in Scripture beautifully conceals the secret of the Great Pyramid at Giza though the text itself appears to be contradictory. This altar is the pillar erected by the Sethites, though the altar is in the *midst* of the land of Egypt and the pillar is at the *border*, there is only a conflict in meaning to the uninitiated, to those having no knowledge of what the pillar truly signifies. Earthly pillars were long ago erected to mark and identify earthly boundaries, but this pillar marks the *border to the Lord*. As this is the dismembered tree of Enoch's vision, this pillar in the midst of Egypt is an axis point linking heaven to earth and earth to the underworld.

The identity of Egypt as being the location of this monument is further validated by Josephus, for Siriad is an epithet descriptive of the land of Sirius worshippers: Egypt. Josephus quotes the Egyptian priest-historian Manetho who wrote that long ago Thoth [Egyptian version of Enoch, scribes of the gods] inscribed all knowledge upon stelae known as the *Siriadic* Columns. The belief was later filtered into Asia Minor and among the Greeks. Plato wrote about these two columns [pillars] in the opening to his *Timaeus*. He wrote that the entrance to Atlantis' temple was guarded by two pillars, one made to be imperishable to fire and the other indestructible by water, both covered in valuable knowledge. These are the same as that mentioned by Josephus, who wrote that they remained even to his day two thousand years ago. The two gigantic pyramids are these monuments, but there is only one Great Pyramid. Only from a distance do these structures appear equal in size. This will be explained more in depth later in this book. These huge pillars upon the Giza plateau are accompanied by a third, much smaller pyramid. According to Scripture, by the testimony of three *witnesses* is a thing established (30), and as will be shown this has never been truer than with the three silent pyramids in Egypt.

The name for the Great Pyramid complex today is Giza, an ancient title of uncertain origin and an etymological relic from an extinct language that is amazingly partially preserved in the *Secrets of Enoch* text as *Achuzan*. Among the oldest languages in the world the phonetic hard consonants *ch* and *g* were interchangeable. Achuzan resolves to A[Guza]n, prefixed by the 'A' because this merely denotes a geographical location or area. Several centuries ago the site was called Ghizeh and it appears to be derived from the Hebrew *geza*, or "the stock of a tree," [pillar] which is akin to the Semitic gazit, a word remarkably meaning *hewn stone*. (31) It is an amazing revelation to find that this phonetic fossil survived the translation from the elder pre-flood script, probably Sumerian, into Akkadian or Babylonian cuneiform and eventually Hebrew to the Greek and Latin but ultimately into Slavonic in the space of millennia to be compared with what the area is called today with little difficulty: Giza.

The Giza complex with its three massive pyramids, two of them truly colossal, was built from divine instructions imparted to mankind through Enoch before the Great Flood in an effort to preserve the holy writings of the antediluvian patriarchs. Giza contains the altar of God at the middle of the earth that serves symbolically as the pillar that marks the spiritual boundary that all men must one day pass through. This is further evidenced in the almost prehistoric root word for both Achuzan and Giza [guz], which means specifically *to pass along*. (32) As it is written, we are sojourners here, and so also is Giza a place of passage.

Giza protects a silent message of universal importance that is only now being decoded and understood. By his translation from earth to heaven Enoch's life and disappearance embodied the hope of all men, to be *redeemed* and raised up in resurrection. His writings and the myriads of variant beliefs concerning him have left behind mysteries, entire occult systems, creeds and whole religions. This pre-flood prophet gave us the key to the Scriptures in the visage of stone – monuments that protect the greatest secret in the Creation.

Mystery of Zion

The patriarch Jacob was given a new name, Israel, which his descendants adopted as the name for their nation. Though they were ultimately the direct descendants of a Chaldean, Abraham, a sage of immense wisdom who had studied in the house of Noah long after the Deluge, the nation of Israel had its beginning in the land of Egypt.

From the careful preservation of very old traditions antedating even Abraham and stretching back to the pre-flood world, the Israelites maintained a deeply rooted belief in a future paradise world, an enormous and holy city of God represented in the sacred writings of their forefathers as a great mountain wherein the eternal righteous will dwell when the heavens and earth are renewed by divine fire. This majestic mountain city will be the Capitol of Creation containing the Temple of the Living God and within its walls would be found the Tree of Life and rivers of living water. It was simply referred to in Hebrew lore and Scripture as mount *Zion*.

When the Israelite families in their infancy in the 17th century BC suffered through the famine in Canaan they found refuge and food in Egypt. They settled in Goshen near Memphis, a region located around and to the north of the Great Pyramid site. The monument had been erected by their Sethite ancestors and the site was already considered as holy. In the Exodus the Israelites quite naturally could not take mount Zion with them so they transplanted the ideal and for this reason we discover a most unremarkable mountain group as being called Zion in Scripture.

Upon settling Canaan the Israelite noted that a mountain cluster situated at the southern terminus of the Anti-Lebanon Range had three peaks close enough together to serve them as a substitute for the Giza Complex's three great pyramids. This mountain group was named Zion. (33) This region was venerated by the early Canaanites and their Phoenician and Aramaic neighbors. According to the Deuteronomy text, the it was called Sirion by the locals, which was special to the Sidonians. It was also called Mount Shenir by the Amorites and was also known as mount Hermon. (34)

Hermon means a sacred or consecrated mountain. The names given to this particular mountain group in northern Israel with its three peaks covered in white snow revealed that they shared a common belief with the surrounding peoples, a remote memory of a similar place important to their ancestors. As migrating cultures often do, the Canaanites, Phoenicians, Aramaeans, Amorites and the Hebrews affixed place-names from their history and legends to distinguishing landmarks in their newly occupied territories.

The earlier title of Shenir was probably a reflection of an ancestral homeland called Shinar in Genesis where the human family after the Flood quickly grew into a populous mass. Sirion appears to be related to *Siriad*, an old designation for Egypt as seen in Josephus' account concerning the two great pyramids identified as the Pillars in Siriad. As Hermon we see that this place was identified with Hermes, the god of *boundaries* identified with the Greek god Terminus according to the authors of *Ancient Symbol Worship*. (35) Terminus represents the end of a measured area. Hermes is known also as Mercury, the Messenger of the Gods, Scribe of the Gods, this deity having developed from very old stories about Enoch who ascended into heaven. This ascent is recalled in the imagery of Mercury who had *wings* attached to his boots. Also, Hermes was the god of pillars.

Because this mountain group marks the general division between Israel and the northern Canaanite nations it was called Hermon. In *Ancient Symbol Worship* we learn that the earliest forms by which Hermes was represented were a ". . .a large stone, frequently square," or the "triangular shape was preferred, sometimes an upright *pillar*, and sometimes a heap of rude stones." Greeks called these monuments hermae or Hermean Heaps and they were used as landmarks. (36)

When the Israelites occupied Canaan they called the mountains Zion though the actual place of Zion and its knowledge antedates the Exodus and Conquest of Canaan which occurred in 1447 BC in the year 2448 from Man's Banishment. Even at such a distant time in history the writings of Enoch were known and his vision of the Blessed Land with three Divine mountains was remembered throughout the Old World before and after the diluvian catastrophe. Enoch was remembered by many different names and as we shall discover, one of these was Hermes.

Earlier we found that before the Flood Enoch laid a testimony upon the earth that was to survive the ages of mankind and the flood as well, to be rediscovered and comprehended by future generations of people toward the end of the present world concerning the judgment that would soon befall the entire world. This testimony laid by Enoch was the monument erected by his sons and kin, the Sethites, who preserved this knowledge in the form of the pyramids knowing that these structures due to their center of gravity and sealed white limestone casing blocks that weighed twenty tons each would be able to withstand the might and violence of the chaotic floodwaters. This testimony was specifically designed to warn the world to come of the *second* flood that would transpire in the Last Days, a deluge of fire.

In the exact same passage where this testimony of Enoch is mentioned in the *Book of Jubilees* we read that ". . .there are four places *to the Lord* on the earth; the garden of Eden and the hill in the east in it; the hill of Sinai [where Moses received the Law]; and the hill of Zion." Concerning this fourth place holy to God on earth, Zion, the *Jubilees* text continues with a statement that Zion will be—

> . . . .sanctified in the new creation for the
> sanctification of the earth; through it the
> earth will be sanctified from all its sin and
> its uncleanness from generation to eternity.
> (37)

This passage identifies Zion as an *altar* for it is at the altars where the blood of sanctification purifies the uncleanness from the sinner. Thus, Zion is the altar promised to Adam who had repented of his sin. Zion is the altar in the land of Egypt, at the border *to the Lord* described as a *pillar* by the prophet Isaiah. By claiming that it is one of the four holy places on earth that will be sanctified exhibits to us that it is an actual site in the world today and *is not complete* and will not be until the new creation. The real mystery of Zion is that no one has yet discovered that it is simply the name of the Great Pyramid.

The word is a compound of both a Hebrew and an Egyptian root word. In Hebrew *zi* denotes a barren place, like a desert. *On* was the ancient name for the Egyptian city of Memphis, later called Heliopolis located only a few miles from the Great Pyramid and in the heartland of Goshen. This combination of Hebrew and Egyptian, zi and on, means *Holy Place in the Desert*, according to Moustafa Gadalla in *Historical Deception*: The Untold Story of Ancient Egypt.

The geographical location of Zion is also described in the *Book of Jubilees*, which further identifies it with the Giza monuments. According to this account shortly after the Flood while Noah was still alive and very old, this aged patriarch assembled his sons, grandsons and families. They numbered seventy patriarchs of all the clans on earth and they divided the world by drawing lots which signified where these men would take their families to build their cities and nations.

> And there came out of the writing as
> the lot for Shem the *middle of the earth*,
> which he and his children should have as
> an inheritance for their generations unto
> eternity . . .and he [Noah] remembered his
> word which he had spoken with his mouth
> in prophecy for he had said, Blessed be the
> Lord God of Shem, and may the Lord dwell
> in the dwelling of Shem! And he knew
> that the garden of Eden, the holy of holies,
> the dwelling of the Lord, and mount Sinai,
> the center of the desert, and Mount Zion,
> the *center of the navel of the earth*, these
> three, opposite one another, were created as
> sanctuaries. (38)

This passage is very important to our understanding of Giza. The Israelites as an infant nation were born in Egypt, living in an area of the Delta region called Goshen where the Hyksos authorities permitted concentrations of Semitic peoples to occupy as they ruled over Lower Egypt from Avaris. At the southern border of Goshen lied the Giza complex which has been shown by many authors to be the center of the earth's landmasses. As Eden was a sanctuary to early man protecting him from the harsher conditions of the wild earth, Goshen was a sanctuary to the Israelites and other peoples who had taken up residence in Egypt during the Great Famine in the 17th century BC. Goshen further protected the Hebrews from the terrible plagues and ecological destruction that led to the Exodus, the same year they surrounded the sanctuary of Sinai and received the Law inscribed initially by the finger of God. The land of Canaan Later became their sanctuary, a land believed by many to be the site of the pre-flood Garden of Eden, a region that even in 1447 BC according to the report of the Israelite spies was full of gigantic grapes and produce. The land of milk and honey.

These three points, opposite one another, form a geometrical triangle. The Israelites, who represent all true believers, have not yet completed the triangle, for they have yet to *return to Giza*, to return to the Altar of the Living God to receive sanctification and eternal cleansing. The identity of Zion has always been a mystery. In Scripture it is mentioned so many times that it becomes redundant and easy to overlook, rendered commonplace and therefore unimportant. But for those who seek there is to be found an undercurrent of ancient theology embedded in the passages concerning Zion that are profoundly linked to the history and ministry of the prophet-king Enoch.

Coptic Traditions of the Pyramids

The Alexandrian Library was founded by the Egyptian ruler Ptolemy, a Macedonian formerly a general under Alexander the Great some time between 319 and 313 BC. This library became the largest repository of ancient texts in the entire world, containing half a million writings on clay tablets, stelae, wood tablets, papyrus rolls, parchments from the Near East, Phoenicia, Syria, Asia Minor, Greekdom, Judea and from Egypt and Libya.

Many of these texts were all that remained of the archaic cultures that left them behind, some being in languages not even the Alexandrian scribes could decipher. This vast archive of historic writings was assailed by the Romans, later by fanatical bishops leading Christians, purging's of the Papacy with the greatest loss of texts in 642 AD by Muslim conquest. As we have seen, the *Book of Jasher* among others were secreted away before the Library was totally lost.

In religious fervor the Arabians destroyed the majority of the writings that had not been filtered out throughout Asia Minor, Babylon, Persia and Europe but there were scholars among the Muslims that also stashed away particular books that interested them in much the same way as the Dominicans and Jesuits of the Inquisition publicly burned thousands of books banned by the Papacy only after they had themselves secured their own copies. Unfortunately, many people were burned with the forbidden books they had been caught with. The Vatican Library is a collection of writings that were obtained in this way.

What had intrigued the Arab scholars more than anything else in the halls of Alexandria were the records concerning the Great Pyramid. The history of Egypt and the construction of the Giza complex were unknown to them and they had always assumed that it was the Egyptians who had built them, an assumption passed off as fact today by established academia. But this is not what is conveyed in the earliest records.

We are especially grateful to these early Arab historians for their careful preservation of the Coptic records, great men of learning such as Usted Ibrahim Ben Wasyff Shah, Soyuti and Mohammed Ben Ayas who had written a book called *The Wonders of Different Countries* still extant today in the British Museum as Manuscript No. 7503. Also found in the British Museum is Manuscript No.7861, called *History of Egypt.* Two other significant chroniclers were Akbar Ezzman and Yakut, the latter having his record preserved today in the Bodleian Library. (39) These writings and others were all compiled by Arab scholars of late antiquity like the famous Masoudi who died in 967 AD leaving behind an incredible text that concerns none other than Enoch himself:

> Surid . . . one of the kings of Egypt before
> the Flood, built the two Great Pyramids . . .
> that the reason for building the pyramids
> was the following dream, which happened
> to Surid three hundred years previous to the
> Flood. It appeared to him that the earth was
> overthrown, and that the inhabitants were
> laid prostrate upon it; that the fixed stars
> wandered confusedly from their courses,
> and clashed together with a tremendous
> noise . . . in another vision he saw the fixed
> stars descend upon the earth in the form of
> white birds, and seizing the people, enclose
> them in a *cleft between two mountains,*
> which shut upon them. Early in the
> morning he assembled the priests from all
> the nomes of Egypt, a *hundred and thirty*
> *in number*; no other persons were admitted
> to this assembly, when he related his first

and second vision. The interpretation was
declared to announce 'that some great event
was to take place.' (40)

At this assembly was discussed several of the dreams that the priests were
having as well, in particular, one of a "deformed people," that was invading
from the east to ruin them. This revelation is consistent with the several
accounts about the mutant and hybrid gigantic peoples of the nations called the
Nephilim, later in Scripture referred to as the Anakim, the Rephaim, Emims
and Zuzims. These were the offspring of the Anunnaki, or Watchers called
the Nephilim in Genesis 6, ancient giants that terrorized mankind prominently
found over and again in the *Book of Enoch*.

These giants were a contributing factor leading God to destroy the entire
planet's surface with water. After the departure of Enoch the power vacuum
was filled by the Nephilim peoples and the world sank into a mire of anarchy,
debauchery and violence. Their fathers, the Anunnaki, or *Those Who From
Heaven To Earth Fell*, are the subject of this author's books *Anunnaki
Homeworld* and *Descent of the Seven Kings*. They indulged in forbidden
hybridization programs using human females to sire their sons, programs
involving even animals and plants. The histories of the giants are the central
theme to the oldest writings in the world, including the Epic of Gilgamesh,
they are the foundation of Greek lore, the war of the Titans and Giants, in
Beowulf, and they are found in traditions around the world. The history of
the Sethites before the Flood, the Israelites after the Flood are filled with
giants as found in the *Book of the Watchers*, other Enochian writings, *Jubilees*
and *Jasher*, the Testaments of the Patriarchs and many other extracanonical
texts. Though the Nephilim are not the focus of this work we find here that
the Coptic records are very consistent with what we already know concerning
the civilization after Enoch's departure, the pre-flood world.

Masoudi's account is astonishingly similar to the story of Enoch in the
Book of Jasher. Surid, being a Coptic Enoch, received his prophetic insights
from a dream and was served by 130 priests just as Enoch ruled over 130
kings and princes. Further, Surid dreamed of two great mountains that were
involved with a judgment from heaven just as Enoch in a vision beheld two
great mountains near a third one of lower elevation at a site the prophet was
told was a *place of judgment*. Both Surid and Enoch beheld a cleft, or valley
between these mountains where the damned were cast. This vision was of
Giza before its construction by the Sethites after Enoch's disappearance.

Surid, having witnessed the same vision . . .

> . . .ordered the Pyramids to be built, and
> the predictions of the priests to be inscribed
> upon columns [pillars] and upon the *large*
> *stones belonging to them* [the pillars]; and
> he placed within them his treasures, and
> all his valuable property, together with the
> bodies of his ancestors. He also ordered
> the priests to deposit within them, written
> accounts of their wisdom and achievements
> in the different arts and sciences . . .the
> writings of their forefathers; likewise, the
> positions of the stars, and their circles;
> together with the history and chronicles of
> times past, and that which is to come, and
> to every future event. . . (41)

And with this excerpt from Masoudi's text is our proof that Enoch was remembered as Surid by the Copts. Enoch received divine instructions that commanded him to preserve the writings of his ancestors Adam and Seth, both patriarchs having received revelations directly from the Creator. The pillar motif is again employed in this text and even described as having been made up of large stones, this being descriptive as we will see in Archive Three as being the gigantic white limestone casing blocks anciently covered in writings along the monument's base. The burying of their ancestors is a reference to the burying of Adam where he was to be deposited at the *middle of the earth*, as well as Seth. This identifies the Great Pyramid as being the altar of God promised to Adam built in Egypt.

These moments were specifically constructed to withstand the force of the Flood, to carry their ancient secrets and knowledge into the newer world after the predicted cataclysm. Mere pillars as we understand them today could not have been sufficient for such a task for the world of that time was full of ordinary pillars and none of these have survived. Only monuments the size and weight of the pyramids would have survived.

There are some other intriguing statements found in the Coptic records that provide additional details not found in the Hebrew writings. The Egyptian Copts wrote that underneath the pyramids at a depth of forty cubits (approximately 66 ft.) were subterranean halls containing ". . .all manner of wisdom, the names and properties of medicinal plants, the sciences of arithmetic and geometry; that they remain as records, for the benefit of those who could afterwards comprehend them." (42) Also, these Coptic traditions mention that the pyramids were assigned a *guardian*. (43) If indeed the pillars of the Sethites are the Great Pyramids of Giza then somewhere close by we should find some architectural evidence of their protection in the form of a statue or monument that would serve them as a guardian. As we know, this has been found. The Sphinx, as the largest surviving statue from the Ancient World, is also on the Giza plateau with the pyramids, facing east. Much more will be revealed about his mysterious guardian later in this book.

It is the opinion of many scholars that Surid was not an Arabic invention. Historians and scholars have long noted the remarkable ability of Arabic historians and chroniclers, translators who took it upon themselves to perfectly preserve hundreds, if not thousands of texts originally found or housed in Alexandria, Egypt into their Arabic. It has been shown that the Arabian scholars passed down the traditions of the Great Pyramid complex with little or no deviation from the parent sources for over a *thousand years*. (44) Even today it is difficult to maintain historical annals and keep them unchanged from decade to decade. As older books are reprinted inconsistencies are introduced as modern misconception taints the texts.

Over a hundred and twenty years ago Gerald Massey in his *The Natural Genesis* wrote that Surid was a title possibly derived from *serit*, an Egyptian designation for *keeper, measurer, builder*. (45) Massey also cited Josephus concerning the pillars of the Sethites built in Siriad in his colossal work entitled *Ancient Egypt Light of the World*. He wrote that Siriad may have derived from *seri*, an Egyptian word meaning *south*. (46) With either Babylon or Jerusalem the seat by which scribes and archaic chroniclers composed their histories, the South was the old designation for Egypt. The North was Assyria, the East the designation for Persia and Elam before that. The West was the sea or those Western Semitic peoples along the Mediterranean coast and the isles.

Whatever Surid actually means it is apparent that the Copts recorded traditions passed down from predecessors in Egypt concerning a famous builder in their history. This we know from Hebrew-Judaic texts as Enoch, a prophet, historian, chronicler, architect, astronomer and keeper of the secrets of God. It may be inferred that by calling the builder of the Great Pyramid complex as Surid the Copts did not actually know his name, that Surid is merely the personification of the geographical designation *Siriad*.

Though it is Masoudi's record that follows the Hebraic records the closest concerning Enoch and the monuments, other Arab historians had much to say about the Gizean relics. An early Arab writer named Jafer Ben Mohammed Balkhi, an astrologer [same as astronomer in those days] wrote that the pyramids were built for refuge against an approaching destruction of the world which was foreseen by wise men previous to the Flood. (47) Abou Mohammed Al Hassan Ben Ahmed wrote, "The pyramids were antediluvian, and they resisted the force of the Great Flood." (48) Ben Ahmed relied upon the records of Makrizi, an Arab chronicler largely believed to have been Masoudi himself.

Probably the most persuasive argument for the pre-flood origin of the Giza pyramids was simply stated by Mohammed Ebn abd Al Hokm when he wrote that the pyramids were built before the Deluge, ". . .for that, if they had been after that event had taken place, some positive and certain accounts of them would have remained." (49) And with this in mind we shall peruse the many other fragments, both Egyptian and Greek, of the origin of the Great Pyramid and the history of the person of Enoch.

Graeco-Egyptian Fragments

Because the foundation of the Alexandrian Library was from the Macedonian rulers of Egypt beginning with Ptolemy, a considerable amount of Greek traditions and records ended up in the halls of the famous Library. The scholars that spent their days translating these texts and accounts immediately perceived in them the parallels between the Greek memories and those of ancient Egypt. An old Egyptian deity having fallen into disrepute but anciently venerated was Set. This was an early Egyptian memory of Seth, who with his kin erected the pyramids at the disappearance of Enoch. Later Egyptians having contact with the Greeks saw in the god Hermes all the attributes formerly attributed to Set. This discovery led to the borrowing of chronicles, and soon, within the space of a few centuries an entire genre of Graeco-Egyptian literature was born that was early on used as a source for much of the Coptic and Gnostic writings and beliefs.

As time passed and newer texts were assimilated into this growing genre, other historic and mythological characters were found to have the same characteristics and histories of Set and Hermes. Such comparative studies gave birth to a species of study and wealth of literature now called Hermetical and one of its most famous contributions was *The Divine Pymander*. This book was believed to have been written by Hermes who allegedly lived prior to Moses, and is laden with astronomical and astrological information, esoteric lore and wisdom. (50) The figure of Hermes came to be regarded as deity but many writers long ago admitted that he was an ancestral figure. Cicero is his *De Natura Deorum* Lib. III wrote, "Although a man, he was of great antiquity, and he built Hermopolis." (51) Hermopolis is Greek for City of Hermes and thus identifies him as a builder. *The Divine Pymander* reads:

> Hermes, he understanding all things, who
> also saw the whole of things together, and
> having seen, considered them, and having
> considered them was powerful to explain
> and show them. For what he understood
> he committed to characters, concealing
> the most part, being silent with wisdom,
> and speaking opportunity, in order that
> in all the duration of the world thereafter
> should search out these things; and thus
> having ordered the gods, his brethren, to
> become his escort, he *ascended towards the*
> *constellations.* (52)

And thus we have the Hermetic Enoch. But this is not a new revelation discovered of late by this or any other modern author but was known even as early as Syncellus, who wrote that Hermes erected stone stelae before the flood that contained the arcane knowledge of astronomy. (53) Also, in the *Syrian Chronicle* of Bar Hebraeus we find that Hermes invented letters, types of architecture, built cities, established laws and taught astronomy and the true worship of God. (54) In fact, Bar Hebraeus (which means Son of the Hebrew) even refers to Hermes as being the Enoch of Scriptures.

Around 1050 AD a monk named Cedrenus studied apocryphal writings that were attributed to Hermes, who he associated to Enoch, who, foreseeing the destruction of the world, had inscribed the science of astronomy upon two pillars; one of stone to resist the element of water, and the other of brick to withstand fire. (55) This is noteworthy, for Cedrenus lived contemporary with some of the Arab historians who were in possession of the Coptic traditions concerning Surid and the traditions of the Great Pyramid. Even then Cedrenus linked these pillars to the person of Enoch, the pillars having been mentioned by Josephus in the same way. The Arab historian Makrizi also linked Hermes to Enoch. (56)

In every way Hermes was to the Greeks what Enoch was to the early Hebrews. He was the first master of the arts and sciences, called Ruler of the Three Worlds [heaven, earth & underworld], the Scribe of the Gods and the Keeper of the Books of life. (57) Works attributed to Hermes were therefore priceless to antiquarians.

One such man was Cosimo de Medici of Florence, Spain who sent out agents all over Europe to search the libraries of old monasteries for forgotten writings of the ancients. In 1460 one of those agents by the name of Leonardo of Pistoia discovered a Greek manuscript, a codex containing fourteen treatises attributed to Hermes Trimegistus, or The Thrice-Great. This was the nucleus of the *Corpus Hermeticum*. (58) In book three of *Corpus Hermeticum* we read that shortly after the creation when men began to multiply upon the earth:

> . . .the gods sent forth many souls clothed
> in flesh, so that men could survey heaven,
> the paths of the heavenly gods [planets],
> the works of God and the activity of nature;
> so that they should know the signs of what
> is good, the power of God, and the turning
> fate of good and evil things and discover all
> the *marvelous works of good men*. So men
> began to live and understand the destiny
> assigned to them by the course of the
> circling gods . . .leaving *great memorials*
> *of their work on earth*; their name remains
> until the darkening of ages. (59)

This obscure Hermetic fragment seems to preserve elements of the Edenic story of clothing mankind with mortal bodies, antediluvian astronomy, the interactions of heaven and earth and the memory of great architectural memorials erected by the first men. Note this curious phrase— ". . .their *name* remains until the darkening of ages." Because the actual name of the people that we call Sethites, after their patriarch Seth, son of Adam, is long lost, we see in this statement a more hidden meaning. The passage tells of ancient memorials of their work and interestingly, the Semitic word for *name* is shem, which can also be translated as *monument*. Thus, ". . .their *monument* remains until the darkening of ages." The association in antiquity between the concept of one's name and the preservation of one's memory by the erection of a pillar or memorial, both called *shem* in Hebrew, offers us a penetrating glimpse into a body of ancient mysteries that will be explored in this book.

Just as the Greek peoples were a composite culture of many, the Ionic, Doric, Danoi, Achaeans, Spartans, Thracians and Macedonians with many subcultures throughout the Aegean and Mediterranean, so too was Egypt divided by many peoples who supported its many cults and priesthoods. Even

Egypt was divided between the factions of Upper and Lower Egypt. In Upper Egypt to the far south were the temples and cult centers of Luxor and Karnak in Thebes, and Dendera and Abydos which were all in a sort of theocratic competition with another and with the northern priests of Memphis in Lower Egypt. These rivaling factions of the Two Lands knew of Hermes by his older Egyptian titles of Set, of Thoth and of Imhotep.

The Greeks highly venerated the strange god Thoth for in him they saw their Hermes. The early form of Thoth was as Taut, a title associated with Set. On the *Inscription of Tahtmes* upon the Stele of the Sphinx we learn that the epoch of the First Time, or Zep Tepi, stretches back to the primordial era of Sut who was regarded as the inventor of astronomy. (60) This is a condensed form of Seth, or Sethites, whom Josephus wrote were the inventors of astronomy. Amazingly, the ancient Egyptians held that Taut erected two pillars and according to the Egyptian historian Manetho who studied at Alexandria, these two pillars were to be found in the land of *Seiriad*. (61) These things were not unknown to the earliest Egyptians for it was they who wrote the *Inscription of Tahtmes* at the feet of the Sphinx toward the end of the second millennium BC when the Sphinx statue was excavated from out of the desert sands. Their own writings identify Giza as being that of Siriad and no matter how unrelenting the modern Egyptologist continues to be, the Egyptians themselves never claimed to have built these amazing structures at Giza and we have no authority upon which to rely but the records they specifically left behind for future generations to find.

There are many fragments that could be extracted from the vast amount of Egyptian records that are relative to this study—too many to expound upon. But of particular interest is the person of Imhotep. This man was a prophet, healer, sage, mathematician, architect and artisan, an astronomer and virtual master at anything he set out to accomplish. He lived before the pyramids were built but during his life he received the plans on how to construct them in a dream he was given from heaven (62), in the same way that Enoch received the divine instructions on what the Blessed Land looked like with its two tall mountains and third mountain of lesser elevation [Giza]. The two pillars cited in these traditions are no doubt references to these two gigantic pyramids. This belief in the import of the Two Pillars is of extreme antiquity and was the inspiration for the erection of two lofty pillars at the city of Heiropolis. In *De Dea Syria* Lucian claims that these pillars at Heiropolis were connected with the Greek myths of Deucalion and the Flood. (63) Deucalion was the Greek Noah, builder of the ark and survivor of the Flood. The stories of him were connected to these two pillars demonstrates the merging of traditions with the passage of time, for the Two Pillars at Giza were designed to survive the Flood, a feat which they accomplished just as the faithful Noah survived as well.

The rivaling Egyptian cults and priesthoods gave birth to secret societies and underground occult movements that later resurfaced in the halls of the Library of Alexandria and from there spread throughout the Mediterranean coasts, the Aegean isles, into Spain, Italy, Sardinia, Crete, Libya, Arabia, Judea, Greekdom, Asia Minor, the Near East and Persia, as far as India, to the west at Carthage and ultimately into the hands of Christians spread throughout Europe and Muslim scholars accompanying the armies that spread Islam far and wide. With the Roman Empire fallen and fragmented the Vatican became the central authority over religious thought that emerged into one of the most powerful political forces to have ever ruled Europe.

The Vatican became a knowledge filter and the Inquisition served as its tendrils of censorship as Dominicans and Jesuits set out over all lands under Roman Catholic authority and confiscated all those texts that brought enlightenment outside the fold of traditionally accepted Scriptures, the Holy Writ itself denied the people. Scripture was for the clergy, in Latin and not to be spread among the people's language. Only at Mass were the people to be exposed to the Word of God, and in a language few of them knew. During these centuries of intellectual oppression of the Dark and Middle Ages the subversive and clandestine secretive societies thrived and their memberships swelled with people hungering for more than what the official Church offered. These grew under Church tyranny into full-scale underground movements that gave rise to such popular orders known today as the Freemasons and Rosicrucians, two organizations that held Enoch in esteem and protected manuscripts about him and his achievements. Even the system of degrees of Masonic hierarchy recognizes this in the Royal Arch of Enoch degree, identifying him as an architect. The icon by which the world knows the Masons today is the Great Pyramid.

As the Protestant movement spread across Europe and wrested away the Roman Church's power over the Holy Writ, the need for these secret societies abated. What was once done in hiding among the faithful in fear of Church persecution was now done openly and the Word became widely published for the Protestant movement unfolded in tandem with the invention, mass production and wide-scale use of the printing press. No longer having to transcribe literary works by hand, the Word of God spread through books across the face of the earth.

Like the Egyptian priestly factions, Protestants too split among themselves into various orders and denominations as interpretation of the Holy Writ varied among its adherents. The publication of the Word and emergence of many churches outside the Roman fold greatly diminished the need for these underground movements. But as churches became more puritanical, even fanatical, the old texts that had fueled the faith of those originally oppressed by the religious authorities were now found to be obsolete. Admittedly not a part of Scripture the common people regarded these texts little to none at all and it was now the clergy, even Roman officials, that preserved them as they became rare and discarded.

We can thank the Freemasons for the preservation of many of these writings. And what they have saved among their own archives is nothing less than astonishing.

Masonic Records of Enoch

Masonic historians have preserved traditions concerning Enoch, recording that the prophet before the Deluge had a dream that inspired the building of a nine fold temple. This monument was built with the aid of his father Jared and son Methuselah, both Sethites, but no one in those days understood the strange purpose to this temple except Enoch. (64) This is consistent with what we have thus far seen, and the *Jasher* records insist that Jared was alive for centuries after his son Enoch vanished.

Masonry is divided into two distinct bodies of teaching, or rituals. The Ancient Rites and the Modern Rites. The 13th degree is among the Ancient Rites and according to the *Book of the Ancient and Accepted Rite of Scottish Freemasonry* the 13th degree is interestingly called the Royal Arch of Enoch, or, Master of the Ninth Arch. Under this degree the initiate is taught that Enoch built monuments before the Flood, one structure erected to hide a cube of agate with a golden triangle that in itself contained the secret name of God. After building this temple, Enoch then built around and over it another structure of great stones. He is also taught to have erected two pillars before the Great Flood, one of granite and the other of brass. The granite pillar has inscribed upon it the description of the subterranean vaults laid by Enoch but it was washed away in the Flood. The brass pillar contained ". . .rudiments of the arts and sciences," and was later found after the Flood by Noah. (65)

One of the earliest Masonic manuscripts concerning these two pillars is called the *Inigo Jones Document* from 1607 AD. This text was considered one of the Ancient Charges of Freemasonry that was destroyed in 1720. The only surviving copy was found in the *Masonic Book of Constitutions*. This book details that before the Flood the sciences of geometry, masonry, music, metallurgy and weaving were preserved because of the coming of a great catastrophe:

> These children knew well that God would
> take vengeance for their sin either by fire
> or by water; wherefore they wrote their
> sciences that they found on two pillars, that
> they might be found after Noah's Flood.
> One of the pillars was marble, for that
> will not burn with any fire, and the other
> was laternas, for that will not drown with
> any water. Our account next is to tell you
> truly, how and in what manner these stones
> were found whereon these sciences were
> written. . . (66)

This document reveals that these antediluvian pillars erected by Enoch were found and excavated after the disaster during the reign of a king called Ninus, who, as we learn from the erudite Alexander Hislop in his penetrating work entitled *The Two Babylons*, was merely an Assyrian title for the person remembered as the Babylonian king Nimrod. So we have it related that it was during the infamous Nimrod's rule that the Great Pyramid was rediscovered. This discovery of the location of Giza was made in the year 2076 Annus Mundi.

As this is not a work on chronology this author has endeavored to restrain himself from dating every single historical event mentioned in this book in the interest of brevity. For those seeking a chronology of events involving the pre-flood and postflood histories, see *When the Sun Darkens*, *Anunnaki Homeworld* and *Descent of the Seven Kings*. All three of these books are works on chronology.

But for our purposes here in exploring the Masonic history, the Annus Mundi chronology was developed in Alexandria in response to the plethora of writings and chronologies studied there that all seemed to refer to a beginning date which was represented as Year One of the Hebrew Chronology. Annus Mundi literally means Year of the World, but this was only conceptual. The ancients believed the calendar began with Creation, thus the description *Annus Mundi*, whereas the Hebrew narratives began with the *curse*. The calendar began with the banishment of mankind from Eden. As found in this author's other works, the date of the Flood is *astronomically* fixed at 2239 BC and independently verified by other dating systems and chronological studies having no relation to the author's other than the fact that the arrived-at date for the Flood was 2239 BC.

In the Hebrew narrative the Great Flood occurred in the year 1656. Again, many chronological works and scholarly studies independently relate this fact. So, if 2239 BC of our calendar was the year 1656 Annus Mundi [Hebrew Reckoning], then 2076 AM was 420 years after the Flood, or 1819 BC. As can be found in the books mentioned above, both Nimrod and Abraham were alive in 1819 BC. At that exact date Nimrod ruled under the throne name Amraphel, the dynastic name Hammurabi and the Sumerian title AMAR.UDA.AK which was conveyed in Babylonia as *Marduk* [Merodak]. And during this time Abraham according to the Genesis record was in *Egypt*. Such an account of the post flood discovery of writings that antedated the Deluge is consistent with another historical account as found in the pages of the *Book of Jubilees*.

> And Kainan grew, and his father taught him
> writing, and he went to seek for himself
> a place where he might seize for himself
> a city. And he found a writing which the
> forefathers had carved into a rock, and he
> read what was in it, and he found that there
> was within it the science of the Watchers
> by which they had seen the astrology of the
> sun and moon and the stars and all the signs
> of heaven, and he wrote this down and
> did not say anything concerning it, for he
> feared to speak to Noah concerning it, lest
> he be angry with him on this account. (67)

Prior to the Babel catastrophe the Sumerian culture thrived, having been descendants of the original survivors of the Flood. Before the language rifts occurred Sumerian was the universal language and the oldest near Eastern texts found to date are in Sumerian ideograms. The learning Kainan received was in Sumerian and any old writings that survived the floodwaters were also Sumerian. Such a conclusion was made by the Masonic historians as well. The *Wood Manuscript* dates from 1610 and is believed to be more reliable that the *Inigo Jones Manuscript*.

This text begins by relating to all the sciences akin to masonry and declares that geometry is the greatest of all sciences. It also mentions two pillars after Noah's Flood that still existed. One of these pillars was found to still have writings on it of all the secrets and sciences of the Old World that was destroyed, in Sumerian, from which the Sumerians developed a moral code that they passed on to the Egyptians through a Sumerian man named Abraham who travelled to Egypt. (68).

The legend of Enoch's Pillar is derived from these traditions, a myth that asserts that there is a pillar of knowledge built by the prophet that contains all the secrets of the world. While this is partially true, referring to the Great Pyramid, some groups in the past have taken the pillar angle too literally that they claimed to have found it in the object of some old dug up relic. Such was the case with the Knights Templar, who claimed that long ago they had discovered a small artifact in the form of a pillar broken into three parts which they claimed was Enoch's pillar. (69)

There are fragmented memories of Enoch and the pyramids from all over the world. Many of the secret societies obtained writings that drew upon these sources. Philo Alexandrinus took such information from the older Phoenician annals which were rich in Semitic histories that state that the first two inventors of the human race were brothers named Upsouranios and Ousous, who consecrated two pillars long ago, one to fire and the other to wind. (70) Diodorus, relying on older books claimed that the Great Pyramid was constructed by one called Chemmis. He claimed that the monument had been there for thirty-four centuries. (71) Even the Arab historians had borrowed much of their information from the old Sabaeans, a people of high antiquity and civilization spanning back to the days of Job in the mid-second millennium BC. These people left records claiming that the Great Pyramid was a tomb housing the bodies of the patriarchs Seth and Idris [Enoch of the Quran]. (72)

Enoch is a constant character and his life the theme of many arcane writings and annals. His name has been found upon stone tablet texts in cuneiform from the Near East, discovered upon the archaic King-lists of Sumer and heard from the tongues of even primitive peoples who still pass on his histories though they long lost the meaning of what they relate. But there is much more to this story. The Gizean relics were not made merely as repositories of ancient information to be gleaned by post apocalyptic survivors of a Flood, but this monumental area serves another purpose.

One you will never forget.

Archive Two

Symbols of the Godhead Upon the Earth

Arcane Images of the Divine Pillar

The Great Pyramid's identity as the *Altar of God* in the land of Egypt built for the redemption of a lost humanity by architects before the Flood is evident from so many corroborating accounts. But the numerous references to the pyramid complex being a *pillar* from so diverse sources requires an intense scrutiny into the mindset of belief systems no longer extant today. In order to understand the pyramid's origin, function and future purpose we must first comprehend how certain images became attached to it.

The ancients widely held that an immense pillar was fixed at the middle of the earth. It served at an earthly marker to the border of the Lord and was God's earthly witness to the world of His promises made to the first men concerning humanity's terrestrial death and future resurrection, an event that will occur only once this planet is sanctified at this *altar*.

This monument according to the prophet Isaiah was a *sign* located in Egypt. Amazingly, the prophet Jeremiah also confirms this indirectly, writing that the Lord "has set *signs* and wonders in the land of Egypt, *even unto this day.*" (1) Evidently the 8th and 7th century BC Hebrews were aware of the Giza monuments and their connection to God. An Egyptian text that may refer to them also was cited in Davidson's epic work entitled *The Great Pyramid: Its Divine Message* on page 371 which reads, "The God of the Universe is the light above the firmament; and His *symbols are upon the earth.*"

The word pyramid is of rather late construction and was not used in distant antiquity in referring to the Giza monuments. Pyramids were originally called *pillars* before and after the Great Flood for reasons that can only be explained by careful analysis of the truly fundamental characteristics of the pillar as a necessary item of architecture. In 1939 an antiquarian named Robert B. Stacey-Judd wrote that in ". . .seeking the origin of the stone column [pillar], we learn that its prototype was a wooden member, such as the trunk [stock] of a tree." (2) And such was the development of all primitive cultures, to build

43

with the wood of trees before acquiring the skills of masonry to erect pillars of stone. To early man the tree itself was a symbol of profound mystery, a vertical bridge between heaven and earth and earth and the underworld. Its boughs and branches high in the air typified the heavens and sky but these were attached to a support, the stock or trunk of the tree which was firmly placed on the ground, burrowing deep with roots stretching into the underworld. The pillars of temples long ago represented the trees of sacred groves. Long prior to Mohammed in Arabia the pillar in the tent, at the oasis or sanctuary served to identify the holy tree. (4) The pillar even anciently was the continuation of the symbolism of the mysterious tree.

Though the majestic stone pillars erected by the Sethites over 48 centuries ago were one thing, esoterically they were something else. This is best explained in the Hebrew word for pillar, which is *matstsebeth*, meaning "monumental stone; something stationed," while also meaning"... stock of a tree; pillar." This word is akin to matstsebah [memorial stone; pillar] or masseba, a stone erected to be a marker. (5) There are some authorities that even assert that the Hebrew words here mean *architectural structure*. (6) Not much has changed in that part of the world, even the Egyptologists term the oldest stone structures related to pyramids as *mastabas*, a word derived directly from the old Semitic words for pillar. Mastabas are box-shaped buildings that serve as lids over the top of well mouths (7), roughly pyramidal in shape.

Here we delve yet deeper into the layers of symbolism. Those peoples living before the Great Flood cataclysm were very aware of the prophecies widely spread concerning the diluvian disaster. Because it was thought that the world would be flooded from waters issuing forth from the underworld, early man maintained the custom of keeping massive stone lids atop wells to prevent the Flood. So profound a fear was this belief of waters from below that even after the Great Deluge the tradition was renewed and practiced. (8) Even in the oldest book of the Holy Writ, the Book of Job, we read, "The waters are hid as with a *stone*." (9) It cannot be left unmentioned here that far below (10) the Great Pyramid is a *well* of uncertain depth, now filled with rubble. The monument was not constructed over it casually, but the entire architectural passage system descends directly to the underground chamber where the well is located. The two largest pyramids at Giza are indeed the two pillars of the Sethites, a fact seemingly remembered by the Sumerians. This incredibly advanced and archaic civilization maintained clearly in their records that their history was divided between time periods both before and after The Flood.

Their memories of the erection of the colossal pillars may be reflected in their term for twins, which ultimately mirrors the old Semitic words just examined: MASH.TAB.BA. (11)

From the remotest times the pillar was used to identify something upon the earth. But they served also a dual function. They supported ceilings as architectural pieces while also displaying artwork, precious objects and idols. But the most common use of the pillar long ago was the preservation and conveyance of messages. Pillars were covered in writings and pictures that gave elaborate testimonies concerning histories, conquests, the reigns and deeds of kings, laws of the land and they were frequently used to mark boundaries while they were ornately covered with the inscriptions that affirmed land ownership and deed transactions. In essence, pillars have always been used to display *knowledge*. In the 2nd millennium BC Near East property was marked by pillars with inscriptions and sometimes pictorial representations. In Hebrew the word gebul, usually translated as *landmark* actually means *border*, or boundary. The erection of a pillar to mark someone's boundary was long regarded as divine law. Even the biblical Book of Proverbs reads, "Remove not the ancient landmark which thy fathers have set." (12) According to the authors of *Ancient Symbol Worship* the pillar was used to consecrate a special geographical place. (13)

The Sumerian King-List was inscribed upon stone columns and pillars, called prisms, records of rock concerning the cities, kings, their reigns and other particulars of interest both before and after the Flood as well as the various sages that served them. The most famous one is preserved in the Ashmolean Museum at Oxford, England. (14) One of the greatest historical centers of learning and knowledge in the world was at Egypt under the Macedonian regents, at Alexandria. The renowned library there housed replicas, translations and copies of texts from pillars taken from all over the Greek-touched world. Epigenus recorded that the Babylonians made records of celestial observances dating back to archaic times carved into pillars (15), a practice they learned from their Sumerian predecessors. Moses of Chorene wrote that a book had been discovered at Nineveh in Assyria which was translated from the Chaldaic into Greek by order of Alexander the Great which contained historical records of the distant past, histories that were found engraved upon a pillar. (16) Archeologists excavating Babylonia from under the arid desert wastes have uncovered a memorial stone of Merodach Baladan I (1320 BC) that calls upon the infernal deities ". . .all the gods on this stone tablet whose emblems are seen, violently to destroy the name," of he who moves this boundary stone. Among the emblems upon the stone is that of a winged dragon. (17) Remember this discovery for it is a window into the ancient mindset. To destroy one's *name* was to completely end the one who retained it, a person *was his name*. The connection between memorial stones and dragons is one that will be seen as this study continues.

The two pillars of the Sethites were built after Enoch received the divine instructions that he had passed to his relatives before his departure. There are many who believe, and with good reason, that the references to two pillars has a more important meaning. It is held that there may have been two entirely different architectural complexes having pyramids that were by the Sethites and that the Great Pyramid complex in Egypt is only one of them. We recall the traditions that one pillar was to remain for a thousand years until the Flood which would destroy or bury this architectural relic, and the other was to survive the violence of the diluvian cataclysm and be an enduring sign and witness to future generations that the world would be destroyed again, by fire. A flood of fire.

Bearing these things in mind we shall now examine the enigmatic etymology of the word pyramid. In the Old Testament books the Hebrew word for pillar most commonly used was *'ammud*. (18) This is akin to the Arabic *'imad*, which means both column and pillar. It was the Greeks who first merged this older Semitic word with their own root word for *fire* to create the word *pyramid*. (19). The Greek root pyr (pur) is an old root for which other modern words developed such as purge, pure, purity, purify and impure. It is a word simply meaning fire. (20)

The Platonists likened the symbol of the pyramid as their symbol for the element of fire. (21) This symbol △ has been recognized as the universal *image* of fire in ancient India and the nations of the Near East and even in more contemporary times occultists and witches employ the symbol in their representation of fire. (22) The Greeks considered the pyramids to be *pillars of fire*. In the old text, *Divine Pymander*, Hermes asserts that fire was the chief medium by which the Creator made the world. He reasons that flames are in the shape of a pyramid because of the way they burn, the flame tips pointing upward forming points. (23) The Hebrew writings tell us that before Solomon's temple stood two pillars called Boaz and Jachin. The biblical meanings of these two titles are "He shall establish," and "In it is strength," (24) but these are esoteric interpretations for the actual translations of Boaz and Jachin are different, perhaps remnants of the forgotten phonetics of an elder speech already extinct as a mode of communication by the days of David and Solomon. Boaz is constructed from roots meaning haste, motion (bo) and fire (az), while jachin derives from jarac, a root for *moon*. The sun and moon. Masons have long held that these two pillars withheld a great deal of secret knowledge. (26) These pillars were a mystical reminder that the sun and moon, as computers for time, were designed as *signs* for the constant observances of men.

The use of twin pillars representing mysteries of the Deity was also discovered at the ancient temple of Heracles at Tyre in Phoenicia where one stele was in the form of a pillar and the other as an obelisk. (27) There is little difference. The obelisk is a unification of the pyramid and pillar, being four-sided like a pyramid but elongated like a pillar. At its base is a foundation stone and its summit bears a miniature pyramid. Most often upon obelisks the pillar surface is covered with hieroglyphic records and inscriptions. Over two hundred years ago the mystic Francis Barrett wrote that the ancients ". . .were willing to deliver great mysteries in sacred letters, and explain them in certain symbolical figures . . . pyramids and obelisks to the *fire*." Harold Bayley in his exhaustive work *Lost Language of Symbolism* (1912) wrote that the pillar symbol represented the gateway to eternity. (29) The author of *Nature Worship* (1929) identifies the obelisk as a shrunken, vertically thin pyramid that seems to embody a secret that was ". . .ancientest among the ancients." (30)

We do not think in terms of words and phrases. The activity of the human mind thinks in *images* and pictures. Early sages recognized this and naturally employed the usage of familiar symbols to represent the images that they knew and conveyed. This scribal art made it easy for a writer to conceal his subject matter beneath a veil of normal images while also delivering deep truths to those who understand the dual application of the imagery. Symbols are thought-fossils enabling the masterful scribes of old to weave arcane things under modern guises.

Porphyry wrote that ". . .the ancients were willing to conceal God and divine virtues, by sensible figures and by those things which are visible, yet signifying *invisible* things." (31) The invisible things were those of the spirit, which to the initiates were the only things that were actually real. Everything on earth known to men were only copies, reflections of something spiritual. Stobaeus in the 5th century AD cited Hermes as saying, "All things then, those upon the earth. . . are not truth, but *imitations* of the truth." (32)

The use of the word pillar for pyramid is no exception. The ideas attached to the image of the pillar are very old and embody a forgotten theology lost to the modern world that requires a delving into the oldest writings on earth to remember.

Not even is mankind exempt from being a mere imitation of something greater. The Holy Writ declares that we are made in the *image* of God, and after

His likeness. But the physical world is only a reflection of the inner belief systems mankind holds as true, and for this reason God is viewed as black to the Ethiopians, as Asian to Orientals or white in the occident. One of the images by which early man depicted or imagined God was as the sun for it provided humanity all the things needed to live comfortably on the earth. Diodorus Siculus wrote that ". . .they adored the sun as expressing the likeness of the Deity." (33) The sun was a constant, daily reminder of the presence of the Creator as it emerged to begin another day. Not only the sun, but the planets too were regarded in like fashion. The Greeks watched the heavens religiously and claimed that the regularity of the passage of the planets and the stars in their cycles (orbits), "beginning ever where they end," was a modular *image of eternity*. (34) In considering that our study involves a monument of God in the land of Egypt at Giza it is a profound thing to realize that in the text called *Hermetica* we find that ". . .Egypt is an image of heaven. . . all the operations and the powers which rule and work in heaven have been transferred to the earth below." (35)

Francis Barrett was a researcher of old occult studies and writings over two hundred years ago. In his work called *The Magus: A Complete System of Occult Philosophy* he wrote, "The wise ancients knew that in nature the greatest secrets lay hidden. . . but as in these latter days, men gave themselves almost wholly up to vice and luxury, so their misunderstandings have become more and more depraved; till, being swallowed up in the gross senses, they became totally unfit for divine contemplations and deep speculations in Nature." (36) God in His infinite wisdom designed the mundane mechanics of our world we all take for granted as similitudes and images of far more important spiritual truths. The sun sets bringing the dark as the world is immersed in shadow, presaging death and ruin, but the moon as a lesser light provides an unspoken hope of a greater light to come, another day. Then the sun emerges and vanquishes the darkness foreshadowing the hope of resurrection. For this reason was Christ titled the Sun of Righteousness. (37) Even our planet's history serves as merely a type. Mankind was made from the elements of the earth, and this Old World because of the rebellion of humanity was destroyed and *made over* by the violence of the Great Flood which resulted in the birth of a new world where men could start over just as the sinner's total immersion under the water of baptism symbolize their new beginning and walk with God. In the future the world will be made to burn in terrestrial fires caused by a celestial cataclysm just as the people of earth will pass through divine fires of the Spirit. And it was for this purpose that Enoch was given divine instructions to have a *pillar of fire* [pyramid] built on the earth to warn future generations of the apocalyptic fires that will destroy the world by the very element by which He had created it.

A common denominator between the widely divergent pyramid traditions discussed throughout this book is that they were covered in the inscriptions of the knowledge of the pre-flood world in an effort to preserve this information for people after the Deluge. These writings concerned the past, the present histories of those days and future. This alludes that the information was of divine origin, for it is by inspiration that one can know the future. Like the pyramids, the oldest writings in the world have all been found on stone. Stone is a symbol of permanence (38) and it was used for the inscriptions of the Sumerians, on stelae, prisms, tablets, pillars and temple facades be the stone natural rock or of human manufacture. Later Babylonia, Akkad, Ugarit, Ebla, Assyria, Mari, Mohenjo-daro, Egypt and many other cultures left to us today many writings because they had been preserved in stone. Had only wood, parchment, vellum, skins or some other perishable mediums been employed our knowledge of the ancient world would be nil.

Our idea of a book in these modern times is very different than that of early man. To them a book was any *container of knowledge*. A temple room exhibiting four walls covered in hieroglyphic texts was a book to them no different than a series of colophon-connected clay tablets in cuneiform telling of the creation of the world. The series of tablets was a book. A man could choose one of the heavily scripted pillars in a temple complex and spend a long time reading the text just as another man employed attendants who dutifully unfurled an old leather scroll as he patiently read the material. To both men they were reading books.

Quite literally, the pillars of the Sethites were books upon enormous monuments of stone, tiny writings along the lower courses being tantamount to entire editions of modern encyclopedias. These *books* were left so that people in the future beyond the Great Flood could learn that there was indeed a Creator and that He had a plan. Today we refer to the Scriptures as the Word of God. But where exactly did it come from? There are twelve definitive colophons in the Genesis narrative that demonstrate that at one time the Genesis text was divided between twelve *tablets*. It will be shown in this book that much of the biblical material found in the Scriptures today actually came from the surface writings once adorning the Great Pyramid. That someone after the Flood visited Egypt and copied the texts that later found their way onto the pages of our Bibles does in no way infer that they were not inspired writings. On the contrary, if they are Enochian in origin then they must have been truly inspired. Could the pyramids be an earthly symbol of the eternal Word of God made of permanent stone, an *image* of the enduring reality of the truths of Scripture? Francis Barrett was close to the mark when he wrote, ". . .and in *stones* the character and images of celestial things are often found." (39)

The stones at Giza in the form of the Great Pyramid are stacked upon each other level upon level reaching slightly over 480 feet forming the *largest book on earth*. It is also the oldest. As we will learn throughout this study not only was the Great Pyramid actually covered in millions of tiny inscriptions studied and copied by the learned of bygone ages, but the architectural designs of the exterior and interior areas of the monuments convey deep spiritual truths hidden for millennia.

Another layer of the pillar symbolism must also be explored here. The prophet Isaiah wrote that the pillar in Egypt was a *sign* and a *witness*. The use of stones to witness some historical event is virtually timeless. The *Book of Jasher* provides us with one of the best examples. Jacob, later renamed Israel by God, was in love with one of Laban's daughters and they came to a verbal agreement that he would labor for Laban seven years to earn her hand in marriage. Jacob fulfilled his word but Laban did not and the former agreed to another seven years, Jacob receiving two wives but only one that he wanted. After fourteen years and a conflict between Jacob and Laban in the presence of witnesses they raised a heap of stones, and Jacob said, "This heap is a witness between me and thee." (40) The site became the famous Gilead. This heap of stones, like a cairn, was a witness to others that Jacob and Laban settled their differences and it was a reminder that the two men had made a *covenant* [binding agreement]. The institution of a covenant is integral to understanding the purpose of the pyramid.

Also in the *Book of Jasher* we learn that when Abraham was taking Isaac to the mountain to sacrifice his son at the request of God, Abraham looked from a distance over the land and saw a *pillar* of fire upon the mountain that extended into the sky and the Glory of God was seen in the cloud. Abraham was astonished and asked the others in the group if they too saw these things, but only Isaac could see them. He deduced from this that the phenomenon was a sign from God that Isaac was an acceptable offering. (41) Fortunately the act of sacrifice was not God's plan, and Isaac lived and fathered Jacob, but God used the event to establish a covenant between Abraham and all of his future offspring and Himself. Thus, the sign of the pillar was the sign of the *covenant*. The pillar of fire. This was confirmed in Genesis where at the heap of stones erected by Jacob and Laban, Jacob also ". . .took up a stone, and set it up for a *pillar*." (42) Jacob was then told by God to move to Bethel and build an *altar*. At Bethel the lord visited Jacob and renewed the covenant between Abraham's seed and Himself. It was then that Jacob underwent a profound transformation, albeit, symbolically. His name was changed to Israel. In commemoration of the event Jacob erected a pillar of stone at Bethel to witness that this covenant was permanent. (43) This pillar of stone was the altar that Jacob built at Bethel, which means House of God, just as in Egypt the pillar [pyramid] according to Isaiah was an *altar* of God. A pillar and altar. A covenant and *name change*. . . these are the elements to an incredible arcanum involving the identity of the Great Pyramid. Remember them.

This was not the first time that Jacob had erected a pillar to commemorate some important event. He had a spectacular vision ". . .of a ladder set up on the earth, and the top of it reached to the heavens; and behold, the angels of God ascending and descending on it." (44) In this vision the Voice of the Lord promised him that He would renew the covenant that he had made with his father and grandfather Abraham. When Jacob awoke in the morning he was terrified, took the stone he was using for a pillow and made a pillar because he believed the site was the Gate of Heaven, saying, "And this stone which I have set for a pillar, shall be God's house." This association between the pillar and ladder motif is very important, as the ladder is the symbol of ascension. In Ancient Symbol Worship we learn that in the early history of mankind the pillar became the universal symbol of the Deity. Also we discover that the artificial hills of stone so commonly found around the world were used to represent the dwelling place of God serving as a witness to the people that He lived among them. Joshua erected a great stone pillar before the leaders of the tribes of Israel before the Conquest of Canaan to show them that their covenant with God was renewed and King Josiah almost eight hundred years later stood beside a pillar when he made a covenant with the Lord. (46)

The pillar as a symbol is a more condensed form of the Divine Tree, typified by the architectural column. This alludes that there is a hidden meaning in the Genesis record concerning the Edenic paradise wherein stood two trees, one of Knowledge and the other of Life. The pillar [pyramid] of the Sethites symbolized the Tree of Knowledge for it was covered in the knowledge of the history and science of the Old World. Enoch witnessed in vision the Three Mountains of the Blessed Land represented in the image of a dismembered tree, which by extension identifies the pillar. But there is yet another layer of the archaic symbolism of the pillar we must explore.

Pillar . . . Or Divine Mountain?

The Sumerian writings tell of a mysterious mountain somewhere here on earth that was called Mashu. This is made more intriguing by the geological fact that there are no mountains in the lands of Sumer in southern Iraq. Concerning mount Mashu these texts read, "On high, to the celestial band it is connected; below, to the lower world it is bound." (47) Here is a belief in a mountain that linked heaven to earth and earth to the underworld. According to the *Herder Dictionary of Symbols* this Sumerian mountain had *two peaks*. It was this World Mountain that the realm of the dead could be accessed. The celestial band refers to the 12 zodiacal constellations along the ecliptic plane, the path of the sun and moon and other planets.

This precession of images told an ancient story, a prophecy. Even the individual stars of the various constellations were given significant and meaningful names that contributed to this stellar theology. Those not initiated gazed upon the heavens and saw only stars and patterns attached only to legends and lore, mythologies that *covered* knowledge rather than divulged it. The history of the future was recorded in this way and the story behind the original zodiac is so profound that it is discussed with meticulous detail in this author's other work, *Descent of the Seven Kings*. Perhaps it is this

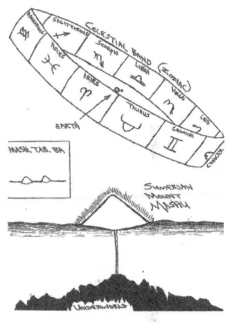

same mountain referred to in this very old Sumerian Temple hymn: "enduring place, light hued mountain which in artful fashion was founded. Its dark hidden chamber is an awe-inspiring place; in a field of supervision it lies. Awesome, its ways no one can fathom." (48) This is an adequate description of the Great Pyramid as any given today. Those Sumerian scribes that had written this were those descended from people who had survived the Deluge. Originally, the Great Pyramid was in "artful fashion," covered in large 20 ton blocks of white limestone facing stones that were covered along the lower third of the monument is writings, texts *burned* into the highly polished stones rather than etched in by tools. A field of supervision is one that is guarded, or protected. We recall here that Surid, before the Flood, had appointed a guardian to the Great Pyramid complex, one we identify today as the Sphinx.

This mountain of the Sumerians is no different in function than their Tree of Life. This tree was also called The Pillar and served ". . .as a ladder that connected the underworld with earth and heaven." (49) In their mythology it was the goddess Inana who rescued this ladder from the Flood. She had also descended into the depths of the underworld by virtue of this pillar. The protector of this Tree was a guardian of the Underworld demons and the sentry before the Gate of Anu [heaven]. His name was Lord of the Good Tree, or Ningishzida. (50) A variant reading of his name means Lord of the Trees of Life. Incredibly, this etymological artifact popularly known as *Giza* today is descended from this epithet: Nin [lord], gishzi [tree], da [good]. Nin[*gishzi*] da.

The Sumerian tree of life was little different from that of the early Germanic people who called it Irminsul, which was to the Vikings known as Yggsdrasil. Irminsul is a pillar that supports the world, a bridge between heaven and earth. The name Irminsul derives from that ancestral hero called Irmin, or Irminus. Great wooden pillars were erected in his honor and by all accounts this figure was none other than a Germanic Hermes, or Enoch. Irminsul was the pillar of the universe, the polar axis that also supported the Pole Star and was important to the order of the cosmos because it kept the stellar foundation. (50) To the ancients the space in the heavens between the Great Bear constellation, the Seven Stars, and the pole star they revolved around which they considered as the Cosmic Tree, was known as the *sampo*, or the "many-ciphered cover," an allusion to knowledge hidden among the stars. John Major Jenkins in *Galactic Alignment* records that the word sampo is derived from Sanskrit, from skamba, or *pillar*. As will be seen in this book, the surface writings that covered the Great Pyramid long ago indeed served as a many-ciphered cover.

The Norse version was Yggsdrasil, the World Tree or tree of life, which was also the pillar that connected heaven (Asgard), the earth (Midgard) and the underworld's own three departments. It was a ladder by which the mystic masters could ascend and descend into the spirit world. This tree was watered by a *well from the underworld* and the tree was also referred to as a *sacred mountain* (52), two elements that directly link it to the Great Pyramid. At the base of this tree stood the Three Norns, three goddesses that represented the past, the present and the future, all being descriptions of the knowledge placed on the Great Pyramid.

Yggsdrasil was represented by two Nordic runes that bind together to form the runic glyph for the World Tree. The Life rune merges with the Death rune to form the symbol for the Great Tree Yggsdrasil. The three branches of this tree form aspects of the City of the Gods, which was supported by the pillar, or earth, above the three roots, which represented the three departments of the underworld: the Land of the Dead, the Land of the Black Elves and the Land of the Giants. (53)

The merging of these two runes forms a symbol so old that even writers as early as the first millennium BC mistook it for a representation of a lightning bolt which later contributed to its use by ancient artisans who created masterpieces depicting Zeus, Thor, Hinum of ancient America, Ninurta and a host of other deities holding this symbol in their grasp. Historian and translator A. Smythe Palmer, in his 1897 *Babylonian Influence on the Bible and Popular Beliefs*, wrote that the glyph used by Merodak to defeat the Chaos Dragon named Tiamat symbolized lightning, the same weapon found in Genesis 3:24 described as a "flame of the turning weapon," that prevented access back to the Tree of Life after mankind had taken from the Tree of Knowledge. (54) While Palmer's assertions are very consistent with later interpretations of other antiquarians who had also misunderstood the symbol, is found not only in reliefs at Sumer, Babylonia and Assyria, but even in early India, China, Japan, Greece, Gaul, Egypt and as mentioned, in early America. No doubt that future excavations will yield forth many more examples of this symbol's importance to the earliest artisans. It was not a lightning bolt. In every instance the symbol conveys that its wielder holds the *power of Life and Death.*

One incredible example of the employment of this symbol is found in the famous painting of Nagarjuna now housed in Japan. (55) It is over a thousand years old and depicts the Chinese hero and esotericist Nagarjuna with distinctly non-Chinese features holding the

Incidentally, this name derives from a Sanskrit title: naga (dragon) and Arjuna, an Indian hero.

The sacred mountain motif is one of extreme antiquity found among the earliest cultures and is directly related by all to the divine tree. The Todas peoples told of a mountain called Makurti which stands at the Navel of the Earth, a towering rock upon a tableland, ". . .of which the souls of the dead assemble for the leap into the abyss of waters that lies between them and the mount of heaven." (56) This "tableland" is the great plateau on which rests the Great Pyramid. Again we have here a connection to waters below the structure. Old Miztec traditions tell of the appearance of two gods who by their immense knowledge and omnipotence made ". . .a great rock, upon which they built a very sumptuous palace, a masterpiece of skill, in which they made their abode on earth. This palace was upon a mountain. And the rock was called the Place of Heaven," according to Gerald Massey in his *The Natural Genesis.* (57) The Aztec Nahautl myths tell that the enormous pyramids at Teotihuacan were also built by gods long ago, by, ". . .knowers of occult things, possessors of the traditions," and that they were built *before a disastrous catastrophe*. (58) Truly the Aztecs did not know who built the pyramids they found in their country or the ruinous cities of living stone that had been occupied by the earlier Toltecs who did not know their origin either, but they merely affixed their own cultural memories to the sites because of their obvious mysteriousness and connections to the pyramid motifs.

The Aztecs were certainly not alien to the secrets of the pyramid. Their god of death was called Mictlan, who lived in a region where the dead repaired after life at a place named Tlalxicco at the *navel of the earth*. (59) Lewis Spence in *The Problem of Atlantis* shows that the Aztecs believed that their Lord of Fire named Xiuhtecutli dwelt at the navel of the earth and entered the Blue Stone Pyramid. He was the Old God, older than the present gods, who lived prior to the foundation of the present world.

Like the Germanic and Viking traditions, the Huoron and Iroqois told the first Christian missionaries that the underworld could be entered by crossing over a deep and swift river by means of a bridge made out of a *tree*. (60) In fact, many Native American groups had beliefs very similar to these and those of the Aztecs. The same can be said of the Chickasaws concerning the great mounds and pyramids of the Mississippi Valley who believed the area with its extensive earthen ruins was the *center of the earth*. (61) This means that these people had retained ancestral memories going back *millennia* to a time where they as a people knew of a place at the center of where the earth stood massive architecture. There have been excavated pyramids in North America, Mexico, several in the Yucatan regions and even in South America. All of the cultures having come in contact with these ruins maintain similar ideas concerning their origin, often identifying them with some primordial holy mountain. This remains cogent evidence that somewhere in the dim past all these people shared a common ancestral link fragmented by the passage of time.

The Zoroastrian beliefs of Iran tell of the Cinvat Bridge which connects this world to the next. Souls judged worthy to pass over enter Airyana Vaejah, the Domain of the Immortals, a paradise world curiously centered at Khvaniranthra, the center of the earth's landmass. (62) But as the dead who are adjudged wicked attempt to pass over they are dragged down into the depths of the darkness. Traditions of Airyana Vaejah concern two divine trees, and in Azerbaijan even Enoch is remembered as associated to Airyana Vaejah. (63) In Andrew Collins' meticulously researched book entitled *From the Ashes of Angels: Forbidden Legacy of a Fallen Race* we learn that Persian scholars accept that Iranian mythological locations were often changed to suit the landscape in which the stories were told. (64) Collins' research has yielded forth two significant finds relative to our study. One, in the *Genesis Apocryphon* found among the Dead Sea scrolls we learn that Methuselah sought for his father Enoch when Noah was born, journeying to a place called Parwain where the patriarchal prophet was residing with angels. Collins discovered that Mandaean traditions mention both Anush (Enoch) and Mount Parwan, a white mountain derived from the root parswana, which means *frontier*. (65) This white mountain is none other the Great Pyramid in its original architectural condition covered with white limestone casing blocks which were discovered in 1837 AD by Col. Vyse, a monument according to the prophet Isaiah was located at the border (frontier) to the Lord. Secondly, Collins wrote that Mandaean traditions tell of the souls after death that go to a heavenly realm called Pthahil, a god of the dead, after flying over a white mountain called *Sur* where souls adjudged righteous journey on to the Pole Star. (66) Collins believes that Pthahil means *the god Ptah* of Egypt, which is probably correct, for mount Sur is merely an abbreviated form of *Siriad*, where the Great Pyramid was erected according to ancient Arabic texts.

The old root Sur is also found in the Islamic traditions of the bridge Al Sirat where the faithful pass into paradise, which is situated in the 7th heaven, a bridge over the abyss. Burmese mythology has the same imagery with an upper world, a middle world and an underworld. The middle world has at its center a flat area where stands a very high mountain on which stands a palace of the superior spirits. No mortal can pass beyond these central borders. Incredibly, this majestic area is covered by dust but beneath the dust is very hard stone, which remarkably is sustained by water. Under the water is an open area full of air. Like mount Meru of the Hindus this mountain extends from heaven to earth and earth to the world below. (67) Harold T. Wilkins in *Secret Cities of Old South America* recorded that the old Hindus stated that the pyramids in India and Egypt were merely copies of the primordial mountain at the center of the world called Meru. Mount Meru was guarded by a dreadful dragon [the Sphinx] and Daniel Boorstin in *The Discoverers* cites that Buddhist traditions hold that mount Meru lies between the Four Worlds, divided between the four cardinal directions and that it was *square at the bottom*. Anyone who has seen a pyramid from an aerial view can easily find its base to be square.

Other elements of the Burmese beliefs need be reviewed here. At the base of the mountain on the flat area [plateau] were three enormous rubies and around the mountain are seven concentric circles of lesser mountains which feed seven great rivers that water the earth. The earth consists of four continents that lied at the four cardinal directions. As rubies are precious stones, these three are the three gigantic pyramids at Giza, the two largest being the Great Pyramids, which is perfectly aligned with its faces positioned facing north, east, south and west. The reference to seven rivers is an obvious memory of the Egyptian *Delta*, for the Great Pyramid plateau lies at the apex of this branching out of seven rivers.

Other distant cultures isolated far away from Egypt preserve these same ideas. Without interrupting this work to examine them all we will finish with one of particular interest. The Chamulas Indians of Guatemala thought of the present world as a *square island* riddled with underworld caves that were inhabited by demons and Earth Lords, but the sky was a multi-tiered pyramid supported by a gigantic *tree*. As will be shown, beneath the Giza surface is a maze of tunnels, galleries of rock and chambers, most now filled with water and closed to the public. Though the more primitive peoples have retained less information we are very fortunate that curious antiquarians long ago as well as secret societies and religious sects have recognized the importance of these truths and have preserved them for future dissemination. Among these are the Kabbalists and Gnostics, Jewish esotericists and the Egyptian Christian mystics. Supporting the Guatemalan traditions we learn that the Kabbalists believed that the Tunnels of Set beneath the dayside of the Tree of Life was where dwelt evil spirits called the oliphoth. Though Set is the older Egyptian deity, it is merely a memory of Seth, one of the chief builders of the Great Pyramid complex before the Flood.

The Kabbalists maintain that there is a heavenly and an earthly paradise, an Eden below and above. The erudite Gerald Massey wrote, "The two are united by a fixed pillar called Strength of the Hill of Zion, somewhat like the colossal pillar Irminsul which bears up the heavens. The souls that enter the dwellings of the lower paradise are permitted to ascend by this pillar. . ." (68) Massey had not connected all of the seemingly random universals from around the world as has been done in this study so he probably did not comprehend how profound this statement truly was. He was writing about the Great Pyramid in Egypt and didn't even know it. The Hill of Zion [pyramid] is the pillar called Strength by the Kabbalists, and the pillar before the door to Solomon's Temple had an inscription upon it that was translated, ". . .in it is *strength*." Additionally, according to the *Jubilees* text, Zion was at the center of the navel of the earth. (69) This was a piece of evidence that lead to the conclusion that the Great Pyramid was a type of book, so we should not be amazed to find this curious passage in the *Book of Jubilees* concerning the future judgment by fire:

> And on that day of cursing and turbulence,
> He will also burn with devouring fire, as He
> burned Sodom, thus also will He burn His
> land and His city and all that is His, and he
> [the condemned] will be erased out of the
> book of the discipline of the sons of men,
> and he shall not ascend into the book of life
> for he shall be destroyed and shall depart to
> the eternal curse. . . . (70)

And with this gem we return to our theory presented herein that the Great Pyramid, constructed to warn the world of a far distant future flood of fire descending upon the earth from the heavens, is indeed a stone book, even an image of the eternal Word of God. . . the Book of Life. And this is the greatest secret among the historic Gnostics, a sect of Egyptians with very Christian like beliefs that knew that the deeper things of God were discernable and learned through the teachings of the Logos, the Greek name for the Word. According to the Gnostic work entitled *Pistis Sophia* Enoch was taken into heaven where he stood in the presence of God while the *Books of Jeou* were dictated to him. Another tradition holds that he learned the holy *Books of Jeou* when he visited a holy mountain. (71) Jeou is a Gnostic variant of a truly archaic rendering of the Hebrew title of God as *Jah.* In fact, the epithet Messiah used to describe Christ is a compound of the Egyptian word *mess* (rebirth) and the Hebrew iah [Jah]. (72)

According to the Gnostics, Jeou declared "...it is necessary for men to gain knowledge of the mysteries which are in the books of Jeou, those that I caused to be written by Enoch in paradise, when I spoke to him from the tree of knowledge and tree of life. And I caused him to place them upon the rock of Ararat: and I set up Kalapatauroth the Archon who is above in Gemmit, him who is under the feet of Jeou and who makes all aeons and all destinies revolve. That same Archon I set over to watch the books of Jeou, to protect them from the flood and also that no Archon, seized with jealousy about them, might destroy them." (73)

Somewhere on earth upon a mountain were engraved the books of Jeou, which are at the site protected by a Watcher [Archon] that protects them from being destroyed. The reference to the trees of life and knowledge return us back to the rich symbolism of the pillar and its function as a ladder between heaven and earth. The Watchers are found numerous times throughout the *Book of Enoch*, an order of angelic beings that due to some primordial controversy concerning the existence and destiny of humankind separated into two factions. Some among the rebellious Watchers went even further and directly intervened in the affairs of men and descended to earth, having been imprisoned by the Creator when the world was destroyed by the Deluge. Then there were others, like this Kalapatauroth, who remained faithful to the Creator protecting His interests on earth. The Watchers were popularly known in antiquity as guardians of portals and entrances between worlds. They were keepers of the ancient wisdom (74) and it was a mighty Watcher that stood at the gates of Eden preventing the first humans from going back into Eden after they were banished.

The Egyptian Coptic translation of the *Pistis Sophia* is merely the translation of an older translation. The earliest known copy of the text was in Greek, naturally as it was an Alexandrian writing, and this is easily ascertained due to the abundant Greek words left untranslated in the Coptic manuscript. (75) In fact, the majority of ancient manuscripts extant today are but translations of translations and rarely are texts found in their original language.

The *First Book of Jeou* reveals that IAO dwells in the center of heaven as the aeons revolve around Him. He is the First Mystery, and from His position at the Treasury of Light was a gate to the regions of the Three Amens. (76) Amen signifies the Hidden One, here represented by the number three. The Gnostics cleverly called him by the acronym of IAO. This is the combining of [A]lpha and [O]mega prefixed with the determinative for the Hebrew Jah [I:Jeou].

The *Pistis Sophia* claims that Enoch learned the *Books of Jeou* at a holy mountain, but then also that he learned them from the Tree of Gnosis (Knowledge). Disparity, or an admission that both are one and the same? As there stand two gigantic pyramids at Giza in alignment with one another geometrically and geodetically with the cardinal directions we find that there are only two *Books of Jeou*. While there stands a third member of the Great Pyramids at Giza, the third is fundamentally different than the two gigantic ones. It was called the Red Pyramid, is much smaller with less mass. It was covered in beautiful limestone with inscriptions like the other two. It must also be noted here that in the Genesis account the Tree of Knowledge was of good *and evil*. The Fall of Man was partially due to a newfound awareness of evil and man's capacity to succumb to it. But this acquisition of information was not entirely to our detriment for God provided a balance, a gnosis of good and evil knowledge, the good concealed in divine mysteries that serve to aid the diligent researcher in getting to the Tree of Life, the embodied Word of God.

The mysteries of the Gnostics lead us to the *Book of the Secrets of Enoch* wherein we discover that the tenth heaven was where God dwells, which in the Hebrew tongue is called Aravat. (77) This is probably the rock of Ararat mentioned in the *Pistis Sophia* that is protected by an Archon. The mountain commonly known as Ararat is not in Egypt at all, but Armenia, and modern Turkey, popular for being the landing place of the ark of Noah after the Great Flood. Ararat may have been the actual name known to the pre-flood peoples given to the Great Pyramid, and as Noah would have known all about the monument, which was still being constructed when he was born, he may have named the mountain Ararat when the vessel came to a stop.

At Giza the primary architectural features are the two huge pyramids, the third and smaller Red Pyramid, the Sphinx; but there are seven other smaller pyramidal structures alongside the Great Pyramids. Altogether on the Giza plateau are ten pyramids, a sum very significant to the Hebrew mystics which held that it signified perfect completion and was the number for God. Remarkably, ten is the third and most important *triangular number* of the Kabbalists and Pythagoreans. Early methods of counting led to a discovery. Different amounts of stones put together formed various shapes. The numbers 3, 6 and 10 form triangular numbers and are derived themselves from unique mathematical formulae. (78)

$1+2 = 3$

$1+2+3 = 6$

$1+2+3+4 = 10$

Ten was considered the supreme and divine equation. Philolaus of Tarentum wrote that this number was the embodiment of perfection and the shape of the triangle was believed to contain the "Unutterable Name of God." (79) Though we have seen how the word pyramid means "pillar of fire" the Coptics went so far as to claim that this was derived from *pirimit*, or, "a tenth part of numbers." (80) The reference here to the Name of God hidden within the shape of the triangle calls to mind the early Masonic records earlier examined that claim that Enoch built a temple before the Flood that contained an agate triangle that hid the Name of God. This tradition was no doubt borrowed from the exact belief of the Greeks. (81) Some of the reasoning of the old writers may have been slightly warped, such as Philo's opinion that the number ten was perfect because the tops of mountains after the Deluge, being pointed, appeared in the number of the decade [triangular] (82) but this alone does not negate the significance in the parallels between various texts and cultures in the belief of this number's importance and relation to God. Because our most remote ancestors refused to call God by an earthly name, the pyramid served as the perfect glyphic representation of the Deity because it was a three-sided figure, an *image* of the holy mountain. He was simply referred to as the Nameless, and titles like El, Jah, Adonai, the lord, and the Eternal or Maker were merely employed to *describe* Him. In the very old writings of India known as the *Rig Veda* we read, "Though One, He is called by the learned by many names . . ." His name was so sacred that it could not be uttered by the human tongue so our earliest priests and prophets fashioned epithets to describe Him and artisans molded wonderful glyphic representations. Among one of the most curious of these symbols designed to represent the "...name of the Great Giver of Light," (83) among the Egyptians, Mexicans and other civilizations spread abroad looked like this:

 One of the most intriguing aspects early theologians attached to that of God was that He was a *door*. For this reason the symbolic representation of the Name of God △ also took on the meaning of a gate or door. In the Hebrew and Phoenician alphabets the △ (daleth) also meant *door*, being the fourth letter, a symbol also found on the famous Moabite Stone. (84) The Egyptian determinative for door was the same, being △ (mr). (85) Because gates and doors connect different areas some cultures affixed different meanings to the glyphs. According to the *Imperial Dictionary of King Hi* the △ is a sign of *union* in ancient China. (86) It was Jacob who erected the pillar of stone and called it the gate (door) of heaven, the pillar identifying the more expansive symbol of the Holy Mountain that *unifies* heaven and earth. This mountain is the door, represented by God, who alone provides access. The Egyptian *mr*, also MER, seems to have been preserved throughout the lower Pacific ocean in Melanesia, Polynesia and Micronesia where are found numerous pyramidal structures on the island chains universally known as marae as found in John Macmillan Brown's research in *The Riddle of the Pacific*. Again, the similarity with *Meru*, the mountain at the center of the world, cannot be ignored.

That a divine mountain connecting our world to both the heavens and the underworld, a place that was accessible to us long ago, is a constant theme of the ancients. Such a location is also alluded to in the second millennium BC texts known as the *Enuma Elish*, or seven tablets of the Babylonian creation epic. The Babylonian hero was Marduk who went to battle against a powerful demonic lord named Kingu, a war deity allied to the Chaos Dragon Tiamat who resided in the Deep. Kingu robbed the Lord High God then named ENLIL of the Tablets of Destinies that contained the eternal truths of the past, present and future, but the hero Marduk wrested them away from the demon lord. Marduk would later destroy Tiamat with a weapon that looked like this:

 After defeating Kingu, Marduk then made a *gate to the deep* so the hordes of demons and Kingu could not steal from ENLIL again. He bolted the gate shut and set a Watchmen (Watcher) guardian over it to ensure that the evil waters of chaos would not rise again. (87) Here we have the retold, albeit earlier, story of the prehistoric theft of the heavenly know—ledges and their restoration on earth. The tablets of Destinies is akin to the Tree of Knowledge, or the *Books of Jeou*, and the Watcher is the Archon named Kalapatauroth represented by the guarding Sphinx, the same guardian placed there by Surid before the Flood, our Enoch.

This gate to the underworld is also found within the writings of the Jewish historian Josephus, who 2000 years ago wrote that the Sethites erected the pillars in Siriad (Egypt). Josephus wrote concerning the lake of unquenchable fire and where it lies hidden that ". . .there is one descent into this region, at whose *gate* we believe there stands an *archangel* with a host: which gate when those pass through that are conducted down by the angels that are appointed over souls. . ." (88) The archangel would again be identified as the Sphinx, which was long ago known to be the composite of a lion, bull, man and eagle, identifying the Tetramorph, or Four Divine Archangels of the *Book of Revelation* that usher in the Apocalypse. The Sphinx with the face of a man, body of a calf (bull), paws of a lion also long ago had painted along its flanks the wings of an eagle.

Josephus does not claim that this gate to the underworld is the Giza complex, but nor does he cite where this descent is located. As a historian borrowing his information from many older sources available to him two millennia ago, we must consider these fragments in light of other glimpses and fragmented texts because all accounts of the Great Pyramid complex have been passed down from times after the Flood by cultures that in themselves only preserved various parts of the whole. Because today we have access to so many of these fragmented beliefs we are beginning to put back together the pieces of this astonishing arcanum, parts of the whole even found within the Holy Scriptures among the particular old Psalms:

> Who *shall ascend into the hill of the Lord?*
> Or who shall stand in His holy place? He
> that hath clean hands and a pure heart: who
> hath not lifted up his soul unto vanity, nor
> sworn deceitfully. . . Lift up your hands, O
> ye *gates*; even lift them up, ye everlasting
> *doors*; and the King of Glory shall come in.
> Selah. (89)

Mysterious Relation to the Number Seven

The $\triangle$ was also used by the Egyptians as a numeral, the hieroglyph representing the number *seven*. Because the symbol is a representation of the three-dimensional triangle, or pyramid, we find the Egyptian glyph simple yet sophisticated. The triangle had three sides, but the pyramid has *four* faces and the imagery combines here to account for the seven. (90) This number was considered divine, a holy number that identified *time* itself. The phenomenon of time was linked to the motion of the celestial bodies, perfectly understood by the Egyptians. They religiously watched the movements of the planets, called wanderers and gods, for it was believed that their movements affected things on earth such as droughts, famines, invasions, periods of peace, victory or even death. Their own beliefs in this respect were no different than those of the Near East and abroad. Diodorus wrote that the Chaldeans believed ". . .that every event in the heavens has its meaning, as part of the eternal scheme of divine forethought." (91) During those early epochs astrology was a type of religious astronomy and the universal mode of communication understood by all the sages and scribes of different cultures was by *numbers*, a language of universal application.

The number seven was of particular importance to these astro-theologies. There were only seven known celestial bodies in the Creation not among the fixed and unmovable stars. These were the Wanderers, the planets of our solar system and the sun and moon. The five known planets were thought to be divine beings because they on their own volition moved against the backdrop of starry hosts that seemed implacable and fixed and their passing close to earth or their conjunction with another planet often signified great portents or divine revelations. The sun and moon were used to tabulate the more popular calendrical systems, but lesser-known time-keeping methods recording the cyclic conjunction of the planets were employed to record the approach and passing of the Great Year, a 600 year period fully explained in *Descent of the Seven Kings*. The Chaldeans of Babylon pictorially represented their concept of time being symbolized by the number seven which was divided into three distinct parts: solar, lunar and stellar, like this Chaldean Star depicted in the illustration. (92)

This geometrical calendar demonstrates how time, though measured in *sevens*, is continual. The end of the seven day cycle of the week here depicted by the sun, moon, and five planets ends with the seventh planet, however, the seven pointed pattern in not complete until the eighth day is reached. Which, incidentally, is the *first* of the seven days of another calendar. For this reason the number eight for at least three thousand years in the Mysteries and by numerologists has been the number for *new beginnings*. The *one* and *eight* are synonymous when the number seven is geometrically depicted.

CHALDEAN CALENDER STAR

DAYS OF THE WEEK

SATURN 7.
JUPITER 5.
MOON 2.
MARS 3.
MERCURY 4.
SUN 1.
VENUS 6.

We find this maintained even as late as the Christian apocryphal writings such as the *Epistle of Barnabas*, which reveals that after the seven ages of the world pass, God says, "I shall begin the eighth day, that is, the *beginning* of the other world." (93) Perhaps this is but a memory of the older *Book of Enoch*, which conveys that there are 7 weeks (ages) of earth history followed by an 8th week of universal peace and harmony. In the Genesis account the world was renovated from the ruin of chaos in six days, but the seventh day indicated the rest (inactivity) of God. However, it required an eighth day (which is actually the first now) in order for another week to follow. The Babylonian *Enuma Elish* was written in cuneiform upon seven tablets and tells of the seven stages of conflict that resulted in the creation and establishment of Marduk as supreme among the gods. But an eighth stage clearly must follow to verify that anything was indeed established. Though the number ten is holy and heavenly, the number seven seems to refer to perfection on *earth*. We were made from elements of the earth and on earth the spectrum of light as perceived on the human visual bandwidth is divided into seven primary colors, what we call the rainbow, the glass prism dividing ordinary sunlight. Even in music the completion of seven tones brings one back to the exact same note, but an octave higher, the Latin root octo meaning *eight*. (94) It is not without design that our present numeral for the number eight appears in such a way as to have no beginning or end:

The deeper we delve into the secrets of nature and the mechanics of God's creative work we find that numbers indeed provide us many amazing revelations. Not only did God create or renovate everything in seven days, but according to the *Revelation*, He shall destroy the civilizations of the world by the repetitions of seven. The seven seals, seven trumpets, seven mysterious thunders and the seven vials (bowls) of wrath will be effected against earth and the seven-headed dragon of chaos (symbolic for Seven Demonic Kings) will be vanquished at the end of the Seventh Age before He ushers in the eighth age: Millennial Earth. Thus, the number seven is a *terrestrial* number relative to humanity and the world we live in, a number embodying the concept of time.

The seven-pointed calendar star was also known to the Norse and Celts. Amazingly, their depiction parallels the seemingly older model used by the Chaldeans and employed the use of runes. Runes were a part of the sacred alphabet that the Norse believed was a gift from the gods of their ancestors and they were believed to have divine properties. For this reason they were used sparingly. The Celtic Calendar (95) mirrors the function of the Chaldean one perfectly. The two are identical and conclusive evidence that they shared a common belief, if not a common origin. The seven points represent the seven days of the week and their runes identify other properties, real or imagined that were enjoyed by the days they signified. One thing of interest concerning the Celtic version is the rune of the *seventh* day, a rune encapsulated within a pyramid symbol. This is beyond coincidence. The Celtic priests, be they Druids or others, must have related the triangle to the concept of *time*.

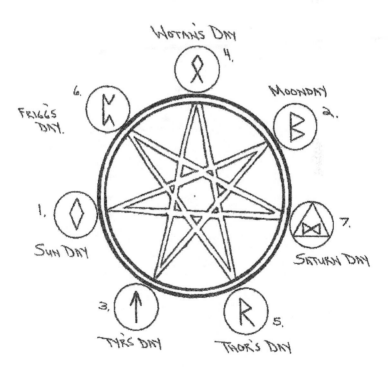

In *Lost Language of Symbolism* we are shown old symbols representing the spiritual fire of the Universe, which, startlingly, is associated with the soul's *goal of ascent*. See Figure A. (96) The spiritual fire is shown to have seven points of flame connected by a thin pillar of three dots. In the next Archive and later in this book the significance of this symbol will become more comprehensible as it reveals a connection to three stars and the inner architectural alignments of the Great Pyramid. See Figure B. for a similar motif which has been described as a bull's head. (97) While this could allude to the import of Taurus in the zodiac, this author is convinced that the effigy is actually that of a *dragon's head*, which would link this to the stellar dragon, Alpha Draconis – the pre-flood Pole Star in the Draco constellation. A circumpolar constellation. The horns artistically, be they of a bull or dragon, identify the two pillars that mark the path to the entrance to eternity. This is why this representation must be that of a dragon. The pole star was considered the celestial gate to God and the realms of heaven, and Draco had dutifully guarded that area of the heavens whereas Taurus' horns are nowhere near the ancient pole star. The stunning alignments within the Great Pyramid as seen in the next Archive make this the more plausible interpretation.

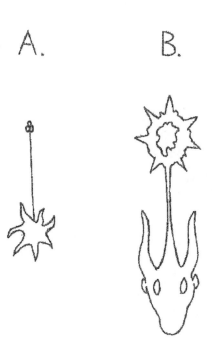

A.   B.

The very earliest appearance of the seven-pointed star is found upon an archaic Assyria-Babylonian seal that depicts a man in reverence to a *pillar* that stands upon a solid foundation. The pillar has a *ladder* painted upon it and the pillar has above it a seven-pointed star-glyph. (98) Intriguingly, the ladder has *eight* rungs. This symbolic ladder, seen in the illustration, is the same as that venerated by the Mystics called Scala Perfectionist or Ladder of Perfection, the favorite emblems representing the roadway to the gods. (99) This ancient seal conveyed that somewhere on earth (typified by the foundation stone) was a gateway possibly in the form of a stone monument (typified by the pillar symbol) that opened up to heaven (typified by the ladder) which would open at a designated *time* (typified by the seven-pointed star) known only to God (inferred by placement of star over pillar). This seal, which was a visual description of the personal faith and belief of the owner, probably depicts himself as the man shown. He knew that time itself must reach an eighth part before he could obtain this hope of gaining access from earth to heaven.

ASSYRIO-BABYLONIAN SEAL

EIGHT RUNGED LADDER UPON A STONE
PILLAR ON A FOUNDATION BLOCK
BENEATH A SEVEN-POINTED STAR

The monument alluded to in the seal is the Great Pyramid, the stone image of the terrestrial number seven. It is the pillar, or gateway that will one day open, merging the world we know now with that which will come. So it should come as no surprise to learn that the standard measurement used in the geometry of the pyramids at Giza was *time* itself.

In a unique work entitled *Beginnings: The Sacred Design*, author Bonnie Gaunt exhibits a startling discovery. An avid researcher into the mysteries of numbers and biblical gematria and how they coincide with features of the Great Pyramid, Gaunt made the connection between the exterior and interior passage angles of the Great Pyramid's surfaces which are sloped at 52°. The Ascending Passage and the Descending Passage are both angled within the monument at 26° and from one another at 52°. Startlingly, the elusive 52° angle can only be produced by one geometrically perfect symbol: the heptagram, or seven-pointed star. (100)

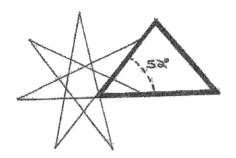

EXTERIOR PYRAMID ANGLE

GREAT PYRAMID

The exterior sloping angle of the Great Pyramids at 52° was a problem for the ancient Egyptians. After the completion of the Giza structures *no other pyramids in the world* replicated this 52° angle. Egyptologists are at a loss to explain away this discrepancy, fancying to ignore all evidence that promotes the view that the Giza monuments may not have been erected by the ancient Egyptians as we have been force-fed to believe for so long. There were many attempts to copy the angle but all met with disastrous results. Many are the mounds of stone along the Nile river that were once pyramid projects, some never even finished. A couple of these projects were documented to have collapsed during construction. The unit of measurement employed in the laying-out of the Giza pyramids was a *solar unit*, meaning, that the unit of measurement employed in building the Great Pyramid was earth-sun commensurate. Presently it takes our planet 365.25 days to encircle the sun, always travelling along the orbital belt at an average distance away from it of about 93,000,000 miles. This is a vast ring we travel, one we call a year, and when we divide 365.25 by 52 we get 7.02. Thus, 52 days is the duration by which it takes our planet to move one-seventh of its distance around the sun. This alone should be cause enough for the serious consideration of a non-Egyptian origin for these structures. Men may have built the Great Pyramids but they did not design them. A Greater Intellect was at work here, One that gave divine instructions to Enoch and his people. The sun is the unit or medium by which we measure days and years and it is vitally important to the earth and all living things. If there be any who have read this far and still believe that men of old on their own initiative could have designed this colossi, the next Archive was written for you. The Great Pyramid was erected in such a fashion as to *never* be duplicated. Ruinous pyramids around the world are an enduring testament to mankind's inability to replicate the works of God.

The seven-pointed star according to Gerald Massey as published in his *Lectures*, page 235, was the *Sign of the Pyramid* and was known to the early Egyptians, who called it Har-Khuti, or Lord of Lights, sometimes as Lord of the Glorified Elect. It was related to the Egyptian concept of the *Eternal Word*.

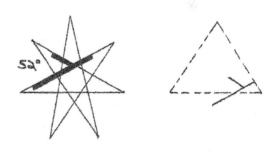

It would indeed be a remarkable thing to believe that the Great Pyramid was a stone prophecy of the redemption of mankind filled with innumerous geometrical mysteries and when translated into rectilinear timelines accurately depicts all of the major events of human history with precision, to find it not mentioned at all in the Holy Writ. This would be a severe blow to this thesis. The fact that the internal architectural geometry is actually a world history timeline has been the subject of several books dating back to 1860 AD but these earlier authors were led by intuition and inaccurate chronologies of world history or inaccurate measurements, so they were forced to fit facts where they "should" have been, as opposed to where they are. If the reader seeks to examine the utterly fascinating proof that the Great Pyramid is a calendar of man's past and future, a large book packed with illustrations, see *Chronotecture: Lost Science of Prophetic Engineering.*

But as to the biblical records and their apparent silence concerning this monument, this is untrue. As seen earlier, Zion was a direct reference to the Giza Complex and indirectly the pyramids are mentioned as pillars in the scriptures. But there is one reference that conclusively refers to the Great Pyramid and no other. In the book of the prophet Ezekiel (29:10) we read of the north-south dimensions of Egypt. God reveals that in the future (long after the 8th century BC) Egypt would be laid waste, the entire country, ". . .from the *Tower of Syene* even unto Ethiopia." The Tower of Syene actually translates to the Tower of *Seven*. Additionally, the stone which was quarried to build the Great Pyramid has long been known by geologists to have been taken from the *Syene quarries*, thus, the description, the Tower of Seven in the scriptures reveals also the source of the stones themselves. The ridiculous argument put forth by some critics that the Tower of Syene is a reference to the Pharos Lighthouse off the coast of Alexandria is anachronistic. The *Ezekiel* text is ancient, antedating the construction of the famous Lighthouse by centuries. The geographical borders of Egypt of old were from the Giza area including Memphis all the way south past Thebes (old Waset) to the borders of Ethiopia.

The more we learn about this monument the more we are confronted with deeper mysteries. This was acknowledged by some unnamed sage long ago, for inside the pyramid someone had written, "I am the herald and witness of God. He created me with human feelings and deposited a mystery within me." (101) This was not an original inscription belonging to the monument, but placed there by someone evidently aware of the purpose of this architectural marvel. There is much more we are not told about the Great Pyramid, information concealed by historians and scholars because what they found was not consistent with what they had been taught, or employed to propagate. There is a nigh impenetrable mystery about the Gizean monuments that begs the question: Why is there so little known about them?

Archive Three

The Great Pyramid of Enoch

Writing on the Wall

At Achuzan in Siriad before the Flood the Sethites erected the Gizean monuments, covering them with texts of the wisdom, discoveries of their time and the knowledge of astronomy and the future. The Great Pyramid was a type of time capsule that protected and concealed an advanced yet original theology that was taken for granted by mankind in the antediluvian civilization. Upon the colossi were placed writings ordained by the Creator, given through Enoch, for the purpose of surviving the destruction of the world. These were the secrets of the distant past, the present, and the worlds to come after the Deluge and far beyond even into the years of the Apocalypse and Millennial epoch. As the largest book in the world it has remained virtually intact even forty-eight centuries after its construction.

The Greek and Roman historians, geographers and writers two thousand years ago and before perplexed over these monuments, gigantic works in the desert of Egypt. Many of them left to posterity their observations and writings. Their findings greatly contribute to our understanding of how the Great Pyramid originally appeared before it was defaced. By the testimony of ancient writers the lower portions of the structure were covered with millions of tiny inscriptions that by the time of the Greeks were already impossible to translate. Most of the information we have studied concerning the writings up the faces of the Great Pyramid have come from Hebraic, Egyptian and various other traditions but they are made believable by their correspondences, and we are not without substantiation from even more credible authorities.

As far back as 440 BC the Greek historian and traveler Herodotus of Halicarnassus eventually wandered into Egypt after traversing the Near East. He sought whatever knowledge he could gather from the antiquarian priesthoods of Egypt. It was there that he in awe beheld the majesty of the Great Pyramid. The account of his visual scrutiny of the edifice conveys that the casing stones were polished and white and covered in writings. He marvelled that these casing blocks were perfectly fit together and polished.

(1). Herodotus wrote that the joints between the casing stones were so close together as to scarcely be seen at all. Almost 400 years later another famous scholar travelled to Egypt, Diodorus Siculus, who wrote that the Great Pyramid was indeed covered in beautiful white casing blocks. He further remarked that the structure possibly lacked a capstone. (2) A few decades after Diodorus, the historian Strabo visited Giza in 24 BC and was struck by the enormity of the magnificent building. He too claimed that the monument was encased in white casing stones. Strabo wrote that the Great Pyramid was ". . .like a building let down from heaven, untouched by human hands." (3) This is a startling statement, for in his days the structure was already over 27 centuries old.

Strabo also wrote that the Egyptian priests knew of a secret door in to the monument, a curiously hinged door disguised among the casing blocks on the north face of the structure that led into a descending corridor. Though this entrance has been rediscovered there is evidence that the Egyptians had long before forgotten where it was located. This evidence is in the fact that there has never been found any authentic ancient Egyptian writings, relics or objects *inside* the Great Pyramid. This is a topic for a later section. That the secret entrance could have been easily lost is now known because of its obscure placement on the north face, high up on the sloping face and not centered so as to prevent detection. Evidently the priests for a long time passed down the tradition of the secret entrance though they had lost its location. The Egyptians also told Herodotus that there was a chamber below the pyramid that would fill up with water from the Nile but this too is but an elder knowledge passed down from earlier times when the secret door's location was known. As will be shown, many pyramid-building cultures preserved this knowledge-that a well or water-source lied beneath the structure.

Strabo's observation concerning the pyramid's appearance as a building let down from heaven is a very accurate description of the optical illusion created by the size of the monument when viewed from a great distance. Long ago when it was covered by the gleaming white limestone amid a barren landscape of desert yellow and brown the heat of the daytime sun on the dead earth visibly obscured the lower portions of the monument. Far away the pyramid appeared to be floating above the solid earth, disconnected to it. As one drew closer to the structure it would literally descend on to the plateau until the observer was close enough that he could see that it was indeed firmly set upon the ground. The highly polished and precision-placed white casing blocks and the nearby reservoirs of water channeled in from the Nile amplified the effect. Pilgrims and visitors were always amazed to discover that the mountain they witnessed from such great distances was actually covered in innumerous smooth white stones seemingly appearing as if they were one gigantic rock. From even up close the Great Pyramid once looked like it was all hewn from a single immense white stone. (4)

Before the diluvian catastrophe that ended the Ancient World the geographical area of what was to become Egypt was the center of knowledge, learning and Sethite civilization in the world. In a unique parallel, *after* the flood this region again became the center of knowledge shrouded in the most arcane mysteries. The Sethites encoded divine secrets into the architectural alignments inside and outside the Great Pyramid, the lesser structures, the Sphinx and huge temples. They inscribed myriads of texts upon its surface and also concealed an ancient library of important writings below the Giza plateau. Though the Egyptian people had been conquered by Amalekites, by Hittites, Amorites, Babylonians, Assyrians, Elamites, all through their history the Nile civilization was still venerated for having cultural centers of learning in their various temple-cities that had no parallels in the rest of the Near East and Mediterranean worlds. This status remained true even until the Macedonian occupation of Greece, Asia Minor, the entire eastern Mediterranean, Persia and Egypt. Egypt as a center of learning flourished under the Ptolemys, also Macedonian and after Alexander the Great became king of Greece, Tyre, Babylon, Persia and Egypt the city of Alexandria was constructed on the Mediterranean and made famous for its incredible library that housed over half a million texts and records. Alexandria became a cosmopolitan admixture of Egyptians, Ionian Greeks, Greeks, Romans, Syrians, Cartheginians, Persians, Jews, people from India and even Romanized or Grecianized Celts and Gauls. Strabo studied there among the halls of 750,000 texts all very meticulously numbered and catalogued according to Manly P. Hall in his thought-provoking *Wisdom of the Knowing Ones*. (5)

Many of the writings preserved in the halls of Alexandria were actually old cosmographies and writings copied from copies, translations of translations that find their ultimate origin as tiny inscriptions once adorning the lower casing stones of the Great Pyramid. An entire Archive later in this book has been devoted to show this. These writings were translated and copied during the life of Abraham, holy scriptures and books of wisdom and prophecy preserved by various cultures and known today as the religious writings of dozens of archaic cultures around the world.

The Roman historian Ammianus Marcellinus, a Greek by birth (4th century AD) wrote about the Great Pyramid claiming that its builders knew of a great flood coming on the world so they dug out deep fissures to preserve the memory of their ceremonial knowledge. (6) His statement was not novel, but the general consensus of all Alexandrian scribes, who had access to histories and chronologies of the world no longer extant.

It was at Alexandria where scholars produced, through patient labor, the famous Septuagint translation of the Books of Moses in the 3rd century BC. These was the books Genesis, Exodus, Leviticus, Numbers and Deuteronomy. By the 2nd century AD they had completed a translation of the entire Old Testament into Greek. Later the Romans destroyed much of the Library but Marc Antony, famed lover of Queen Cleopatra, built the Library of Pergamene at Alexandria afterwards which held over 200,000 texts. (7) Many since then are responsible for the library's ultimate demise, from invasions of Romans, Visigoths, Christian religious purgings and fanaticism and even Muslim occupation of the city. During these tumultuous times many of the texts were secreted away by land and sea to reappear in hundreds or thousands of personal caches and smaller libraries in Europe, Asia and Arabia.

The scholars of the Arabians that filtered into Egypt to study the pyramids and their later counterparts also left us records of their findings that verify the observances made by the older Greek and Romans writers. Masoudi left us the Coptic traditions of Surid [Enoch] studied earlier concerning the building of the pyramids. However, this scholar also conducted his own research of the Giza site. Masoudi's manuscript is preserved in the British Museum as Document 9575 which tells that the faces of the Great Pyramid were inscribed with unknown and unintelligible writings of people and nations of forgotten antiquity, a fact corroborated by the writings of Ebn Haukal. (8) Another Arab historian whose name has been lost to us recorded that the surfaces of the two gigantic pyramids at Giza were covered in inscriptions from top to bottom and that the lines of text were very close together but nearly erased with time. He claimed that the meanings of the writings upon the casing stones was not known. (9) Such an admission conveys that the inscriptions were very old because the Arab scholars at this time were among the world's intelligencia, versed in Aramaic, Coptic, Hebrew, Latin, Syrian, Greek and some even studied ancient cuneiform and hieroglyphics. Being unable to translate a script is one thing, but not being capable of even identifying the writings is quite another, a fact indicating that the inscriptions upon the Great Pyramid were of one of the truly ancient languages. Probably Sumerian. As will be seen in this book, there is a considerable amount of evidence that the Great Pyramid was indeed covered in Sumerian pictographs which were translated after the Flood in the days of the patriarch of biblical fame called Abraham.

Tiny inscriptions grouped in lines close together over all four faces of the Great Pyramid, possibly over the surfaces of the other pyramid as well, would be the most extensive ancient library in the world. The largest book on earth. Had these writings been in any known post-diluvian language then there would have been many accounts of their contents. Even the Arab chronicler Makrizi wrote that it was not known who built these monuments, and he wrote that everything connected to them was mysterious; the traditions respecting them were various and contradictory. (10) These are the records of respectable historians regarding the writings of Giza. These men saw these monuments as they were intended to be seen and they are to be envied for this privilege. What we behold at Giza today is not comparable to the awe-inspiring majesty of the site they had witnessed. Later historians tell us why.

Beneath the Casing Stones

The great Arabian scholars that have contributed so much to the preservation of many records concerning the Great Pyramid are not to blame for the desecration of this most sacred site. It was their Muslim contemporaries who are to blame for the reason these gigantic pyramids appear naked today. It was because of their hunger for newer building materials that no human for that past six and a half centuries has laid eyes upon the monument as it was supposed to be seen. Today only a bare complex remains, bereft of the glorious mantle of highly polished white limestone casing blocks covered in minute writings that dazzled the ancient pilgrims who journeyed to see it and confounded the learned.

In the year 1356 AD a devastating earthquake toppled many of the buildings in the Muslim city of Cairo near Giza. Muslim engineers had the local populace strip off the immense white limestone blocks from off of the Great Pyramids and then haul them a few miles to Cairo to rebuild the wasted city. The stone was redressed and cut and even today, as late as 2015 AD, some of the white mosques still stand, made from the stolen stone of the world's most ancient sacred site. It took the Muslims several decades to removed all of the stone facing blocks and the work left behind hills of broken rocks all around the monuments. The surface area of the pyramids' faces covered 22 acres and the blocks, 144,000 in number, were 100 inches thick. (11) Almost two hundred years later the Turks were stripping the casing blocks left behind, also after an earthquake that had occurred in 1517. (12)

So completely had these people defaced these monuments that debates centuries later raged among the world's scholars and historians over the existence of these casing stones. The pyramids were laid bare, stripped, and their magnificent covering, being removed, exposed their internal structure to all. Levels and levels of darker limestone blocks. Though the Egyptian hieroglyphic determinative seems to indicate the presence of tiny writings toward the base of the Great Pyramid (13), ...

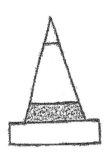

for over three centuries not a single white limestone casing block had been found at the Giza site. This hieroglyphic picture reveals that the pyramid had either a capstone or was intended to have one. The Great Pyramid does not have one. The 52° angle of the monument and the smoothness of the casing blocks would have prevented anyone long ago from climbing its faces. Because the inscriptions were very small in lines packed closely together it is probable that the early Egyptians did not know that these writings ascended to the very top, just as there is also a good chance that they only covered the lower third of the structure's face. The Arabs and Turks left the base of the pyramids buried in rock rubble from their decades-long extraction of the casing blocks, enormous piles of stone refuse and it was not until 1837 that any serious archeological excavation was conducted there. At that time the British Col. Vyse and his crews cleared away the piles of rubble and looked upon the foundation level of the Great Pyramid for the first time in over four hundred and eighty years. They ended the debate, for miraculously, Col. Vyse not only found the Great Pyramid's original base level but also discovered original casing blocks in situ still attached to the structure. The white limestone casing blocks had been buried under the rubble. Their rediscovery in 1837 validates the ancient historians' testimonies. These few blocks were weathered badly and damaged by their burial, but their smooth faces and geometrical perfection demonstrate the unbelievable level of sophistication required to manufacture just one of them. (14)

At this point one would naturally ask, and rightfully, if there were any inscriptions found upon the few remaining blocks. The answer is no. The casing blocks discovered were at the very base of the monument adjoined to the actual limestone plateau. It is not known if the writings were ever on these blocks. However, assuming that inscriptions were present at one time we must also consider that these lowest blocks would have had the most exposure from millennia of sand-blasting, they were within human reach, were under the immense pressure of the rising and moving floodwaters of the Deluge and the runoffs that occurred for years afterward, the flooding of the Nile and Delta and the touching and kissing of the stones by millions of pilgrims that visited the holy site similar to the Wailing Wall in Jerusalem. It is quite possible that over a billion people in the last 4000 years alone have touched the lower blocks. Many others copied the inscriptions they found upon the surfaces and still others had written their own names and dates on the stone.

We cannot ignore that the early Greeks and Arabs wrote that the writings were in their day still perceptible, albeit almost erased with time. These writings were *not* engraved because the casing blocks by all accounts were as smooth as still water. These writings were perhaps burned by some unknown technique or painted. According to Tony Bushby as related in his well-researched work, *The Secret in the Bible*, samples taken from these surviving white limestone casing blocks were sent to the prestigious Norbonne University in France and careful analysis by chemical and spectrographic examination of the fragments determined that there was a film of paint once present on their surfaces.

We have to surmise that the painting used was as sophisticated as the monument itself. These casing blocks were massive, about a 100 inches thick and weighing several tons. William Corliss in *Ancient Structures* wrote that they were ". . .of complex shape, smoothly finished and formally held in a very thin layer of cement of great strength and unknown formula." Even the scrutiny of modern science cannot decipher the mysteries of this monument. We are not much further in comprehending these megaliths as was Herodotus 24 centuries ago.

In Herodotus' internationally famous book The Histories [Book II 124] we read that he was told by Egyptians that the structures were built in three monthly shifts of 100,000 men each and that it took ten years of oppressive slave labor to build the track along which the blocks would be hauled. He was told of underground sepulchral chambers under the plateau, that the pyramid took 20 years to build and was covered in ". . .polished stone blocks beautifully fitted." He was shown inscriptions on the structure and was told by the Egyptians that the writings explained the amount of funds expended in feeding the men that constructed the complex. The entire episode is doubtful. Even Herodotus expressed his doubt in the story. He wrote, "And I remember distinctly that the interpreter who read me the inscription said the sum of 1600 talents of silver. If this is true, how much must have been spent in addition on bread and clothing for the laborers duration all those years the building was going on- not to mention the time it took to quarry and haul the stone, and to construct the underground chamber?" [*Histories* Book II 125].

Mathematicians have estimated that there were 144,000 casing blocks on the Great Pyramid alone. They were several tons each and similar to marble in hardness, though limestone. (15) Though divine, celestial and terrestrial histories and secrets had been written upon the outside of these enormous casing blocks, as well as prophetic destinies and angelic mysteries, it is *beneath* these outer blocks where we discover additional mysteries that even in this technological world today's sages have yet to penetrate and unravel. One of these enigmas is why and how the Great Pyramid came to be constructed of 2.5 million blocks all weighing from 2.5 tons to 70 tons with the heaviest elevated hundreds of feet high in the structure, which stood to an amazing 203 levels of blocks at 481 feet high. High in the structure is the Kings Chamber, roofed with 70 ton megaliths.

Buildings today are made from human manufactured bricks by use of machines. Because of the ease by which bricks are produced we take for granted the extreme difficulty in making them. People today do not grasp the herculean effort expended in the construction of the Great Pyramid. By today's modern standards the blocks of the Great Pyramid are *gigantic* compared to bricks used in our structures. Additionally, these huge blocks are carved from *living stone*. Not a single block was manmade such as clay burned in a mold within a kiln. We burn clay and other materials to make bricks and this method is ancient. Most of the standing structures around the world today, old and new, were constructed of bricks manufactured by men even as early as the ziggurat pyramid-temples of Babylonia. Concerning the superiority of stone-quarried blocks as opposed to mud-bricks structures, Herodotus relates a curious story of an Egyptian king who had a pyramid built to commemorate his own reign, a building constructed of kiln-fired bricks ". . .and on it cut an inscription in stone to the following effect: DO NOT COMPARE ME TO MY DISADVANTAGE WITH THE STONE PYRAMIDS." [Book II 136].

There are stone cities around the world in remote areas of the Yucatan, Central America, in the Andes Mountains of South America, in Mexico, along the equatorial belt through China, India, the Near East and about the Mediterranean. These truly archaic and mysterious cities provided foundations for later cultures that used the sites and built over them. These older cities are unique in that they employed stone blocks and cyclopean building methods stacking cut stones of such size and weight that modern engineers are at a loss to explain how they accomplished these amazing feats. The common denominator between the places of great antiquity is the disturbing fact that they all appeared to have been abandoned abruptly, having suffered catastrophic damage. No megalithic city has remained standing. All have fallen and were reclaimed by the earth and excavated by men, some even restored somewhat but none maintained their original majesty. Only the Great Pyramids can boast this.

The quarrying of millions of blocks weighing tons with a precision that only a laser could obtain, their stacking without damage, cracking, fissures, the transport of this seemingly countless multitude of blocks from the quarry site, their elevation as the courses were built upward, the setting of each block into place and then cementing them all together into one stone with an adhesive 1/50th of an inch thick is *impossible* today. It has been tried by various architects and engineers and the feat even at one-third the scale was a disaster. The most baffling aspect of these blocks is the fact that the builders of the Great Pyramid employed a 0.010-inch precision on the planes of the casing blocks when a 0.25-inch plane would have been sufficient tolerance as it is in modern brickwork, according to William Corliss on page 181 of *Ancient Structures*. This is evidence that the builders of the Great Pyramid strove for *perfection*.

Two thousand years ago Pliny the Elder in *Natural History* under Mining and Minerals 81 remarked that concerning the Great Pyramid, "No trace of the method of building these pyramids remains," and also, "The most significant problem is how the blocks were raised to such a great height." Many archeologists have remarked that not even razor blazes can fit between the blocks. The ultra strong and gossamer-thin cement was applied to every stone, along all of their faces so that 2.5 million blocks became *one stone*. Forty-eight centuries has not weakened the binding between these blocks. Bonnie Gaunt in *Magnificent Numbers of the Great Pyramid and Stonehenge* wrote that this cement can scarcely be seen with the naked eye, and that ". . .the stones themselves will shatter before the mortar will yield." (16) Gaunt is a researcher into the meticulous numbers and numerology of the Scriptures, the gematria of biblical passages and their relevance to the Great Pyramid. It was her discovery that this incredible monument actually identifies itself as the Building of God, for the Hebrew numerical value of HE CREATED is exactly 203, which we now know is the exact number of levels of blocks that make up the Great Pyramid. (17) In fact, the level of blocks (courses) of masonry form an astonishing *calendar* of the Last Days but readers will have to see this author's other works *Anunnaki Homeworld* and especially *Chronotecture*.

Though we mourn the loss of the wonderful white mantle once adorning the Great Pyramid, this loss has turned into a blessing. The white limestone casing blocks had formerly concealed the inner shell of the pyramid's core masonry and hid the monument's only entrance from prying eyes. The removal of the casing stones has revealed to us fundamental characteristics about the Great Pyramid that distinguishes it from all other known pyramidal monuments.

But the greatest mystery of all is that the casing blocks were even applied. These were often 16-20 tons, 100-inches thick and none of them would have fit together so perfectly had any *interior* blocks been misaligned. With a structure the immensity of the Great Pyramid there is supposed to be noticeable defects. Two and a half million blocks. This means that the core masonry, the pyramid itself, had to be *perfect* before the exterior facing was applied. Anyone not baffled by this has never stood before the Great Pyramid. This had to have been effected by an engineering science now lost to the world that perished with the Deluge, perhaps a method of softening limestone to perfect its planes and dimensions. Assuming that 25 men all weighing 200 lbs. all used their own body weight as leverage, these men could only dead-lift one block. This does not consider the movement of these blocks, only a vertical lift. The size of the structure is only a part of its uniqueness.

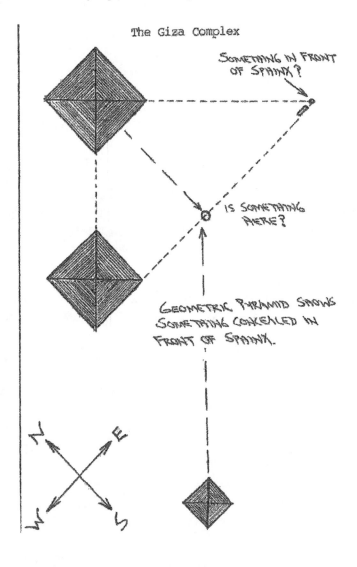

The Giza Complex

SOMETHING IN FRONT OF SPHINX?

IS SOMETHING HERE?

GEOMETRIC PYRAMID SHOWS SOMETHING CONCEALED IN FRONT OF SPHINX.

Enormity of the Great Pyramid

The immense girth and height of the Great Pyramid cannot be adequately realized without comparisons with modern structures and areas. It is the height of a modern 40-storey building, yet it is so massive that it covers a 13-acre area. Or, on another scale, it covers an area equal to seven downtown New York City blocks. (18) This vast monument is heavier than the world's ten tallest buildings *combined*, and according to *Nile Valley Contributions to Civilization* we can build *30 Empire State Buildings* from the stone of the Great Pyramid. (19)

Throughout the millennia of human memory in Egypt, Babylonia, Assyria, Persia, the rest of the Near and Far East up to the more modern civilizations of Byzantium, then Constantinople and now Istanbul, to the European nations, Great Britain and the United States up to 1884 AD, the Great Pyramid was the tallest stone structure ever built on the planet. In 1884 the Washington Monument was raised which stands 555 feet (6660 inches) but this is not a fair comparison because the monument is an *obelisk*, not having the internal passages and chambers so peculiar to the Great Pyramid. But still, atop the 555 ft. monument at the apex of the Egyptian obelisk is none other than a *replica of the Great Pyramid.*

Modern buildings are constructed with the idea of containing things, be they offices, storage areas or housing units. The Great Pyramid was no different, but the size of the chambers and small passages within the courses of masonry compared to the enormity of the structure itself reveals that the monument is virtually solid through and through. Vine Deloria in *God is Red* made an excellent illustration of the impossibility of building such an edifice today. Each stone block was a task in itself but assuming it took the original builders of the Giza monuments an entire day to set in place 20 of these blocks it would have taken *342 years* to complete the Great Pyramid. . . and this estimate does not take into account the actual quarrying of the blocks and transportation time, hewing the rock to precise dimensions and raising them to the courses they were to be set in. Deloria calculated that if George Washington had the fledgling nation begin this project at this rate of production in 1776 then the building would be finished in 2118 AD. (21)

We can more clearly understand why the ancients associated the structure to the World Tree, or Axis Mundi that linked the heavens, the earth and the underworld. In both size and mystery it was unparalleled. It was considered to be in the center of the world, and remarkably, by drawing lines directly east-west and north-south with the pyramid as the prime meridian we find that the Great Pyramid is indeed in the center of the world's landmasses, a fact easily ascertained by looking at a map. (22) The east-west lines drawn from the 30° parallel latitude where the Great Pyramid rests will pass over more dry land than any other possible east-west lines just as the north-south line passes over more dry land than any other north-south longitudinal line. The association to the World Tree and Axis is made also because the four faces of the pyramid face the four cardinal directions of north, east, south and west. The structure geometrically is a wonderful three-dimensional scale of the planet and a geodesic marker that identifies itself as being located exactly where on the world's surface it is found. So precise was its placement on the Giza plateau that the variation of the magnetic needle can be determined by it. (23) Structures built in more contemporary times at 1/100th the scale have not been this precise.

The sheer size and weight of the structure, its cardinal alignments, perfect symmetry and craftsmanship and geographical placement hint of an intelligent design far beyond the capacities of ancient and modern man. Its 52° surface angle maintained to such an astonishing height enduring forty-eight centuries without collapse reveals that it was intended to last, to survive whatever natural phenomena occurred be it storms, earthquakes or even floods. Though this enigmatic building has never been matched among all the structures erected by the kingdoms of men, there are pyramids all around the world that prove by their own existence just how incredible this monument truly is.

Relics From the Age of Replication

There are over three hundred and fifty pyramids around the world. There are thousands of ruinous mounds beneath jungle growth, desert sands, found underwater in lakes and rivers and off of coastlines, many of which could have once been pyramids or pyramidal structures. In Egypt alone are concentrated the most of these ruinous piles of collapsed pyramids. There are between seventy-five to eighty of these heaps in Egypt, some of them largely intact. But there appears to be only one place where true pyramids are found at Giza.

The Egyptian and deeper African pyramids were inferiorly put together, most having collapsed because their builders attempted to amass huge piles of rock refuse as filler. They piled up boulders, dirt and rocks and sometimes broken architecture from earlier structures into large piles that they then attempted to build on top of or cover with facing stones. This method has never served as anything other than a temporary way of erecting outwardly impressive monuments with very short structural durations. After a decade or a century of settling and subsidence the structure then loses its shape. Weight is shifted, internal instabilities occur and the edifice collapses. Such is the story of the ancient Nile civilization and its perplexed architects. Men sought to please their regents with visually impressive pyramidal monuments, and for a while, throughout the life of the Pharaoh the ruse worked but after the passage of time the monuments crumbled to the obscurity we see throughout Egypt today.

The Greeks were they who first called the people of the Nile valley by the name of Egyptians. Originally they were called the people of Khemet. When these early Africans initially found these gigantic pyramids they thought they were the magnificent tombs housing the bodies of great kings or gods and as their own culture progressed they attempted to replicate these colossi for their own rulers. The pyramids built by the people of Khemet at Saqqara, Abusir, Dahshur and dispersed throughout Upper and Lower Egypt and to the south in Nubia never achieved even a fraction of the mastery in engineering that was required for the Gizean artifacts. The various construction methods employed in the now dilapidated ruins that were intended to be pyramids expose for us today the fact that there never really existed any uniform method of pyramid construction by the Egyptians. . . and nor could there have been.

With the Giza pyramids encased within 100-inch thick white limestone blocks hard as marble the early Egyptian copyists had to guess at how these gigantic buildings were erected. Had they have been aware that the inside of the monument was built of millions of gigantic blocks of precise dimensions and phenomenal planes in 203 levels all cemented together with adhesive one fiftieth of an inch thick then these architects might not have attempted to replicate them, or at least, opted to try to copy them more accurately than by using unstable rubble or the more temporal mud-bricks. The fact that rubble was used as filler also demonstrates that the ancient Egyptians did not originally have any knowledge of the Great Pyramid's internal passage and chamber system. So difficult was the replication process that many pyramids in Egypt were never finished, some having collapsed during construction or were laid so incorrectly that their builders became too exasperated to complete the work. The Egyptian pyramids are from 1000 to 1500 years younger than the Giza pyramids, and they are crumbled, collapsed, sinking from unequal weight distribution and are overall visually unremarkable whereas the Great Pyramid complex is still intact even after having its casing blocks purposely removed. Even though the internal structure has undergone stress fissuring from subsidence of upper levels, the unimaginable weight of the mass has not sunk an inch in forty-eight centuries. The greatest architectural achievements of the ancient Egyptians were the temple complexes and palaces of Saqqara,

Abusir, Dahshur and Memphis in Lower Egypt near the Great Pyramid complex around the Delta, Amarna between Lower and Upper Egypt and those of Luxor, Karnak at the metropolis of Waset which is more popularly known by its Greek name of Thebes, and Dendera, Edfu, Naqada and Abydos in Upper Egypt. Also, we must include the Valley of the Kings and the enormous canal works along the Nile. The Egyptians can be credited with these as important and artistic achievements of their culture, however, these are no more impressive than the magnificent ruins at Knossus, Crete, the Lion's Gate fortress of Mycenaea, the majestic walls, palaces, temples and ziggurat pyramids of Babylon, at Angkor Wat in Cambodia, what historians call Mohenjo-daro of the old Harappan civilization bordering India and Pakistan, the ruins of Sumer, Baalbek in Lebanon, and over in the Americas we find the equally impressive ruins of Cuzco, Tiahuanacu, Palenque, Tiotihuacan, Chichen Itza and Tenochtitlan. Truthfully, some of the Egyptian piles of architecture are an embarrassment compared to the relics left behind in Asia Minor, the Aegean and Europe.

The temples, canals and palaces of the Egyptians were awesome edifices because they were *original* designs and projects, not attempts to replicate preexisting structures. Many of their pyramids were mud brick buildings and not made of quarried stone. Stone carved out of living rock has a longevity that mud brick constructions cannot equal. This is especially true when using mud brick as filler. The step pyramids of Saqqara and the 12th Dynasty pyramid of Amenemhet I are a testament to early Egypt's lack of knowledge in pyramid construction concerning the use and benefits of living rock. Amenemhet I even had his pyramid filled with rubble from Old Kingdom buildings. In fact, unlike as with so many other feats of Egyptian engineering, not one architectural tablet or writing has ever been discovered depicting how pyramids were built. (24)

When one thinks of Egypt today the image of pyramids automatically comes to mind. However, the Egyptian pyramids outside of the Giza complex are not only inferior to these, they are not even comparable to those found on the *other* side of the world. There are pyramids on other continents of much more elaborate design and enduring construction in the Americas, monuments that provide us convincing and cogent evidence that their builders not only retained an intimate knowledge of pyramid construction methods but they were also familiar with the idea embodied in the pyramid's origin and purpose.

In North and South America are scores of magnificent and wholly preserved pyramids that have received very little attention by serious historians of the more classical civilizations. These buildings were made of living rock. Because of this they have survived millennia even though the cityscapes around them have not. These areas have been covered by dense jungles and forests. The more famous of these pyramid sites in the Western Hemisphere are Machu Piccu and Tiahuanacu in South America, Cholulu, Teotihuacan and Tenochtitlan in Mexico and those of the Yucatec region and Central America like Chichen Itza and even a particularly ancient pyramid at an Olmec site (25) and those of the North American valley between Ohio and Mississippi. Except for the pyramids at Giza, there are pyramids in the Americas far larger than *any* of those erected by the Egyptians. Also, there are pyramids in the Americas in the most unusual places. High in the Andes mountains of Bolivia is a ruinous city largely carved out of a mountain called Tiahuanacu. No one knows who built the city but archeologists and geologists affirm that it was once a port city that had been thrust into the sky 12,000 ft. elevation since its construction. Breathing at times can be an onerous task and the region is infertile due to the high altitude climate. When the Spanish explorers and conquistadores explored the unusually preserved ruins they were told by the Inca that the city was already present when their ancestors migrated to these lands. (26) Incredibly, even at this isolated locale stands in Tiahuanacu an old pyramid called Lukurmata.

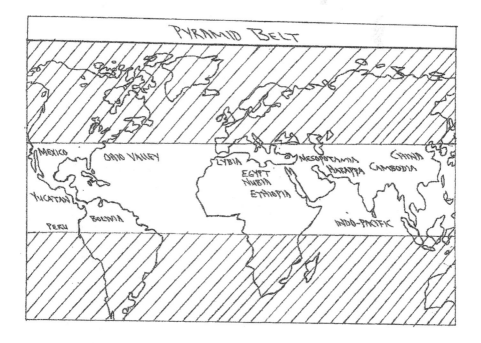

The famous city of the Aztecs outside Mexico City called Tenochtitlan is actually a city built many times over. The Aztecs took up residence in it long after they claim that the Toltecs before them had lived there. They regarded these Toltecs as gigantic men who were very intelligent and knew all the secrets of astronomy and earth sciences. The extensive ruins boast many intriguing pyramidal structures and temples but the real mystery is in why these people called the city Tenochtitlan. This word is a compound epithet conjoining *to send a messenger* [titlan] (27) with *Tenoch*. The latter is also a conjoined term meaning *the man* [te *Enoch* [enoch]. The title of Tenochtitlan carries with it the idea as *Place of the Messenger Enoch*. Though this was not the original name of the unknown city, it was precisely what the Aztecs called it. This could have only been as a result of the careful preservation of ancestral memories and their correspondence to pyramids which were found in Tenochtitlan.

The Aztec glyph for Tenoch was a seven-pointed cactus emerging from a stone. (28) The cactus is the Native American symbol for the *pillar* and interestingly, it is the desert equivalent to a tree. The cactus was a suitable symbol linking the idea of a deity [in this case Tenoch] having the power of life and death with the icon of the pillar.

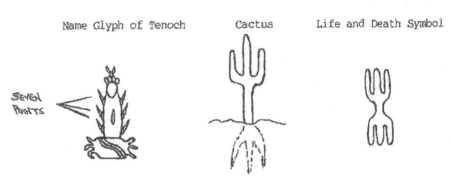

Name Glyph of Tenoch   Cactus   Life and Death Symbol

SEVEN POINTS

Also found in the ruins of Tenochtitlan was a 135 ft. high pyramid with two temple structures at its summit that architecturally identify the twin-pillar concept, linking it to the Great Pyramids of Giza. This is the Great Temple of Tenochtitlan and discovered within it was the stone effigy of Huehueteotl, the old *fire god*. (29) The connection to fire is almost as amazing as the *eye motif* upon the effigy so consistent with pyramid findings all around the world.

HUEHUE TEOTL, OLD FIRE GOD.

EYE MOTIF — DISCOVERED IN GREAT TEMPLE

GREAT TEMPLE OF TENOCH TITLAN

TWIN PILLAR MOTIF

135 FEET

The greatest of all pyramids in the Americas in sheer mass are found in the ruins of Teotihuacan in Mexico where the Pyramids of the Sun and Moon dwarf the surrounding structures. This is an extensive plain full of ruins but its history is obscure, so old that the Spanish conquistadores found the city already buried and the pyramids appeared as hills covered in shrubs and trees. The Aztecs considered the site holy and refused to disturb it. To them it was regarded as the Birthplace of the Gods and they had no recollection as to who built it or when it was destroyed. (30) On the entire face of the earth there is not another ancient architectural site that so closely parallels the Giza Complex in Egypt. This site is on the opposite side of the world from Egypt but it was built with the specific purpose of mirroring the architectural traits of the three Great Pyramids.

At Giza there is an optical illusion that has caused much confusion from those not in the know. The specialist literature always refers to the Great Pyramid but all those who have seen it in books, pictures, video or visually from a distance see *two* Great Pyramids. This is a clever optical illusion causing the beholder to believe both of these pyramids are identical when they are not. There is only *one* Great Pyramid and it stands 203 courses high upon the plateau but the one next to it, thought to be its twin, is actually *elevated* on an artificial platform foundation that makes it look bigger than it actually is. In the ancient Mexican counterpart we find this exact reduplication. The Pyramid of the Sun is gigantic, but instead of being 203 levels of blocks it is *203 feet* high and filled with smaller bricks and rubble. Though it is much larger than the Pyramid of the Moon the latter is upon a raised platform to make it appear equal with the former. (31)

Such a coincidence can only be traced back to some arcane and forgotten tradition mankind shared thousands of years ago, or, perhaps, the builders of this stone city complex in America had actually visited Giza sometime in the dim obscurity of earth's past? Though this is an interesting idea, there is another possibility to consider. It will be recalled that the historian Flavius Josephus specifically mentioned that there were *two* areas constructed before the Flood by the Sethites because they feared that one site might get destroyed by the Flood. Though this association seems purely conjectural we must recall that the site was initially *buried*. Also, discovered at Teotihuacan was an intricate mural of a dragon-serpent lording over two trees with seven branches. (32) These no doubt symbolize the primordial Tree of Life and Tree of Knowledge. Again, notice the prominent eye motif. This serpent-dragon has a protruding tongue, which denotes the power of speech. A talking serpent among two Divine Trees with seven branches below an accentuated eye symbol bespeaks of closer ancestral ties with the ancient Near East than most scholars will readily admit.

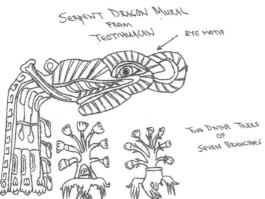

Probably the greatest artifact out of the Americas relative to our study is that gigantic stone disk known as the Aztec Calendar Stone, or, Stone of the Fifth Sun. This mysterious 24-ton relic is an archaic Mexican apocalypse, or Book of Revelation hewn out of rock. Comets, floods, disasters, fires and calendrical motifs all encircle the epicenter which depicts a face with a *sword protruding from his mouth* just as the Revelation text reads that ". . .and out of his mouth goeth a sharp sword, that with it he should smite the nations." (33) We should not be surprised to find that the stylized symbol for *Doomsday* on the calendar stone looks like:

(34) These ideas did not derive from the Spanish but were already existing in the New World before the western European nations began their exploration and colonizing campaigns.

The Americas are not without their poorly made pyramids as well. In Mexico stands the Cholulu pyramid at 215 ft. high but it has a mass covering 45 acres. Except in height it is bigger than the Great Pyramid in Egypt but it is inferior, a heap of earth and rubble covered in bricks, not solid masonry. The pyramids in the Ohio-Mississippi valley are not true pyramids either, more like gigantic mounds of earth and debris where ". . .vast remains of a strange character," have been unearthed. (35)

The American pyramids seem to be older than their Egyptian counterparts. Some even had limestone facing, as did the Gizean structures. In some areas it has been found that pyramids were built over older pyramids, which were in turn built upon the foundations of even older structures. In Volume 1 of Lord Macartney's *Travels*, we read that ". . .in both Americas, it is a matter of inquiry what was the intention of the natives when they raised so many artificial pyramidal hills, several of which appear to have served neither as tombs, nor watch towers, nor the base of temples. . ." (36) This is an interesting comment, and one that Egyptologists have avoided like a plague, not wanting to compromise the sanctity of the ridiculous pyramid-tomb theory. Most of the American pyramids are astronomically aligned with associations with the planet Venus and four cardinal directions. Both the early Near Eastern cultures and the ancient and more contemporary Americas venerated Venus and carefully recorded its movements through the heavens.

The pyramids throughout America are in common with those Egyptian ones outside of the Giza complex in that they did not have interior upper ascendant passages and chambers within their construction as does the Great Pyramid. Many have entrances that descend under the pyramids into chambers, natural rock recesses, well or cisterns. The Great Pyramid was long ago known to have an entrance and it was known that this descending passage went down to a well-pit beneath the pyramid. Civilizations around the world that erected pyramidal structures copied this concept but remarkably *no* one built pyramids with ascending passages and upper chambers, which makes the Great Pyramid a unique pyramid among the many. It was about 12 centuries ago that modern men first learned that the Great Pyramid had these unusual features, long after the Egyptians ceased erecting their own versions and too isolated away from the American cultures which were still building.

This is conclusive evidence that the Great Pyramid was the original, and oneof-a-kind. Such is the principle tenet of Freemasonry—that the Great Pyramid is the archetype, the original, and all other pyramids are merely subsequent constructions. (37) It was the first of pyramids and at the rate by which the others are deteriorating, it will be the last as well. The Alpha and Omega of pyramids. The fact that the entrance to the Great Pyramid remained hidden for thousands of years does not imply that it remained hidden from human memory.

Secret Door to Giza

In the Coptic traditions preserved by the Arab historian Masoudi we learn that the pyramids of Giza had a secret entrance and these accounts give precise measurements in cubits as to the location of this hidden door. (38) This door was designed to yield with the slightest pull, having been ingeniously counterbalanced. But even the force of the Flood and hundred of thousands of tons of pressure could not open it by force.

One of the ancient Egyptian mystery cults highly venerated Amenta, or the Hidden Underworld which was associated to the Hidden One, named Amen, a primordial deity that is mentioned in the older writings of the Book of the Dead. This priestly sect closely guarded the secret of the hidden entrance into the Great Pyramid, called the Door of the Stone. (39) Over a hundred years ago the historian of Egyptian antiquities Gerald Massey wrote in his monumental work *Ancient Egypt Light of the World*:

> The entrance to the Great Pyramid was covered by means of a movable flagstone that turned on a pivot that none but the initiate could detect. This, when tilted up, revealed a passage four feet in breadth, and three and a half feet in height into the interior of the building. This was the mode of entrance applied to Amenta as the blind doorway that was represented by the secret portal and movable stone of later legends. The means of entrance through what appeared to be a blank wall was by knowing the secret of the nicely adjusted stone . . .(40)

The initiates and sages of the Egyptian mysteries truly believed that the Great Pyramid contained a secret entrance to the underworld. All around the world, from cultures of great antiquity and diversity it appears that the universal motif was that there was indeed an entrance to the world below our own, a world of the blessed and righteous dead, and a portal that led into it. However, in this case, it is intriguing to find that the Egyptians believed that this entrance was at the Great Pyramid in Giza. A rationally thinking Egyptian would not have placed such a doorway into another world in any monument that he knew was made by his own countrymen. He would assume that this mystic locale would have been in a sacred place that was *older* than that of his people and culture, as well as their monuments. And this is exactly what we find the world over concerning the cultures that migrated to newer lands to discover stone cities and huge pyramidal structures still intact amongst devastated ruins. These structures were immediately associated to the underworld and its gates. The oldest civilizations on this planet had in common a core belief of the erection of a world pillar which served as the epicenter of Creation that connected the three worlds, heaven, earth and the underworld. All of the pyramidal buildings in the Americas have attendant legends and lore passed down from the indigenous Native Americans concerning their links to the other worlds through these structures. But the greatest link yet discovered is not quite a tale. It is an old petroglyph.

In North America a Hopi petroglyph has been discovered that conveys an astonishing belief. One so old it is unremembered even by the Hopi who still protect it. It concerns an arcane theology involving the ascent to heaven and the likening of this ascent to the image of the pyramid, or artificial mountain with a secret entrance. . . an entrance only accessible *through a god*. A picture of this petroglyph is found in the book entitled the *Book of the Hopi*:

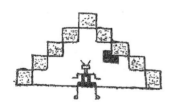
Modern archeologists and historians sometimes have a very warped way of reasoning and view of the world around us when comparing it to that of the ancients. One example of this is the fact that scholars measure the cultures of old America by the standards of western histories and that of the development of the Near East. They assume for instance that because a people may have been nomadic, pastoral or in a primitive condition that this people's mode of communication would have been primitive as well. We are learning today that this is not the case. The ability of a people to become civilized and learn how to communicate using a script language based off of verbal

components does not in any way exhibit that culture's superiority concerning
communication ability. In fact the script writings we use today are inferior to
the ancient pictographic modes of communication utilized by the ancients,
beginning with the Sumerians. We think in pictures. And it's fair to assume
that we would be better off *writing* using these same pictures.

As a culture the Hopi are extinct. Those still claiming Hopi are the
descendants of those who were once a populous civilization. These were a
people who still communicated in the oldest form known to man: by pictures.
The Hopi petroglyph seen here belonged to the Deep Well clan who claimed
that the black square seen within the pyramid petroglyph signified that there
was a secret crypt inside the pyramid. (41) There is no known historical
evidence that the Hopi had even built a pyramid or lived in any region of the
Americas where pyramids had been erected. This memory must be ascribed
to an elder tradition beyond their ability to recall. Preserving these pictures
in the form of petroglyphs has greatly contributed to the longevity of these
traditions.

Of immense significance is that this particular petroglyph was preserved
by the Deep Well clan. This identifies the third link to Giza. First is the
pyramid motif itself. Second is the fact that it contains a secret chamber or
vault associated to a crypt. Third is the preservation by the Deep Well clan,
which infers that they also remembered (or were supposed to) that underneath
the pyramid was a well of uncertain depth at Giza. The Hopi interpretation of
the secret crypt may be true, referring to an as-yet-undiscovered burial crypt
somewhere inside the gigantic edifice. The old Hebraic traditions claim that
both Adam and Seth were buried inside the pyramid complex, Seth having
died in the 52nd year of the construction of the Great Pyramid. The secret
vault may refer to the previously undiscovered ascendant passages that lead
up to the Grand Gallery and the areas now called the Queen's and the King's
Chamber. The mysterious Kings Chamber contained the granite sarcophagus,
though it is known that it never contained a burial. While these are possible
alternatives they are not probable as an explanation for the black square's
proximity on the exterior of the pyramid attached to the facing blocks of the
petroglyphic pyramid. The location of this black square is most likely the
secret entrance into the Great Pyramid, which is not on the surface level of
the plateau but located high up the face of the structure about fifty feet on
the northern face. Additionally, the petroglyphic pyramid's facing blocks are
discovered as if they were painted or had writing on them.

The final piece of this stunning mystery in North America is the name the
Hopi gave to the village where this petroglyph was preserved and guarded.
It is called Winima, or, *The Way Home.* (42) This extinct culture faithfully

preserved a divine secret committed to their trust eons ago. Their distant ancestors knew that *the way home* was by the *ascending* steps of a pyramid that contained a secret entrance that was only accessible *through* a deity who served as a Gate, or doorway into this other realm. . . this door and the ascending corridors of the Great Pyramid were specifically designed by the antediluvian Sethite builders by the instructions of Enoch. The door was to remain hidden until a certain designated time in the future after historical events unfolded that were prophesied to occur before the Flood. These events transpired long after the Deluge. Though myriad traditions from the Old World survived concerning this hidden door and the descendant passages that led to the well beneath the structure, it was the knowledge of the ascendant passages and chambers that remained unknown throughout the entire history of mankind until recently.

Mysteries of the Ascendant Corridors

Over twelve centuries ago an Arab expedition led by the Caliph of Baghdad of Babylon named Al Mamun travelled to Egypt and camped at the foot of the Great Pyramid. They had come for treasures rumored to be hidden within the structure. Others had attempted to tunnel into the structure and had given up. The limestone hard as marble was a deterrent for thousands of years from would-be treasure-seekers.

Abdullah Al Mamun was a unique ruler. He was a scholar and learned in the traditions of his people, the Copts, Egyptians and Greeks. He was an intellectual and collector of accounts about the Great Pyramid. There is every possibility that this builder and innovator was in possession of many of the old writings taken from the Alexandrian library centuries before. The stories he amassed concerned the historical reference to objects hidden within the Great Pyramid and Giza Complex before the Flood. With a sizeable force of engineers, scholars and laborers he set to the task of tunneling into the massive building in the desert having promised every man a share of the discovered treasure. There is evidence that this genius never intended on finding any treasures but was there out of a burning curiosity to learn about the Great Pyramid. More on this later.

The Great Pyramid was in 820 AD just as majestic and imposing as it had been over twenty-six centuries earlier during the life of Abraham, a white-adorned gleaming mountain that was so perfect in its geometrical dimensions and placement that it appeared as an otherworldly construction amid the golden desert sands. Under the direction of Al Mamun the laborers tunneled into the granite hard casing blocks employing various techniques to compromise the integrity of the stone. They eventually penetrated the white limestone casing blocks only to find gigantic limestone internal core blocks of almost equal density. They persevered, though grudgingly. Though the men under his command with every dozen feet grew more and more bitter and distraught believing the structure solid through and through, Al Mamun urged them on.

It was at the point of giving up that something miraculous happened. As the despairing men chiseled and hammered their way into the mountain of blocks a sudden dull thud was heard inside the structure. Something heavy had fallen down. The news spread quickly and Al Mamun and his men furiously tunneled in the direction that the men supposed was the source of the sound. Though hope was renewed Al Mamun's position was volatile. So much labor for so long had produced nothing. The men worked in shifts aiming for the supposed hollow and when they finally broke through they found themselves in a tunnel within the Great Pyramid with absolutely perfect planes that had been sealed off from human wandering and scrutiny since before the Flood. Al Mamun had discovered the Great Pyramid's *ascending* passage hitherto unknown to mankind. Only by the agency of traditions was it known that upper passages and chambers existed in the Great Pyramid, but for thousands of years the Egyptians and other cultures only knew of the pyramid's *descending* passage.

This discovery proves that the Great Pyramid is the *original* one and that all other pyramidal monuments around the world are merely replicas. No other pyramids in the world copied these ascendant passages and chambers in the upper reaches of the structure because *no one had ever been inside this upper area of the Great Pyramid* during those thousands of years when men were building their own pyramids.

The Arab and Egyptian workers soon learned the source of the loud thud that had attracted their attention. Their hammering had caused vibrations sufficient enough to dislodge a massive stone slab that had been concealed in the ceiling of the pyramid's descending corridor. The granite plug was disguised as a ceiling block inserted into the roof of the passage. When the Egyptians investigated the interior of the Great Pyramid and took note of the descending passage, subterranean chamber and well pit below, they walked right under this hidden entrance without ever knowing about it and transmitting the knowledge to other pyramid-building peoples. None of the pyramids throughout Egypt replicate this wonderful feature. The Arabic account holds that they tunneled up and around the granite plugs, a series of three of them, to open up the Ascendant Passage according to D. Davidson in *The Great Pyramid: Its Divine Message* on page 178.

It was this hidden entrance that prevented the engineers around the world from copying the totally one-of-a-kind tunnel and chamber system of the Grand Gallery, the Queens Chamber, the Antechamber and Kings Chamber with the several Relieving Chambers inside the building. The pyramid civilizations as far as the Americas knew of the descending passage with its underground chamber and well and they faithfully replicated these features. It is certain that had they have known about the ascendant passages and chambers then they would have copied these architectural features as well, for the World Pillar, the Axis Mundi or Navel of the World was central to all of their most ancient cosmological traditions. The existence of these upper reaches within the Great Pyramid was a secret maintained by the Sethites that died before the Deluge, a secret probably passed down through the lineage of the survivor Noah and his son Shem, patriarch of the Semitic peoples which later fell in to Abraham's possession, a direct descendant of Shem. In fact, Shem outlived Abraham and personally tutored him, a man born one hundred years prior to the cataclysm when human longevity was measured in centuries rather than decades. The incredible life-spans of the ancients is a subject of *Descent of the Seven Kings.*

By 820 AD even the secret location of the entrance to the Great Pyramid had become lost. It was this expedition that reclaimed it. The Arabs explored the interior of the Great Pyramid venturing down the long Subterranean passage to the chamber underneath the structure deep inside the limestone plateau and found the well pit blocked off by debris. Remember that Herodotus twelve and a half centuries before this wrote that the Egyptians maintained that the well was deep and that it flooded from waters of the Nile. (43) Nothing of value was discovered in the descending passage so they turned their attention to exploring the mysterious upper areas.

The Arabian explorers now searched the areas come to be called the Grand Gallery, the Queens Chamber, the antechamber and the Kings Chamber. These are not the true names of these architectural places, which are lost to us, and nor did Al Mamun's men find anything inside the Great Pyramid. Though no treasures were found these men made the discovery of the millennium. They walked and beheld chambers no humans had seen in over thirty-six centuries.

One of the most profound discoveries concerning the interior upper passages and chambers was not made by the Arabic engineers, but by modern researchers. Salt crystals have been found exuding from the limestone rock from the surfaces of the Queens Chamber, access passage and the lower half of the Grand Gallery. These have now been cleaned out but their presence was recorded by many men who had explored the interior in the last four centuries. These crystals were found to have fossilized microorganisms like protozoa and plankton from the ocean. This was a significant find and one consistent with what we know about the Giza plateau. The common thread concerning traditions about the Great Pyramid is that it was *under the ocean* for a period of time. In the Scriptures we learn that the world was completely underwater for a year. In this author work, *Descent of the Seven Kings*, it is shown that the location of the Great Pyramid complex was unknown after the Deluge until 340 years after the cataclysm when a mighty earthquake rocked northern Egypt. This quake was caused by the raising of the Giza plateau out of the southern Mediterranean Sea that created the unusual delta. Egypt was originally called the *Raised Land*. The original Egyptian civilization was centered hundreds of miles south around Thebes [Waset]. After the quake the raised Delta area, the Nile river run-off created in a flash as seawater created several rivers, the Egyptians found that they were now another 108 miles further from the coast. This new Mediterranean coast is the one we know today.

Several travelers, geographers and archeologists over the years of Giza exploration have noted the abundance of seashells lying everywhere around the Great Pyramid complex. How the salt water seeped into the Great Pyramid is a mystery and this author will not presume to know how. For salt crystals to have appeared in abundance then this indicates a long time immersed and because the Queens Chamber and the lower half of the Grand Gallery were full then the structure would have had evaporating water for centuries. The residual crystals are evidence of this. The facts that no salt crystals have ever been found in the Subterranean Chamber and passage system reveals that the three granite plugs that blocked the entrance to the Ascendant passage were water-tight. The salt encrustation was half an inch thick on the lower Grand Gallery walls and the Queens Chamber according to William Corliss in *Ancient Structures* on page 194. He further remarks that archeologists are hard put to explain how the limestone core blocks of the Great Pyramid retained so much dense moisture content when the limestone plateau and area around Giza is so arid. He too postulates that the pyramid was under the sea.

Inside the Kings Chamber the Arabs found only an empty granite box popularly known as the Sarcophagus. Nothing was found inside of it- no bones, no relics from an ancestral burial, no evidence of anything nor anything even remotely Egyptian. Though this is allegedly the container of some historic ruler according to the Egyptological model, this stone box was found empty. But an incredible mystery lies within.

The Kings Chamber is a mine of enigmas. The architecture is megalithic and imposing. Above this is the Relieving Chamber composed of several vaults divided by slabs weighing 70 tons each. (44) One seeking to enter the Kings Chamber must pass through the antechamber, and in doing so, must bow down or kneel in order to pass underneath the Granite Leaf. Only by this act can one walk into the majestic perfection of the Kings Chamber. The Arabs under Al Mamun found no writings here and no evidence on any treasure. But this does not infer that there are no messages conveyed within this most holy place. The very architecture itself, its arrangement and geometrical alignments are patterned in divine revelations. So many astounding truths are found in the architecture of this structure and the correspondences between geometrical alignments and historical calendars and timelines that this author has provided them in *Chronotecture: Lost Science of Prophetic Engineering*. Only a few more obvious ones are listed herein.

The only piece of furnishing in the Kings Chamber is the granite Sarcophagus, a massive stone box resting on a truly colossal slab of rock that serves as the floor to the Kings Chamber, a massive foundation. One of the most disturbing discoveries concerning this granite coffin-sized box is the fact that it could have never been brought into the room. The doorway is too small to admit the Sarcophagus. This means that the Sarcophagus was *lowered from above* as the structure was still being built. This empty box tells a silent story about something that was supposed to be inside of it, perhaps a body, but is not. Without a lid the box does not have the power to contain. The four corners of the Sarcophagus correspond to the four corners of the chamber itself providing us the sum of *eight*, the number of *new beginnings*. Eight stones cover each end of the chamber and sixteen the sides. (45) The number eight is significant in relation to the earthly time-cycle known as the week. The eighth day is the first of the next series of seven, a new beginning. Eight was represented by a symbol having no beginning and no end. As the terminus defining a seven day week and also the first day of the next seven days that would make another week, the number eight was the Alpha and Omega of numbers. Since terrestrial time is measured in sevens; days, years, 70 day or year periods and the prophetic seven ages of mankind, the number eight signifies the concept of *rebirth* and *renewal*.

The silent message screaming out from the architecture of the Antechamber and Kings Chamber concerns One who was killed but is not dead, One who is accessible to the humble, One who left death behind Who heralds a new beginning to all those who ascend in their journey to seek Him out. The Kings Chamber could more correctly be rendered the Chamber of Man's Inheritance. It is in this chamber that another mystery unfolds.

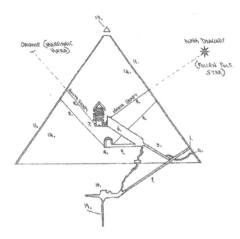

The Great Pyramid: 1) Hidden entrance (Door in the Stone); 2) Al Mamun's entrance & tunnel; 3) Ascending passage discovered by Al Mamun; 4) Passage to Queen's Chamber; 5) Queen's Chamber (Chamber of Angelic Inheritance); 6) Grand Gallery; 7) King's Chamber (Chamber of Mankind's Inheritance); 8) Observation shafts/ air shafts; 9) Descending passage (known to many ancient nations); 10) Subterranean chamber; 11) Original limestone casing blocks; 12) Current outer surface of exposed blocks; 13) Missing cornerstone; 14) Well pit

On the southern face of the Kings Chamber is a small shaft like a telescopic tube cut precisely through 200 ft. of stone, through scores of courses of limestone blocks. The ingenuity required for this laser-precision shaft defies the imagination when considering the fact that the shaft was cut into the blocks *before* they were laid in place and not after the courses of blocks were set. This makes these blocks especially difficult to fashion, their architects seemingly inhuman. Today only lasers could replicate this feat. Archeoastronomers claim that this shaft was originally designed to pinpoint the three belt stars of Orion: Alnitak, Saiph and Rigel. Orion was a type of messianic figure to the ancients. The oldest rendering of the epithet is Urion, meaning "drawn from the water." Orion was the Coming Prince and as a constellation it is the most brilliant in the heavens. It has become a very popular theory that the three largest pyramids at Giza, the Great Pyramids, are aligned geometrically to match the three belt stars of Orion's Belt. Perhaps the theory is older than we think. The Arabian writer Eddin Ben Yahya long ago wrote that each of the Gizean monuments was consecrated to a star. (46)

Opposite the shaft in the Kings Chamber is the one extending from the antechamber and points into the northern heavens at the ancient pole star, Alpha Draconis, or the Eye of the Dragon. Alpha Draconis is far from the zodiacal constellations (47) and it appears to be lording over all the other stars because it was the celestial pivot, a star that did not move as the rest of the starry hosts slowly revolved around it. When entering the antechamber one must turn around looking behind them to see the shaft.

Since 1859 several attempts have been made by serious researchers to demonstrate that the internal architectural measurements of the Great Pyramid are an encoded timeline of the history and future of the world. Unfortunately, not one of these men had an exact chronology to work with and some manipulated historical dates to conform to internal rectilinear measurements within the monuments to fit their preconceptions into their design. Others did not have exact architectural measurements so their dates did not matter anyway. These men were driven with a passion to exhibit this phenomenon because they were inspired to know it by intuition, by the Spirit, but not its particulars. For any who disbelieve that this Enochian superstructure is in fact a gigantic prophetic calendar of the world then they must read, *Chronotecture: Lost Science of Prophetic Engineering* which shows in multitudes of charts the awe-inspiring fact that the descending passage, subterranean chamber, well-pit, ascending passage, Queens Chamber, Grand Gallery, antechamber and Kings Chamber have all been accurately, scientifically measured in minute detail and that these measurements conform *exactly* to a rectilinear timeline we call World History. The Great Pyramid. . . a three dimensional calendar of the future. But because we are now over 48 centuries into its prophetic chronology we can easily see in retrospect how definitively perfect these arrangements are.

By turning backward one looks into the *past*. This is what one must do to see the shaft formerly hidden in the antechamber. To the ancient mindset one looked *into the past* if they looked backwards. This was the chief trespass of lot's wife when Sodom and Gomorrah were destroyed. Though they were spared as a family despite the fact that the inhabitants were left behind to die a fiery fate, she disobeyed the command and turned backward to see the cities as they were destroyed. She could not let go of the past. Her body was burned so fast as she stood in a field of salt from the Dead Sea that she mineralized, turned into an instant fossil composed of salt crystal as organic tissue was replaced with minerals absorbed from the environment.

Hebraic records found at this location among the Dead Sea Scrolls and in the *Book of Enoch* refer to Azazel, an evil archangel that before the Flood was guilty of polluting the heavens for inducing men on earth ". . .to see that which is behind them . . ." This infers that the dark angel appeared to ancient men and taught them the forbidden knowledge and science that caused the ruin of former generations. This belief is traced back as far as the 3rd millennium BC among the Akkadians, preceded only by the Sumerians. The Akkadians claimed that humanity was originally blameless until tempted by the Dragon of the Deep. (48) Prior to this deception the Dragon was the divinely appointed Keeper of Time (epicenter of starry motion) and inside the Dragon constellation was the Eye of the Dragon, the antediluvian polestar. (49) There are Hebrew traditions that link Azazel to another name, Shemyaza, who was judged by Orion and eternally bound for revealing the *name* of God to mortal women. (50) As will be seen, these traditions are also linked to the secrets of the Great Pyramid.

In the most primitive and remote cultures around the world the Dragon was noted long ago to be the appointed guardian and "keeper of hidden treasures on the mountain of the gods; the mount that interchanges with the tree." (51) The dragon archaically symbolizes divine kingship (52) and this concept is as old as Sumer and Babylonia. After the diluvian disaster it became a prevalent tradition which was carried all around the world. The Aztec mural excavated from Teotihuacan with the dragon with a large eye hovering over the Two Trees is merely one of thousands of examples of this idea spread throughout antiquity. In Genesis we find the beginning of the dragon as a serpent that deceived mankind, a serpent that as a terrestrial king becomes a dragon with seven heads toward the Last Days end of the Dragon's reign. Probably the oldest recorded story of the dragon before the Deluge was discovered upon tablets in the famous Assyrian library of Ashurbanipal. (53) He was also called the twisted serpent because of its snakelike appearance in the heavens, a string of stars forming the Draco constellation, which was even mentioned in the ancient Book of Job. (54)

The importance of the Dragon ended with the Flood because of a planetary change. Our axis pointed at Alpha Draconis prior to the Deluge but after the global catastrophe ended the survivors noticed immediately that there was a whole new starry order and that the Dragon had fallen. Now the axis had shifted and pointed at the Great Bear, Ursa Major, which was the new pole star. The Flood that destroyed the world's civilizations was by no means a mere flooding of the land. It was a worldwide cataclysm.

Though this book cannot cover all the details and literature concerning this tragic End-Time event in ancient humanity's past, here is a very concise summary of what occurred. The full accounts are in this authors' works entitled *When the Sun Darkens* and *Descent of the Seven Kings*. About the same time that a large star appeared moving in the heavens with a tail that looked like a divine sword, earthquakes shook the cities of the world. For seven days and nights the people of the earth beheld the approaching sword and brilliant star as the foundations under their feet cracked and the animals became erratic and violent. Volcanoes erupted and pillars of fire shot high into the air and rained ash. The earth trembled unceasingly and entire mountain ranges sprang up as new river systems appeared in days and lakes vanished or others appeared overnight. Whole cities were disintegrated and sunk below the shaking ground while landmasses were thrust upward while others buckled and were buried under new coastlines. It began raining and never stopped. The animals traveled in wild packs, domesticated animals maddened, attacking their masters and children. As the tail of the gigantic burning star enveloped the sky the entire sun dimmed to a dark brown orb barely seen as flames burned across the sky and plasma in the upper atmosphere caused a spectacular display of lightning bolts that scattered across the darkened sky in the daytime and struck the earth in thousands of places. As the passing comet or planetary fragment entered into a full transit between the sun and earth the daytime sky blackened like night, the stars appeared in the daytime, the moon turned the color of blood and gigantic rocks fell from the sky. One particularly colossal meteorite crashed far away and the entire planet shuddered as the whole region we know as the Gulf of Mexico became the burning impact crater. The shockwave literally took apart the entire western hemisphere. The center of Sethite civilization sank below the rising tides and was buried under 40 days of rainfall, the mighty Gihon river raging against the land once fertile covered in woods we call Egypt. The Giza plateau bearing the Great Pyramid suffered subsidence of the entire shelf and was plunged into the depths of the sea we know as the southern Mediterranean, where it would remain at the bottom for 340 years. The violent current during this year-long inundation underwater severely damaged the Sphinx and caused deep water-erosion that the pyramids encased in facing blocks did not suffer. This water-erosion is the source of the erroneous theory propagated today that the Sphinx is older than the pyramids.

A year later the world was a colder place of glacial sheets miles high, covering the upper northern and southern polar regions, extending southward and northward for thousands of miles beyond the arctic and Antarctic circles. The world was filled with mudslides, sink holes, meltwater seas that created vast freshwater lakes. The world continued to settle as decomposing bodies of billions of life forms were compressed under millions of tons of earth. Entire buried land surfaces with broken forests and their occupants formed immense coal deposits and graveyards of pre-flood life forms and flora were burned by pressure, decomposition and radioactivity. The world's oil deposits were created, as were tar pits, and hollowed cavities deep under the ground have filled with natural gases like methane as the world that once was has decayed, fossilized and become gaseous, bitumen, coal, oil or other fossil fuel byproducts. The entire pre-flood world and its once-thriving civilization vanished and the topography of the whole planet was altered. It was literally turned upside down.

It was this global cataclysm that caused the earth to tilt and move its axis away from the Eye of the Dragon. The approach of this object, known to the ancients as *Phoenix*, caused massive geomagnetic disturbances and even several reversals in rapid succession as it was in direct transit between our world and the sun. As the earth was immersed within its parabola and shadow, the gravitational attraction and interference *loosened* the outer layers of our world. People in terror braced themselves as they saw the stars in the daytime. Then the earth rolled, turning over to face the night side and rolled back before Phoenix pulled away and the planet recalibrated. The equatorial bulge was created in an *instant* from this reshaping of the earth's dimensions and when it was all over the new axis pointed at the Great Bear for the *Dragon had fallen.* (55) The fact that the northern shaft in the Great Pyramid points to Polaris [Great Bear] indicated to Gerald Massey over a hundred and twenty years ago that the Great Pyramid was built ". . .to demonstrate the ending of the Great Year and the final overflow of the Dragon." (56) Such a pole shift is found in the ancient text called the *Book of Noah* dispersed among the writings of the *Book of Enoch*. These writings claim that before the Flood the world trembled violently, and the earth became ". . .inclined, and that destruction approached." (57)

The Flood ended the reign of the Dragon, which could no longer control the destinies of mankind. The Noahic Flood was not the cause but an effect of powerful interplanetary dynamics, this other planet not one that travels the plane of the ecliptic like the others but seen in 1764 AD by astronomer Hoffman as it passed over a fifth of the sun's surface in a partial transit and was seen by people all over Europe with the naked eye. Hoffman noted that it travelled on a north-to-south trajectory passing over the ecliptic. This rogue planet on its 138-year orbit has been seen many times and is the topic of *When the Sun Darkens*.

When Phoenix transited it compromised the fragile mesosphere that once protected the earth, a high-altitude water canopy that deflected harmful radioactive particles while creating a wonderful global greenhouse. This water vapor canopy, similar to that like Venus's, collapsed and fell to earth causing the Flood. Genesis is very clear that prior to the Flood the entire world was watered in the morning and evening by a thick mist that emerged from the ground and that *rain was unknown*. The collapse of this mesosphere also caused the drastic decrease in human longevity from centuries to decades. Coupled with this was a decreased metabolic rate due to vitamin and mineral deficient foods due to the infiltration of harmful radioactive particles from the sun that the former mesosphere shielded away. Because of the reign of the Dragon the world had become inferior. It tilted like a pillar falling and the heavens, stars and planets, withdrew from earth visually because the water vapor canopy that had been there magnifying the heavens was now gone. The removal of the mesosphere altered human biology to the molecular level and even now the human genome retains "junk DNA" from those times before the Deluge when we were biologically superior beings.

The Great Bear is a constellation of seven stars revolving around the pole, or circumpolar. What is disturbing is the fact that these stars in no way conform to the shape of a bear but the association to a bear animal was universal among the ancients. (61) These seven stars were a symbol of initiation into the holy mysteries of the heavenly ascent of the soul. (62) As the ascent of the soul was required for resurrection the link to the bear may be due to its hibernation trait during the winter, a type of death during the dead part of the year. The bear emerges in the spring as the cold dissipates in a type of rebirth. It was said long ago that the bears *kept watch* in the stellar stories (63), however, as will be shown, the older beliefs are quite different as to the identity of these stars.

Hindu legends claim that there exists a place on earth where the Lord of Time dwelt upon a transcendent mountain that had a summit that glowed like a tongue of fire at sunset [Great Pyramid with crystal top stone?] and towards where the seven stars of the Great Bear turn their eyes. (64) In old India they were called the Seven Rishis, seven powerful and ancient wise rulers in humanity's distant past that were known as the "seven sons of the Dragon of Wisdom." (65) Max Muller interprets rishi to be derived from a root meaning *to shine*. Before the Flood there was a dynasty remembered by the Sumerians as the Seven Kings. These wicked rulers began their dominion after the departure of Enoch and they were personally responsible for creating the insane conditions and corruption that led to the judgment of God that resulted with the Great Flood. This is the subject matter of *Descent of the Seven Kings*.

The link to the bear may have been due to a phonetic corruption among the nations of antiquity possibly spanning back as far as the Babel holocaust. There is evidence that an initial vowel has been worn off of rishis. Originally the word was Ar-ishas, the ideas behind the star group was not that of a bear, but of *the ploughing of the dawn*. These seven stars were identified as seven ploughing oxen. (67) Phonetically the word bear is the same as baur, or *Father of Light*. In fact, most of the elder languages had the sound of the word bear equivalent to the words for either light or fire. The Latin ursa (bear) resolves into *ur se* (fire light), and the sanskrit riksha (as in rishis) expands into *ur ik isha*, or Fire of the Great Isha. Riksha means bear. (68) These seven stars represented the Gate of Heaven and for this reason do we find in Egypt depictions of a ladder tipped so as to point to the seven stars of the Great Bear. (69) This faith in the divine entrance to the heavens may be why the oldest nations referred to the seven stars as the Sheepfold. (70) As pastoral societies early man envisioned the afterlife as a state of perpetual perfection where he no longer had to worry about mundane needs such as food and protection from enemies. . . things taken care of by the Shepherd of the Flock. And this is the mystery between the Dragon and his enemy, the Shepherd, embodied within the faces and corners of the antechamber, Kings Chamber and shafts.

Below the Kings Chamber, or Chamber of Man's Inheritance, lies the place come to be known as the Queens Chamber. No extravagant Grand Gallery or antechamber system leads into this largely unremarkable chamber. There are two shafts that penetrate through 260 ft. of stone but they do not point at any obvious star groups. As the Kings Chamber concerns the incredible destiny of humankind and their redemption, the lower chamber concerns the other sentient beings in the Creation: the orders of angels known by many names like archons, decans, principalities, cherubim, watchers, guardians and seraphim. What was meant for angelic comprehension was not intended for human comprehension. The angels came before us and entry into the Queens Chamber does not require the travelling up through historical timelines (Grand Gallery, Antechamber, Kings Chamber). The histories of the angelic orders are far more complex than the simplified explanations by theologians. Long prior to the creation of mankind the angels were a part of an extensive civilization, multidimensional with our own solar system being the epicenter of government. The long-held misconception of men crowned in halos with white feathery wings and white gowns is a fiction. Angels are trans-dimensional beings able to transcend our fourth-dimensional reality because they are fifth-dimensional intelligences allowing them to move beyond both space and time. They have passions, allegiances, orders – and have the capacity to disobey them as well. The orders of the angelic hosts have taken sides in a primordial dispute between the Godhead and the first created Archangel, and this led to a devastating war that destroyed planets and billions of life forms. . . all long before anything was ever introduced into the Creation called Man. Our earth is very old with a rich history though in the span of planetary antiquities humanity is an infant.

Humankind was never meant to be. The Godhead made man in His image having an immortal soul, but his body was designed merely as a vessel. The Sarcophagus in the Kings Chamber is necessary because mankind was given over to Death on earth, a scheme designed by his enemies, those angelic entities that rebelled and thought to make war against God through His signature creation. Though the angels were created in the beginning and were never initially subjected to death, being a biological phenomenon, by their own choice did they cast their lots, lose a war and now await the very fate they had initially planned for mankind: death. Though judgment has been delayed it has already been declared. That the Sarcophagus is empty reveals that One had already sacrificed Himself for His flock.

There are some who would object to this analysis on the basis that the angels came first and their own chamber was underneath that designated for mankind. The Great Pyramid is prophetic architecture and alludes to that which will be, not the state of things that are. Angelic beings indeed have deserved a status much higher than those who came later, than humans on earth and scripturally the angels are described as greater in power and might. But this was by God's design. The story of the Prodigal Son is about disobedient mankind going out in the world in defiance of the Father while the other brother (angels) stayed with the Father and did everything he was supposed to. This parable was *for the angels*. When the defiant son returned and begged to enter his Father's house the Father had a great party and feast, gave him a robe and ring and was elated with his return. The faithful brother informed the Father that he had never received these things but the Father replied that it had always been that they were together, but his brother who was lost, had now returned.

It is difficult for people to grasp how humans could be regarded more highly to God than His own angels because people are unaware of the truly astonishing inheritance the redeemed shall receive in the eternal future. According to the New Testament records while on earth we are a little lower than the angels, however, in our resurrected glorified and powerful bodies we will be made in the likeness of Christ, receiving an eternal inheritance greater than that of the angels. In fact, Paul wrote that we will be put into a position to judge angels. (71) Angelic beings were the first Sons of God but some of them fell in distant antiquity, falling from their first estate and became evil terrestrial entities bent on corrupting mankind. Those among men who believe on Him shall receive the Spirit of Adoption, also becoming Sons of God. Created in His image we receive a higher divine status, which is reflected in the internal architectural features of the Great Pyramid. What information is blind to us is evident to the angels. The airshafts of the Queens Chamber are mysterious to us but we do not know what revelations they contain for angelic beings, luminaries that according to the Genesis account were created to be signs to those of us on the earth. (72)

In the *Book of Enoch* we find this a possibility. Concerning the passing of the night sky, Enoch wrote, "I blessed the Lord of Glory, who made those great and splendid signs [stars], that they might display the magnificence of his works *to angels*, and to the souls of men; and that these might glory in all his works and operations; might see the effects of his powers; might glorify the great labor of his hands; and bless him forever . . ." (73) We cannot deny that the angelic mind is one of an *ancient* intelligence with a memory spanning many millennia, perhaps eons before the creation of homo sapiens and most likely with the capability of instant recall. Memory for an angelic entity would not be biologically based with the neural restrictions we possess. What information concerning their own destinies may never be known among men but evidence that our predecessors partially knew of these secrets is found in several Enochian passages. Further, old Hebrew traditions link angels with the pyramid esoterica in that they told that the number of angels that originally fell from heaven and deliberately descended to earth assuming humanlike bodies was 520, and these 520 angelic beings took the daughters of men. This 520 is a duplication of the pyramid exterior angle of 52 by a factor of the pyramid number 10. These angels lusted for human females and sexual experiences and crossed a spiritual barrier that could not be breached once passed through. These angels are forever lost and continually interfere in the affairs of men, maddened with rage and fear. Judgment declared but delayed. Mankind as redeemed is offered the opportunity to pass through this spiritual threshold and take up the offices of those that had disobeyed, inheriting these positions through divine adoption.

Over a century ago various scholars and translators of Near Eastern texts were of the uniform opinion that the ancients believed that humanity was specifically created to fill in the gap left behind from the defection of the innumerable angels who were banished. (74) One of these intriguing finds was the Babylonian *Revolt in Heaven* tablet, which reads, "To those rebel gods [ili: angels] He prohibited return; He stopped their service; He removed them unto the gods [ili] who were His enemies. *In their room He created mankind . . .*" (75) Such also was the teaching of the Gnostics who held that mankind would only replace those Archons, Decans and Principalities that rebelled, becoming a part of the *Inheritance of the Height*. (76) This is none other than a reference to the Great Pyramid, the mysteries of resurrection embodied within its design.

The Hidden One

Though the Great Pyramid is the original of these type of structures upon the face of the planet erected by an advanced civilization buried by the

Deluge, it is itself merely an *image* of what a true pyramid should be. It is a symbol representing an ideal. Even when it had its beautiful white limestone garment of casing blocks with their minute writings the monument was still incomplete. With its over 2.5 million blocks cemented together by adhesive so strong the building is virtually one single stone of many parts it is still only a semblance of a true pyramid and not yet finished. Just as the Sarcophagus whispers to our souls that something is missing, so too does the 30x30 foot platform atop the Great Pyramid hint that something is not quite right.

As a colossal pillar the function of the edifice, at least structurally, was to *support* something of great importance to the earth, and by extension, Man. But this area at the APEX is as empty as the stone box in the Kings Chamber. Architecturally, there should be placed at the summit of the pyramid a cornerstone but there is no evidence that such a gigantic piece was ever set in place. In fact, such a capstone would be enormous, a *true* pyramid because it would be carved out of living rock from a single stone. A cornerstone cannot be a topstone if made of blocks. It would be a true and perfect altar 31 feet high and 48 feet wide (77) and weighing over 100 tons. We know of no other ancient megalithic structure on this planet that requires or has a stone this immense and heavy hoisted up to this 481-foot elevation. If the largest cranes in the world were to attempt to hoist this size of stone to 481 feet over the wide faces of the Great Pyramid it would be a feat unrivalled in the history of human engineering.

The existence of the Great Pyramid alludes to that which is perfect. After its erection 48 centuries ago it was still incomplete because the structure required the placement of white limestone casing blocks to cover the monument to give it the appearance of being a single enormous pyramid. In essence, it was originally designed to appear as an illusion. Only a garment of gleaming white could beautify the body within. Without this clothing of white limestone casing blocks the cornerstone atop it could never set right upon the building. Even if one of the 144,000 casing blocks was off alignment it would have rendered the entire structure an imperfect symmetry. The flawless would have been flawed. But unlike the pyramid structure itself, the cornerstone does not require casing blocks to perfect it. It is already perfect.

If the placement of such a colossal prism is not possible even today then naturally we must look deeper into the symbolism of this pillar. When we look backward to ancient Egypt we stumble upon a profound belief concerning a large stone that fell from heaven shaped like a pyramid. When the Egyptians discovered this rock they found it covered in writings upon its faces, arcane knowledge about the birth of the universe. It was called the benben stone and was linked to *rebirth*. (78) The Heliopolitan cult near Giza at Memphis maintained a Mansion of the Benben and it was held that this pillar was originally made of meteoric iron. (79) To the archaic mind meteoric iron was a heavenly metal holy to God. This stone shaped like a pillar was a spiritual-geographical marker that represented the First Point of Creation, or Place of the First Time. (80) Thus, the true capstone descended, or will descend from the heavens and will initiate a rebirth. Which brings us back to the Empty Sarcophagus in the Kings Chamber.

To the Sethites both before and after this Deluge this monument was the stone embodiment of a prophecy from the earliest times concerning the end of the world and its destruction by fire. It was the fragmented memory of this that gained it the name pyramid, or *pillar of fire*. But this is merely the covering; the surface text to a gigantic book that has remained in plain sight for millennia, an enormous mine of revelations that beckons us to search deeper into its mysteries. We see spiritual truths like as ". . .through a glass darkly," (81) and it just may be that this silent and magnificent monument is a gate to a promise from heaven extended to all on earth who choose to see it.

Secrets of God in Egypt

What the Scholars Have Buried in Siriad

Because the Giza complex is in Egypt it is logical to assume that the Egyptians long ago knew more about the origin and purpose of these monuments more than any other people. Unfortunately, the most ardent enemy against new thinking and reinterpretation of the earliest records from Egypt concerning the Great Pyramid are the Egyptologists. This school of historians and scholars are bent on making all believe that Giza is a cultural relic of Egypt's past, of the Golden Age period of Khufu, Chefre and Menkara, all early dynastic rulers known better by their Grecian names: Cheops, Chephren and Mycerinus. To these men who have a vested interest in having the world believe in the Egyptocentric origin of the Giza monuments it is absolute blasphemy for them to even consider the possibility that the pyramids were not built to house the dead bodies of Pharaohs.

Over the last few decades researchers have attacked the pyramid-tomb theory. These writers are responsible for the rift between the Egyptologists and the wide readership throughout the world that holds that the pyramids could not have been built as tombs. Just as unrelenting as the Egyptian scholarship, these renegade researchers and fringe archeologists are too obstinate to even allow for any other interpretations but their own, none considering that the purpose of the Great Pyramid could be multifaceted with one aspect being the representation of an empty tomb. One, as revealed earlier, that was specifically designed *not* to hold the remains of a body.

One of the battlegrounds between the two differing vantage points concerns the Valley of the Kings. It is hundreds of miles south of Giza and second to the Great Pyramid and Sphinx in popularity. The Valley of the Kings is a royal burial site riddled with tombs, crypts, secret vaults, hidden entrances and deeply concealed subterranean complexes that were once filled with provisions for a Pharaoh's journey into the Afterlife. Early Egyptologists theorized that the Valley became a burial site of their kings in late antiquity because it could not possibly account for all the regents of

Egypt's past. In order to continue their efforts to prove that Egypt was truly over a thousand years older than the other traditional civilizations of the mid second millennium BC, Egyptologists then had to assume that the earliest burials before the Valley must have been within the pyramids. This teaching is propagated extensively when in fact there has *never* been excavated any royal remains from any pyramid in Egypt. Some earlier historians even attempted to place the mummified remains of long dead commoners inside the monuments for others to discover, but these feeble attempts were never persuasive and unusually evidence was found to prove the deception.

The pyramid-tomb theory was simply invoked to explain away the lack of truly ancient burials at the Valley of the Kings site. The evidence taken from the Valley concerning the Pharaohs that were interred there suggests that Egypt is no older than Babylonia, Sumer, Mitanni, Elam, Anatolia or other approximately 4400 year-old civilizations. Egyptian history has largely been molded upon a foundation that lacks authority, ideas born to fill in an apparent void rather than based upon truly existing facts or evidence. Anthropology and archeology as a whole do not support an Egyptian presence beyond 2500 BC. Egypt's great age is only attested to in Egyptian mythology and records of late Grecian antiquity; no other national archives from the Old World support their claims to high antiquity. Such collaboration should have been found somewhere, perhaps in the thousands of ancient stone writings of Ashurbanipal's library, the Sumerian library of Nippur, the Canaanite Ras Shamra library or archaic tablets of the Ebla library, the Amarna documents of Egypt or even the biblical records. Even the Pyramid Texts and Edfu inscriptions speak of a civilization predating Egypt, curious writings that will later be detailed in this archive. Nowhere is Egypt's claim to high antiquity validated.

One of the world's most undisputed authorities of Greek mythology and researcher of the world's oldest theological systems is Robert Graves, who in his epic work entitled *The White Goddess* wrote, "Egyptian texts and pictorial records are notorious for their suppression or distortion of popular beliefs." (1) This is seen clearly in that the scholars today claim that Egypt's dynasties stretch back to 3150 BC to what they term the Early Dynastic Period which lasted to about 2686 BC. The problem they confront is that the burials at the Valley of the Kings merely date back to the Middle Kingdom (ca. 2040 to 1780 BC) beginning with Thutmose I. (2) The historians had no choice but to create an Old Kingdom that buried their kings in pyramids, which is nothing but good ol' scholarly fiction based off zero evidence. As we will see later in this work, the first so-called dynasties of Egypt were actually borrowed, these records mirroring the earliest dynasties of other Near Eastern cultures. Egypt can only truly claim that it is but a part to a whole, sharing a common origin traced back to a single elder civilization.

Egypt's great age is made more dubious by some other important facts. First, there are no known liturgies revealing life beyond the grave until the *end* of the Old Kingdom, about 2155 BC. (3) This is not as it should be. Assuming Egypt is as old as they claim, and at a highly developed state of civilization as to have erected the Gizean monuments, then liturgies should be discovered *everywhere*. Is this not controversial? Is this not hypocrisy to state on the one hand that a culture could have built a monument the size and precision of the Great Pyramid for the purpose of burying a ruler and preparing him for his afterlife journey while also knowing on the other hand that there existed no writings in ancient Egypt at that time depicting a belief in life after death?

Part of the confusion was specifically introduced by the scholars of Egyptology. At a rather insignificant pyramid attributed to Unas, an early Egyptian ruler were discovered what have become popularly known as the Pyramid Texts. This pyramid is at Saqqara near Giza in Lower Egypt. These Pyramid Texts have absolutely nothing to do with the Giza monuments. Because the pyramid of Unas is far inferior to those of Giza the historians and archeologists automatically claim that Unas ruled before any of the Giza pyramid builders basing their conjecture upon the premise that the pyramid building art followed an evolutionary path from small and inferior to the colossal edifice of the Great Pyramid itself. What is truly curious, if not outright suspicious is why Egyptologists do not comment on why the Great Pyramid and its adjacents do not have inferior inscriptions or hieroglyphs. In fact, no writings have been found within the Giza complex pyramids. (4) The real irony is that we are told that Egypt's dynasties are based upon fact, however, it is a fact that Egypt's history was never recorded as a series of consecutive events measured out linearly as we have with the present Gregorian Calendar or older Julian Calendar. In Egypt, each calendar began with the reign of a newer Pharaoh after the death of the earlier ruler. (5)

The records of the Hebrews do not support Egypt's claims either. In the *Book of Jasher*, writings of Jubilees, the various testaments of the Patriarchs, the Torah, Midrashic and Talmudic writings, there is no reference at all to the burying of Egyptian Pharaohs in pyramids. This is a startling fact due to the historic ties these people had with ancient Egypt. In the Testament of Simeon we learn that at his death he was put in a coffin with the bones of Joseph which were in the "tombs of the kings," in Egypt. These tombs were religiously guarded by the Egyptians. (6) All of the patriarchs that died in

Egypt were buried in the tombs of the kings of Egypt because Joseph was highly venerated by the Egyptians, having virtually become one of their greatest rulers, second only to Pharaoh. According to the Book of Jasher the surviving Hebrews in Moses' time were commanded to take these bodies out of the tombs and carry them with them from Egypt to Canaan to bury them with their forefathers, at the city of Hebron. This leads to a very interesting fact concerning Egypt's claims to high antiquity. Hebron was anciently called Kirjatharba in the days before the Israeli occupation of Canaan, named after a legendary patriarch of the Anakim giants who was named Arbah, the father of Anak. In the book of Numbers we learn that the Egyptian city of Zoan was built seven years *after* Hebron in Canaan. This statement has baffled scholars for centuries because it has nothing to do with the text. Biblical Zoan has been identified by Egyptologists as the city of Tanis and this intriguing statement was most likely inserted into the text because even in those early centuries after the construction of Hebron in the days of Abraham's fathers it was a prevalent teaching among the Egyptians that they were older than their contemporaries, an ancientness the author of Numbers sought to show was untrue. The Hebrew records clearly detail how the cities of Canaan were built first, then Egypt was occupied by seven nations all kin to each other that in the 19th century participated in a war for the Nile regions. The people of Khemet won out, successfully ousting cultures that later came to occupy Philistia, Crete, Libya, Nubia and many areas of the Aegean. One of the oldest surviving records concerning this early conflict is found in the writings of Flavius Josephus in his notes on the Ethiopic war. Also we find remnant traditions of this olden war in the fragmented Grecian myths.

Probably the most profound enigma is how the scholars have so adamantly, without any debate or peer refutation, portrayed the Great Pyramid as being the intended tomb of a Pharaoh Cheops. The actual stele of Cheops claims there was already a pyramid at the Giza site prior to his own reign. (7) Incredibly, though this is supposed to be the largest tomb in the world, historians claim that Cheops feared that his own people would desecrate his pyramid and burial site because they were discontented with his reign, so he was secretly buried in an elaborately cut sepulcher a thousand feet away. (8) This is a ridiculous notion, and to think it is actually passed off as serious scholarly consideration. A pyramid the size and majesty of the Great Pyramid was built by a culture that hated its ruler and this regent was then buried in a lesser construction nearby because he feared his tomb would be desecrated and his remains forever lost before they could be granted access to the Afterlife. Preposterous. A hypothesis completely built from a vague reference in Herodotus' writings that claim that the Egyptian people so completely hated Cheops and Chephren that they "...will not even mention their names." One must be invested with a tremendous amount of blind faith to accept the idea that Cheops or Chephren had anything at all to do with these monuments.

Despite the efforts of modern scholars, redactionist historians and archeologists and their united effort to bury the truth in Siriad, there stands today a quiet artifact from the ancient world from before the Deluge that cannot be buried and concealed. There still stands a guardian at Giza that protects over the secret purpose of the Great Pyramid.

Guardian of the Deep

At 240 ft. long and 66 ft. high, carved out of living rock, the Sphinx is the largest and oldest statue from the Old World still intact. (9) Over 2,000 years after the Sphinx was made the Egyptians erected a 68 ft. statue at Thebes (not to be confused with the Greek Thebes), which is now fallen and crumbled. Also, the Greeks at Olympia constructed a seated statue of Zeus (the Roman Jupiter) that stood at 68 ft. in height, which likewise has not survived. (10) It is a testament to the ingenuity of pre-flood engineers that this relic, exposed to weather and catastrophic conditions for over four millennia, that it should remain largely intact though statues built almost a thousand years after the flood have long since perished.

The Sphinx identifies a very old concept recorded in the book of Genesis. After mankind rebelled against the ordinances of God and ate from the Tree of Knowledge of Good and Evil, "...their eyes were opened," and they then knew that they were naked. No longer fit to reside in paradise (the walled garden), they were banished from Eden. Because the Tree of Life by virtue of its fruit could sustain them forever, they were sent out of the garden and at the entrance was placed a guardian cherub with a flaming sword at the east of Eden to prevent them from obtaining access back to the Tree of Life. The Cherub's duty was to protect the interests of God from defilement, for mankind had become unclean (was naked), and now because of the knowledge of sin and rebellion man had to be clothed in a new garment before entering back into the paradise of God. The Sphinx even today faces the east, toward the rising sun, which is typified in many archaic beliefs as the fiery flaming sword of antiquity before the image of these two most sacred *trees* (two large pyramids).

The Hebrew cherubim find their origin in the Akkadian *karibu*, sphinxes that acted as guardians of temple entrances. (11) They were exclusively placed at the eastern entrances of palaces and temple precincts. (12) Interestingly, some Babylonian temples guarded by cherubim were called "...the Temple of the Great Tree." (13) In the Near East these cherubim conveyed a twofold meaning inferring that their presence protected inaccessible areas forbidden to sinful men while also signifying that by passing by them and entering the temple courts that they guarded, the truths of the priesthood and its mysteries were indeed accessible. A further embellishment linking to Genesis narratives is that many temples in Old Babylonia had priestesses in the entrances that enticed passersby to enter by holding out fresh apples in exchange for temple "truths," a ritual in commemoration of the Mother of All Living (Eve) and her taking of the fruit of the Tree of Knowledge, a very old concept known by the Babylonians and their predecessors. Some of these priestesses were charged with having sexual relations with temple visitors in a darkly twisted theology that brought more offerings to the priesthood, for when men accepted the gift of the apple from the female he was admitted into the inner sanctuary of the premises and rewarded by carnally "knowing" the priestess, a practice of sacral prostitution directly linked to the belief in the Genesis narratives. This knowledge of carnal relations with the girl came with a price that was paid to the temple. This sacral prostitution was practiced early on and was a main component to the goddess religions that served to teach men that knowledge was gained through females, priestesses who in turn received divine knowledge from the gods themselves much in the same fashion as Eve received information from the deceitful serpent. As a divine protector, the cherub sphinxes became a very popular household item. Some artisans and merchants made their living by carving and trading miniature replicas of them. In biblical writings they are referred to as *teraphim* (guardian divinities of the gate), named after Terah, the father of Abraham. In Hebraic writings like the Book of Jasher we learn that Terah was a religious worshipper of these idols and although he was a general of the armies of Babylonia and was a Chaldean, he was rebuked by his son Abram who smashed all his idols.

The original tradition associated with the Sphinx was that it was a Watcher. These angelic beings were of an order of heavenly guardians entrusted with protecting the interests of God on earth, but some of them fell and induced mankind to worship them through their forbidden knowledge, as opposed to the Creator. Arabic beliefs seem to be linked to these traditions for the name by which they called the Sphinx was *Abu 'l hol*, meaning Father of Terror. (14) This epithet alludes to the duty of cherubim to terrify men from entering the holy places consecrated to God. The Arabic title derives from the Egyptian word for *guardian* (hu). (15)

The word sphinx is not at all an Egyptian word but was the Grecian title given to the monument that was in itself based off of a false etymology in reference to an old story about the statue strangling a man for not being able to answer a riddle. These people thought the statue bestowed secrets of great importance to travelers in the forms of riddles, which are images of truth artistically concealed within puns, allegories and metaphors. Thus, the Greeks of later times believed the meaning of the Sphinx was "throttler," when in fact, the word actually means *to bind closely together*. (16) This meaning identifies the Sphinx as a Watcher, for in occult writings based off of ancient traditions the Watcher guardian was to protect portals ". . .that link worlds together." (17)

In the Egyptian *Book of the Dead* are torturous guardians of portals in the world of the dead that attempt to keep disembodied spirits from passing through into the Other World. (18) Such protectors were used in Egypt's temple complexes also and were called Aker lions, which were sphinxes placed before doors and gates. The Aker statues were "keepers who open and shut the gates," into the worlds of "yesterday, today and tomorrow." (19) Remarkably, the ancient title of the Sphinx given by Egyptians was Aker because it was believed by them that the gigantic statue stood atop the underworld which was also called Akar. Gerald Massey in his Ancient Egypt Light of the World wrote that the Sphinx protected the secret of earth's beginning from the Abyss (the Deep) and that it was carved ". . .out of the rock at *the center* of the earth to commemorate that sacred place of the creation." (20) Perhaps this is further alluded to in the *Book of the Dead*, which reads, "Hail, Lord of the Shrine which standeth at the *middle of the earth*! He is I, and I am He." Such a shrine would refer to the Great Pyramid which the Sphinx guards. Massey also wrote that an Egyptian text called the Ritual teaches that the mystery of the Sphinx ". . .originated with the mount of earth [pyramid] as the place of passage, of burial, and of rebirth. . ." (21) That it was known that God had set a Watcher to guard this place of passage connecting the Abyss to earth and earth to the heavens seems to be implicated in the book of Job where the patriarch asked, "Am I a sea [yam] or a sea monster, that thou settest a watch over me?" The word chosen by Job to describe the sea, *yam*, literally refers to ". . .the heaven-assaulting sea, the tumultuous primitive Abyss." (22)

The assigning of the pyramid directly behind the Sphinx to Chepren by Egyptologists is directly related to excavations conducted around the statue. Over 3,500 years ago the first recorded excavations were carried out. Thutmose IV discovered an early restoration stela near the Sphinx that claimed that in very remote times the statue was in very bad need of repair. Thutmos was also called Tahtmes, and in the Stele of Tahtmes IV we learn that this gigantic statue belongs to Khepera, ". . .the very mighty, the greatest of spirits, and the most august . . ." Khepera was regarded as the sole power that was worshipped as eternal. (23) This account serves to show that the Sphinx was found by the earliest Egyptians. It was incredibly mysterious, even provoking early Pharaohs to worship it as a god. These old rulers were baffled as to its age. (24) Its existence points to an elder tradition among the Egyptians of a Supreme Being, for *being* is the meaning of the word in Egyptian (25), from a root [khepr] that means *transformer*.

Egyptologists adhere to the assumption that the pyramid behind the Sphinx belonged to Chephren only because the restoration stela bore the syllable *khaf*, a meaningless piece of the text that they claim signifies the name Chephren despite the absence of the necessary cartouche that is supposed to surround a royal or deified name. (27) A single syllable not even qualifying as a hypothetical piece of evidence has evolved beyond theoretical status to become passed off in all the history books as fact, and this, despite that the earliest people calling themselves Egyptians (people of Khemet) recorded that the Sphinx and pyramids were more ancient than Chephren. Even the later Greeks knew the Sphinx was not of Egyptian origin, believing that this silent but colossal statue was solely responsible for killing the ancients, (28) referring to the Great Deluge.

The Stele of Tahtmes declares that the Sphinx was built to commemorate the sacred place of creation, or literally, "of the First Time." This holy site is said to go back to the time of the Masters of Kher, or Kar which, as a divine locality identifies the Neter Kar of the underworld abyss, a place of ". . .exit from Amenta." This Amenta is the hidden underworld, the grave of man's lost world [as Eden is]. (29) It was also where the dead are raised again to inherit a second life. In Amenta it is the duty of the gods to ". . .assign thrones to the spirits, and to banish the damned to a place set apart for them, and to destroy their bodies." (30) In Amenta is located the Great Deep. (31) Taking all of this into consideration we see why the earliest Greeks called this statue a *sphinx*, for it was the duty of this guardian "to bind closely together" the world of the spirit with that of men.

Archeological evidence affirms the extreme antiquity of the Sphinx and the monuments of Giza about it. Seemingly dateless temples near the sphinx and pyramids are enormous and exhibit signs that long ago when they were still old they were restored with great slabs of stone added to their edifices to prevent further erosion but these were again taken by later generations for building materials. Though the Egyptians may have renovated these colossal structures, they did not build them. In 1912 another huge temple was excavated and the stones of its construction were bare of all decoration, one measuring 25 ft. long. This temple was carved out of solid rock. (33)

An inscription discovered long ago by the Egyptians tells us that the temple was discovered by them in a time when the Sphinx was in bad need of repair (as was already mentioned). (34) Colin Wilson in his *From Atlantis to the Sphinx* wrote that these temples have no architectural identifiers linking them to Egyptian masonry methods or designs. Unlike the elaborately carved cylindrical columns seen all throughout Egypt's oldest surviving buildings, the columns found at Giza from beneath the sands are devoid of all writings and are rectangular. This is definitely not characteristic of Egyptian artisanship. Further, these temples around the pyramids and Sphinx are constructed of stones weighing 200 tons each. (35)

Frederick Haberman in *Tracing Our Ancestors* on page 63 wrote that the Sphinx is the most important symbol of Eden on earth that we have left, constituting a link between paradise lost and paradise regained. The Sphinx with a body of a lion and the head of a woman symbolizes nothing less than the prophecy that from the "seed of the woman" shall come the *Lion of the tribe of Judah* to crush the head of the serpent. Haberman wrote that for millennia [49 centuries] it has faced east watching for *His* return.

Giza's mysteries are yielding to the light of discovery. But the Sphinx alone cannot unlock its secrets. The paradox lies in that though the Egyptians did not build these monuments, it is with ancient Egypt's oldest inscriptions that we find the keys to understanding the Holy Mysteries of God and the message and purpose of the Great Pyramid. Sometime in Egypt's obscure past they were visited by one who knew these secrets and he passed to them the meanings of these mysteries, and though later generations had lost the interpretations to these teachings, they had faithfully preserved them for future people to study and comprehend.

Just as Giza is intimately associated with the realms of the dead, so now will we learn from the esoteric and truly arcane teachings of the Egyptian *Book of the Dead.*

Testimony of Thoth

The Egyptian equivalent to the Greek god Hermes was Thoth. As an Egyptian Enoch, Thoth was the Lord of the Divine Books, a mathematician who computed times and seasons, ordained laws for the heavenly bodies, invented the arts and sciences and as the Scribe of the Gods he was known as the chronicler of heaven and earth. (36) The Alexandrian schools regarded Thoth as the author of all the ancient books in the world. (37) Thoth was actually called in the texts as Tehuti and his name meant "the measurer," but others claim it is more accurately rendered as "erecting." (38) Thoth represented divine intelligence, and the oldest rendering of the name was Taut, which identifies him as a god of *pillars*. (39) As Egypt's most popular figure among the earliest gods, Thoth was said to have built the city of Thebes. The Alexandrian Greeks considered Thoth to have been a human. (40) Plato described him as a conveyer of souls and messenger god who invented arithmetic, geometry and astronomy. (41) Incidentally, the two numbers greatly associated to Enoch were also connected to Thoth by the Egyptians, being 8 and 52, sums related to specific secrets in the mysterious chamber now called the King's Chamber. (42)

It has long been held that the vast archives of Egyptian esoteric literature come down to us in the collection known as the *Book of the Dead* were authored by Thoth, which, originally having been inscriptions, date back to the First Dynasty. Wallis Budge in his translation of these writings wrote that the origin of these works were very old even in the reign of Semti, an Egyptian king of the First Dynasty. This collection of texts was originally so incredibly vast that it required extensive abbreviation just to condense the writings into a format usable to early scribes when they covered temple walls, crypts and pillars with these inscriptions. The archive was copied, recopied, added to and abbreviated more and so forth for a period of thousands of years. (43) Budge further speculated that the Book of the Dead antedates even the reign of Mena, first king of Egypt. This is a significant claim for the Egyptian Mena is the same as the Semitic Anam, who according to the Book of Jasher was the first king of Egypt who had a son named Oswiris. (44)

Anthony T. Browder in *Nile Valley Contributions to Civilization* on page 269 declares that the correct translation of the title the Book of the Dead is actually *Book of Life*, and Albert Churchward in *Origin and Evolution of Freemasonry* refers to the ancient corpus of writings as the *Ritual or Resurrection of Life*, claiming on page 169 that it was originally composed *before* the First Dynasty and that it had suffered much editing.

The Book of the Dead contains secrets of the afterlife, burial and rebirth, and the Other World. All Egyptians, whether king or ploughman, queen or maidservant, lived with its teachings and was buried in accordance with its instructions. (45) It is the *origin* of these fantastic writings that is the true enigma for the Book of the Dead contains fragments and concepts that are definitely not Egyptian. Even the earliest Egyptians attested as much. Archeologists discovered within 11th Dynasty coffins inscriptions that specifically claimed that portions of the Book of the Dead had been "discovered" during the reign of Hesep-ti, the fifth king of the First Dynasty. (46) When portions of the

Book of the Dead were found in this remote period it was ". . .as a wonderful object. . . a thing of great mystery, the like of which had never before been seen or looked upon." (47) Because these inscriptions were initially found upon this wonderful object, and these writings were so extensive that they required editorial abbreviation we can easily assume that they were found inscribed upon the face of some monument. While this serves to allude to the discovery of the Great Pyramid beneath the sands of the desert after the Deluge, our most powerful evidence linking Giza to the Book of the Dead are the writings themselves. Even one hundred and twenty-five years ago historians theorized that some parts of the Genesis text may have been taken from ". . .some of the traditional wisdom said to have been contained in the sacred books of the Egyptian Thoth, and the records engraved upon the pillars of Set." (48) These pillars of Set are actually the pillars [pyramids] of Set[hites]. The title Book of the Dead was not the original name of this collection of vast texts. The abbreviated versions of these inscriptions came to be known as the *Book of the Dead* because of the *origin* of these particularly ancient writings. . . from off the faces of a monument built by the ancients who died in the Great Flood. The dead were the authors of these writings.

In *The Secret of the Bible* author Tony Bushby relates that the *Book of Thoth* [Enoch] was taken from off of the surfaces of the Great Pyramid and that an ancient name for the Book of the Dead was Per-am-rhid, the phonetic origin of *Pyramid*.

Though scholars claim Moses authored the Genesis text it must be conceded that nowhere in Scripture did Moses claim authorship. There is more evidence that portions of Genesis formed a larger work detailing pre-flood history than there is to claim that the earlier parts of the text were written in the 14th century BC by Moses. Catholic scholar J.T. Milik made a startling discovery concerning portions of the Genesis record. After researching Enochian fragments from various sources of different translations, Milik, in 1976, published his conclusions in a 400 page tome that shows the book of Genesis contains abbreviated versions of the Enochian records and not the other way around. (49) It has long been theorized that the Enochian books were composed during the Alexandrian era, none considering that it is more probable that scribes and translators at Alexandria merely translated very old copies of earlier copies that span back millennia. It was the seat of the most extensive libraries in the ancient world. Milik's discovery was mentioned in Elizabeth Clare Prophet's book *Fallen Angels and the Origins of Evil* as well as a curious reference to Augustine's work entitled the *City of God* wherein Prophet shows that it was known to the early Church fathers that Enoch did leave behind divine writings but they had not been included into the canon of Scripture because they were so old that ". . .their antiquity brought them under suspicion." (50)

POST DELUGE CRADLE OF
CIVILIZATION [MESOPOTAMIA]
2300 - 1700 B.C.

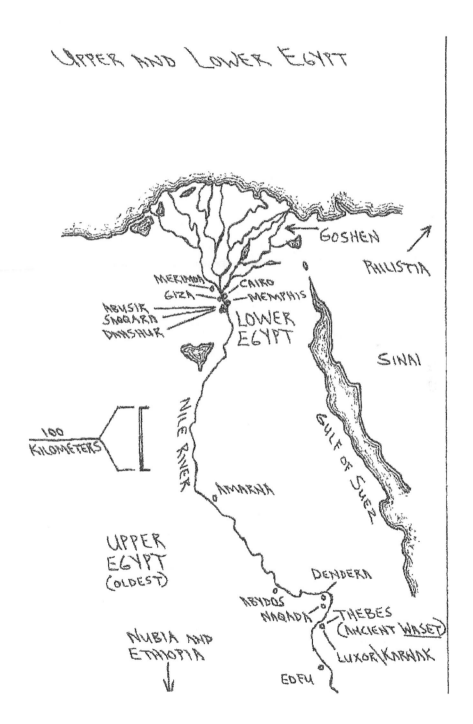

UPPER AND LOWER EGYPT

GOSHEN

PHILISTIA

MERIMDA
GIZA
CAIRO
MEMPHIS

ABUSIR
SAQQARA
DAHSHUR

LOWER
EGYPT

SINAI

100
KILOMETERS

NILE RIVER

GULF OF SUEZ

AMARNA

UPPER
EGYPT
(OLDEST)

DENDERA

ABYDOS
NAQADA

THEBES
(ANCIENT WASET)

NUBIA AND
ETHIOPIA

LUXOR/KARNAK

EDFU

It is within the writings of the Book of the Dead that we see with perfect clarity the origin of the Hebraic beliefs that a pillar was erected in Siriad in the middle of the earth that served as a gate to heaven and a border between heaven and earth. In the pyramid of Teta we read, "When Teta hath purified himself on the *borders of this earth* where Ra hath purified himself he prayeth and setteth up a ladder. . ." (51) This reference to a ladder is also found in the pyramid of Pepi I, where we read, "Hail thee, O Ladder of God; stand up, O Ladder of Set! . . . whereon Osiris went forth into heaven . . . Pepi hath gathered together his bones, he hath collected his flesh, and Pepi hath gone straightway into heaven by means of the two fingers of the god who is the Lord of the Ladder." (52) Earlier we learn that in Genesis the patriarch Jacob saw a ladder whereupon angels ascended and descended upon the earth. This is the only reference to a ladder in the entire Bible! This then exhibits that this arcane symbol was so important that it was not allowed to share its image with any other concept. The two fingers of God are identified here in the Egyptian writing as the two larger pyramids at Giza. The Lord of the Ladder is none other than Egypt's oldest deity: Amen. Lord of the Two Mountains. (53) We cannot but assume that these two mountains are the very same Enoch witnessed in his vision of the blessed land.

This reference to the Ladder of Set in ancient Egyptian writings is profound. As Amen was the name of the Universal Deity in Egypt from the most remote times, so too does Set appear to be nearly as old in Northern Egypt where he was held to be a primordial god. (54) Almost everywhere upon Egyptian monuments the name Set was accompanied by the glyphic representation of a *stone*. (55) This is interesting because the early inhabitants of Egypt invoked the name of God as "Rock of Truth is My Name." (56) The name Set has been studied extensively and its etymology compared with that of other similar words from various cultures. In the 19th century it was believed that Set in archaic Hebrew as well as in Egyptian meant *pillar*, but also, in a more general sense its meaning was "the erect; elevated, high." (57) This serves to link Set with the figure of Thoth. The Book of the Dead also interchanges Set and Tet (Thoth) and some scholars are of the opinion that this relationship identified the two as being one in the same, for Thoth inherited many of the traits formerly associated with Set when the popularity of Set was forgotten. (58) In the 19th century multivolume work entitled *Egypt* by Bunsen we find that up to the 13th century BC the god Set ". . .was a great god universally adored throughout Egypt, who confers on the sovereigns of the 18th and 19th dynasties the symbols of life and power. The most glorious monarch of the later dynasty, Sethos, derives his name from this deity." Bunsen adds, "But subsequently, in the course of the 20th

Dynasty, he is suddenly treated as an evil demon, inasmuch as his effigies and name are obliterated on all the monuments and inscriptions that could be reached." (59) Evidently, Set lost out on the ongoing war between the conflicting priestly factions of Egypt and their competition for the affection of the masses. He was originally a benevolent deity much sought after by the living and the dead (according to Egyptian texts), even up to the 19th Dynasty, but it was the cult of Osiris that prevailed in establishing that Set was the origin of all evil. (60) Set was more easily removed than the elder god Horus, who, after the passage of a couple of centuries became regarded as the son of Osiris. Anciently Horus was called Orus, a messianic figure associated to Orion and known as the Lord of the Pillars, the Light of the World, Bruiser of the Serpent, Conqueror of the Dragon, God of the Pole Star, and Manifester of the Ever-Hidden Father. Horus was the first who arose from the dead and established himself forever. (61) Osiris was a perfect name for the Egyptian cults to build upon because he was a verifiable historical personage who was a real human king. The attributes of vanquished deities and persons were assimilated into the characteristics of Osiris. Thus, the old messianic hero Orus became his son. These are pre-Christian beliefs and epithets that can only be explained by realizing that these people once had access to a large Arcanum of eschatological information largely forgotten over the millennia. And of course, this would be the surface texts of the Great Pyramid, which were said to contain the histories of heaven and hell and the entire *future* of the world and heavenlies up until the time of their collision in what we refer to as the coming Apocalypse.

In the Book of the Dead we learn that the souls of the deceased could not ascend to heaven by means of the Ladder without an adequate knowledge of the *name* of the Ladder. (62) This was the deepest of occult mysteries, for the name of the Ladder was indeed the very *name of God*, and the Lord's name in the most ancient times was Amen. Unfortunately for those not having the answer to this spiritual secret, Amen's name simply meant *hidden*. An Egyptian fragment reads, "Unknown is his name in heaven. Whose name is hidden from his creatures. His name which is Amen." (63) This name also has come to be interpreted as *hidden secret*. In the biblical book of Judges we read that the angel of the Lord told Samson's parents, "Why dost thou seekest after my name, seeing that it is *secret?*" (64) Another Egyptian fragment reads, "His name is hidden from his children in his name Amen." (65) It was the first god; begetter of the ancient gods. He was called in the older Egyptian writings as the One Lord of Heaven and Earth. (66) His name is variously Amun, Amon, Ammon and Amen, a god having no beginning and no end. (67) The Israelites went as far as referring to God as *The Name*.

The question as to the meaning of the title Amen was not for the masses and uninitiated. The cults and priestly classes closely guarded this secret, and evidently there was debate even among themselves as to the correct translation. However, all of the translations of this archaic epithet hint of a body of very old knowledge concerning a belief in a Deity that long ago chose to represent Himself in the visage of a stone upon the earth, a rock that mankind could build upon and grow. His true name has never been known, and this was acknowledged by the Egyptians also. A papyrus in the British Museum reads: "His abode is not known. No shrine is found with painted figures of Him. There is no building that can contain Him. Unknown is His name in heaven. He does not manifest His forms. Vain are all representations of Him." (68) The word Amen has become so commonplace in the dialogues of modern Christianity that its true significance has become obscured. We end our prayers over food, at night before sleeping, at the hospital with loved ones, at funeral ceremonies and at Church with *Amen*. We have preserved this tradition from our Christian forefathers who in turn adopted it from the Hebrews who have in their Psalms various passages that end with Amen. Today it is popularly believed that Amen means "and may it be so," but this definition is the result of its traditional use and does not at all have anything to do with its original meaning.

In Egyptian Amen has come to be understood as meaning "to come," or "coming One," and was originally designated phonetically as "aa" being represented hieroglyphically as $\triangle$ (69). Further, the root *men* means "architect," or "builder of all things." (70) As we saw earlier the name of God to the Egyptians was akin to *stone* and they called him the Rock of Truth. This may be why the early Hebrews derived 'amen to mean "firmness," from a root meaning "to believe." (71) Incidentally, the Celtic root *men* means stone (72), a phonetic relic from an extinct elder language similar to the name of God according to Kurdish beliefs that hold that God's name is Haqq, which synonymously means "truth." (73)

Later in this research we will explore the fascinating parallels between rock and spiritual faith and what Christ revealed concerning them. The permanence of stone and the unyielding faith of those who believe in Him are integral to one's ascent upon the Ladder of Set. Because as humans we cannot enter into His presence in purity, and further, He knows we are unclean and without a garment to cover our nakedness, there exists an old concept attached to the title Amen . . . debt cancellation. Amen was the expression used when one excused another for an outstanding debt. The speaking of this word to a debtor signified that his debt was forgiven and cancelled. As time passed the name Amen to the Hebrews became simply a designation for the truth (74), and in Egypt Amen later merged with another popular deity to become Amon-Ra, principally worshipped at the Karnak complex in Waset (Thebes) in Upper Egypt to the south. This connection to Ra, a solar deity, is very intriguing for Ra was worshipped as a *stone* shaped like a pillar with a pyramidion atop it that stood upon a base of masonry. (75) An obelisk. Though found numerous times in the Old Testament, the name Amen is found only once in the New Testament. In the Book of the Revelation the Son of God is called the *Amen*: "These things saith the Amen, the faithful and true witness, the beginning of the creation of God." (76) Amen is represented by the image of the pyramid; the pyramid in Siriad was designed to be a *witness* at the border of the Lord in Egypt according to Isaiah the prophet. . . and this witness was fulfilled with Christ, Who is the *image* of the invisible God. (77)

The purpose of the Giza monument is twofold. One, the stone monuments and their guardian conceal in geometrical mysteries the name of the Creator while also silently promising the diligent that this mystery will one day be made manifest. Giza's other function just may be a *literal* gate between heaven and earth and earth and the underworld. This is purely conjectural, but taking into consideration that this monument was built specifically with the intent of warning future generations of the last day's judgment upon the earth, could this complex actually have some physical engineering function with its descending passage and subterranean pit for a purpose known only to God on Judgment Day? It is on this Day that the Creator becomes Destroyer, and not of the world only, but even the very fabric of the souls of men will on that Day be condemned. The purpose of Giza was to hide something of grave importance to humanity, a secret guarded so closely that it is unimaginably obvious to the extent that we are blinded by its truth. Almost suspiciously, the stele near the Sphinx reads, "Thou hast built for thee a place protected in the sacred desert, with hidden name." (78)

There is something spiritually compelling about the Giza monuments that drives men to travel great distances just to look upon its outer surfaces. For thousands of years people have come from lands at the edges of the world to see the pyramids. Some of these people compelled their cultures to attempt to replicate these buildings and soon after these lesser monuments became centers of pilgrimage. Several hundred pyramids wrap around the world within the geographical area known as the Pyramid Belt, extending from China all the way to the dense jungles and high mountains of America. Pyramids within this belt have even been discovered on dozens of seemingly insignificant islands and even under the sea. This massive pyramid-copying campaign ended abruptly with massive geologic upheavals and flooding all along the equatorial zones of the Pyramid Belt, tremendous earthquakes and volcanism that has occurred periodically since the Great Deluge.

In Abu Feda's *Historia Anteislamitica* it is stated ". . .that Syria was one of the earliest inhabited countries, and that the Syraic language was the first that was spoken; that the Sabaean language was established by Seth and Edris (Enoch); that there was a town called Haran, to which pilgrims resorted, as they did so to the large pyramids of Ghizeh, one of which was said to be the tomb of Edris . . ." (79) This was confirmed by another Arab writer who said that pilgrims made trips to visit the Great Pyramid. This was Abn Allatif, and he claimed to have read in the books of the Sabaeans that one of the pyramids was the tomb of Agathadaemon, the other of Hermes. Agathadaemon was the person of Seth (80) and Hermes would herein be Enoch. Edris, the Enoch of the Arabic Quran was not buried there but the mentioning of his name in reference to the pyramids at Giza serves to show that even the Arabian religious writings, at least in part, were ultimately borrowed from a parent source.

Haran was the land of the Chaldeans and is the origin of the people historians have come to call Hurrians. It was also where Abraham lived with his father Terah. Abraham lived during the reign of King Nimrod, who was several years earlier the king of Akkad and is identified on Sumerian records as AMAR.UDA.AK. Actually, the Hebrew patriarch Abram was also of direct Sumerian descent, as was most of Babylonia. He was called a Hebrew, meaning *sojourner*, and as such he lived up to this name for he travelled and spent years of his life in Canaan, Philistia, Egypt and Syria. Too many today assume the early Hebrews were racially different than the Babylonians, and such is false, for Abram was Chaldean, a holy man separated from his culture by a fervent yearning to obey the will of God. Of great interest to this study is that Abram went to Egypt according to Genesis, and other Hebraic records tell that he travelled to Egypt more than once. The Book of Jasher reveals that Abram was famous throughout Babylonia and Canaan for his testimony against the evils of the king of Babylon, Nimrod [AMAR.UDA. AK] and for his part in the defeat of the Elamite Confederation recorded in Genesis 14 when the people of Sodom and Gomorrah were taken captive and then returned safely by the valor of Abraham, his household servants trained in war and his Amorite allies in Canaan. He was raised in the house of Noah, who was at that time very old and looked after by the Semitic peoples living in Canaan. Under Noah's tutoring Abram became learned in the secrets and sciences of the antediluvian world. He became a student of pre-flood astronomy and was initiated into the hidden mysteries of time keeping under the earlier Draconian Calendarical systems and the newer post-apocalyptic modified systems and all scribal lore and chronological histories. Noah and Shem taught Abram firsthand the history of the world before the flood and the prophetic writings of their forefathers concerning the end of the world and the return of God to earth. Abram also studied the writings of Enoch (81) which were at that time inscriptions also studied by his great grandson Simeon. (82) The Quran tells that Abraham left behind a book of writings himself. (83) Much of the teachings of Noah were from the books that he preserved upon the ark. (84) Noah's wisdom and knowledge was immense. Having lived under the pristine climate and atmospheric conditions of the world prior to the Deluge he was a man born under better genetic circumstances that allowed him to live so long. He was already 600 years old at the cataclysm and if the Sumerian records are true, Noah was a king of the city of Shurrupak long prior to the flood. Having spent forty years learning from this ancient man Abram himself was a remarkable repository of information. He was the *only* man on earth 350 years after the flood when Noah died to fully grasp the vast spectrum of the mysteries of God both before and after the Deluge. Abram visited Egypt and it is the author's belief that such an incredible man could *never* have left Egypt unaffected.

Hebraic traditional writings hold that Abraham went to Egypt and taught the astrologers and wise men of Pharaoh's court great secrets of God hidden in the stars and celestial motions. Such a claim is also confirmed in the Masonic document called the *Wood Manuscript*, which dates from 1610 AD. The Wood Manuscript claims that the sciences and knowledge taught by Abraham had been derived from one of the pillars that had been discovered, and that as one learned in the scribal mysteries of the Sumerians, Abraham understood these writings and related them to the Egyptians. (85) This pillar was one of the Giza pyramids covered in minute inscriptions from the pre-flood world seen by the baffled Greek and Roman historians almost two thousand years later.

The Masonic *Inigo Jones Document* cited the same information, however, Abraham here is substituted for Hermes. It is clear that Abraham is the subject of the context however because the text claims the antediluvian writings were found upon excavated pillars that were translated by a minister to "Oswiris king of Egypt," during the reign of Ninus, who was Nimrod according to the Assyrians. (86) Alexandrian historians identified two distinct Hermes figures. The first was the builder of the pillars and the second was much later. It was the second Hermes that found the pillars and *translated* them according to Iamblicus, who wrote that this second Hermes lived after the Flood. (87)

And this would no doubt be Abraham, who according to this Inigo Jones Document taught the ancient Egyptians the Zodiac and the secrets of the stars, hieroglyphics and diverse sciences. Such is further substantiated in the book of Jasher, which states that in the days of Abraham the king of Egypt was *Oswiris, the son of Anom* [Mena]. (88) The Jasher account extensively outlines Nimrod's life and reign and even his personal experiences with Abram, the son of one of his favored Babylonian war generals. The connection between Osiris, second ruler of Egypt and Nimrod of Chaldea is nothing short of astonishing. But even more incredible is the evidence that this "minister" to the Egyptian ruler was in fact Abraham.

Cyrillus Alexandrinus in *Contra Julianum* (89) wrote that long ago a powerful Chaldean visited Egypt, a man of immense wisdom. Such a historical reference would not have been recorded if this stranger had not left a powerful impact upon the Egyptian people at such a remote time in their culture's infancy. Many Chaldeans have visited Egypt. If such an incredibly wise man of learning did visit Pharaoh's court then such an event could not have remained unacknowledged in Egypt's archives. Setting aside the apparent anachronisms so prevalent in interpretations of Egyptian history, we learn that an Egyptian record called the *Westcar Papyrus* does tell that during the reign of Khufu a foreigner visited Egypt, a venerable man of 110 years in age who was believed to be able to perform miracles but was known greatly for his vast wisdom. Of particular fascination to the sages of Pharaoh's court was the fact that this stranger to Egypt was ". . .acquainted with the mysteries of Thoth [Enoch]." (90) Abraham was a Chaldean by birth and a savant of the mysteries of Enoch through Noah and Enoch's inscriptions upon the tablets kept safe by the Sethites after the flood. At age 110 Abraham was living among the Philistines at the eastern borders of the land of Egypt so it is not improbable that he could have spent a considerable amount of time translating these pillars [pyramid inscriptions at Giza] for the Egyptians.

The Greek historian Herodotus may have inadvertently recorded this as well. Concerning the pyramids at Giza he wrote that they had been built by one called Philition, which merely is a Grecian title meaning *native of* [ion] Phili. He was also called Philistis, a shepherd who frequently fed his flocks near Giza. (91) In *Civilization or Barbarism?*, Cheikh Anta Diop on page 281 wrote that it was Philistis who brought the secrets of the calendar into Egypt. . . exactly what is said of Thoth, Hermes and Enoch. The Westcar Papyrus reveals that this 110 year old man knew the number of the *Chambers of Thoth*, some Egyptologists interpreting this to mean "secret chambers of the primeval sanctuary" according to Zechariah Sitchin in *The Wars of Gods and Men*. This visitor to Egypt of old claimed to know where the *Plans-With-Numbers* were hidden. This no doubt was what Abraham found inside the "primeval sanctuary," or Great Pyramid. It is quite possible that he did not build these monuments, but because of his own fame he later became identified with them. All of this further identifies Abraham, who was a shepherd and a nomad who was living in that area at the Philistine city of Gerar when he was 110. It is obvious that after the passage of so many years the historical accounts of different scribes and records would have become slightly confused. It is not a stretch of the imagination to assume that the Egyptians would have later credited this stranger with building the monuments if he had been remembered as the one who translated the mysterious writings found upon them.

All evidence points that the enigmatic writings of the Book of the Dead as well as some of the older biblical records and the ancient writings of *many* early civilizations merely borrowed their source material from the inscriptions preserved through the flood that were engraved into the faces of the Great Pyramid. Though Egyptologists claim that the writings that constitute the Book of the Dead were so extensive that they required editing and abbreviation into shorter works to be adequately used, this appears to be the case with *most* of the world's oldest historical writings. This is especially the case with the little understood and mysterious Edfu wall-texts. Discovered in Upper Egypt to the far south of Egypt was an archive of ancient glimpses into an even earlier past that appear to have been unique to Edfu. Even more peculiar is that the Edfu writings tell of the plans for a great temple that predated the other temples of Egypt that dropped out of heaven near Memphis and that Imhotep built this edifice according to these plans. (92) Memphis is the area of the Giza plateau, only a few miles between them. What's interesting is that these Edfu records were found on the far side of Egypt to the deep south, on the edges of Nubia instead of near Memphis. These plans are the "divine instructions" received by Enoch concerning the architectural dimensions of the Great Pyramid.

The Edfu inscriptions tell of a distant history of Egypt concerning the First Time [Zep Tepi], the primordial Sages, primeval gods, the abyssal waters of the Nun that existed prior to the creation of our world, of alien gods before the Egyptian deities, an Enemy in the visage of a Serpent and a great conflict that brought this earlier world to a devastating end. Linking these writings to the Book of the Dead and Great Pyramid is the fact that these writings are attributed to Thoth. Andrew Collins in *Gods of Eden: Egypt's Lost Legacy and the Genesis of Civilization* cites these strange writings and goes on to write that all of the inhabitants of this earlier world perished and when the world was brought back out of the darkness of ruin the world contained the ghosts of this earlier civilization. The only relic to have survived this judgment was a single djed-*pillar* located in the field of Reeds. (93) This would serve to identify the Delta area and surrounding regions where Giza lies for the Field of Reeds is adjacent to the Sea of Reeds, commonly referred to in the Scripture as the Red Sea crossed by the Israelites fleeing Egypt.

The story is the same the world over, but the more it is told the more fascinating the parallels become. The Babylonian historian Berossus wrote that the god Kronus bade Xisouthrus (Noah) to set down a writing of the beginning, middle and end of all things before the flood. This god told his earthly servant that after the deluge he was to "recover the writings" and publish them for men to see. The account reads that these writings were located after the catastrophe and dup up. (94) Assuming arguendo that these were merely small books then why not just take them upon the ark? This author believes these books were not small nor was it possible to have taken such a vast archive of knowledge through the cataclysm, but that they were meticulously inscribed upon the Great Pyramid, and that there were originally four of these gigantic books that corresponded to the four faces of the monument just as there were four Gospels giving men different versions of the same Messianic story and there stand four Watcher guardians around the throne of God. Though embellishments crept into this account the exaggerations focused on localizing the tradition to Babylon rather than on the material facts that collaborate the hundreds of other legends and myths from other nations in antiquity. We find additional collaboration in India, where again the same operable facts remain the same but the traditions are centrally focused within the subcontinent.

There is an immense aura of mystery attached to India. Its culture is an enduring one and recently research has shown the apparent relationships between the Indian and Sumerian pictographic languages. (95) In fact, no other civilization exists today aside from India that so closely mirrored ancient Sumer. They have maintained their traditions for millennia, beliefs derived from the mysterious Sanskrit and Vedic writings whereas those nations surrounding them have almost entirely succumbed to the relatively newer Islamic faith. India is a window into the past. The Vedic scriptures are commonly believed by those in India as being eternal having existed in the mind of the Deity since the beginning. They were considered the knowledge of God Himself, divine information imparted unto the Rishis who in turn took this knowledge and wrote the four Vedas from the four mouths of Brahma [the Creator]. The Seven Rishis took this knowledge and wrote it down for the benefit of mankind. Brahma was believed to have four faces, which this author believes is a signal characteristic that links the Creator to the Great Pyramid symbolism. Even in the book of Revelation the Throne of God has four faces.

The Great Pyramid does not factor in anywhere in the Vedic writings however, the ideas of which they embody is clearly seen in these arcane texts. The four Vedas of Brahma are said in these writings to have sprung from the Gayatri shortly after Brahma finished framing the world. The most sacred metre in the Vedic texts is the Gayatri, a metrical speech consisting of three times eight syllables. The Aryans believed that the syllables of words could be measured out in the form of divine speech. The Gayatri speech is associated to fire and expressed the idea of Brahma. Interestingly, the Vedic man had to employ this sacred metrical speech when attempting to acquire ". . .sacred knowledge, and the thorough understanding of all problems of theology." (96)

Like the Egyptian Book of the Dead which was clearly copied from an older source from an entirely different language, so too were the original Vedic records in a alien language very different from the Sanskrit that they have presently survived in. Translator Ralph Griffith wrote in his *The Vedas* (1892) that ". . .the language of the Vedas is an older dialect, varying very considerably, both in its grammatical and lexical character, from the classical Sanskrit. Its grammatical peculiarities run through all departments." (97)

For the critic who still remains unyielding to such a connection between Giza and these most ancient writings from India and other classical civilizations I defer now to the actual Sanskrit in order to banish any further disbelief. The Great Pyramid was designed to convey *knowledge* and was long ago called an *altar* by old Semitic cultures. With this in mind we find it an amazing parallel to learn that the Sanskrit word for Veda is in fact *knowledge*, which incidentally, is a very old word etymologically related to the Sanskrit vedi, or *altar*. Further, like the Book of the Dead writings discovered and excavated by the early Egyptians, the Vedic beliefs were that the gods long ago *dug up the Vedic writings*. (98) This too is the testimony of the Hindus who assert that their holy books long ago were recovered ". . .from the bottom of the ocean," *after the flood* as found in the classic research of Ignatius Donnelly in *The Antediluvian World* on page 303. Also, the most sacred of the holy books was the Rig-Veda, which has exactly 10,800 verses in Sanskrit. . . ancient scriptures told to correspond to the 10,800 bricks of the Altar of the *fire* god Agni! (99) This altar is that spoken of by the prophet Isaiah that stands in the land of Egypt.

Abraham was an initiate into this Arcanum. He knew of the altar of God in Egypt and its hidden identity as the pillar of Enoch that represented the holy mountain of Heaven and its function as a terrestrial gateway between heaven and earth and earth with the underworld. He translated these mysteries for the Egyptians and wrote his own records as well which have been preserved in Genesis and within obscure passages in the oldest Psalms. There is every possibility that he discovered the writings of the Apocalypse upon the faces on these stones of the pyramid. The Revelation record as recorded by John is truly a masterpiece of ancient symbolism and extinct motifs. It was written in Greek but the Greeks nor Hebrews could have understood it two thousand years ago because the language of *symbolism employed is specifically of* Sumerian *origin.* The end of the world was written in the signs, motifs, symbols and language of imagery that could have only truly been comprehended by those who lived in the *beginning* prior to the Deluge. Unfortunately, this shocking and informative study is the subject of an entirely different book and is not the objective of the present study. Suffice it to say that we infer this from the fact that according to the manifold sources already cited in this book, upon the faces of the Great Pyramid was written the past, the present, and the *future.* The knowledge, *Vedas,* was revealed by Abraham and after centuries passed, the priests of India preserved his name in the name they referred to as God – Brahma, which had its origin in [A]braham. That Abraham of Genesis is alluded to there can be no doubt. His wife was Sarah, just as the Vedic god Bramha was married to *Sara*-Swati.

Abraham's ministry to earth's earliest post-apocalyptic civilizations was no accident, for the work of Abraham's translation of these holy mysteries to the world was the result of an Enochian prophecy foretold almost a millennium prior to the Flood. The Book of the Secrets of Enoch reads that after the flood ". . .shall arise another generation, much afterwards. . . he who raised that generation [Abraham] *shall reveal to them the books* of thy handwriting [Enoch's], of thy fathers, to them to whom he must point out the guardianship of the world, to the faithful men and workers of my pleasure, who do not acknowledge my Name in vain." (100) The early Egyptians learned through the wise Abraham the contents of the glyphic writings at Giza and immediately incorporated these mysteries into their theology. These translations often meant nothing to the Egyptians other than that they were of divine importance and were words and phrases needed in the afterlife. Egyptologists admit that it was often the case that even Egyptian scribes long ago meticulously preserved hieroglyphic texts even though they themselves did not quite understand the meanings of the texts themselves. These inscriptions were placed inside tombs, upon temple walls as walk-in books, within coffins, on artwork, on beads, inside crypts, and on obelisks that were erected everywhere throughout

Egypt. One can read the Book of the Dead, which is a compilation of these texts from all over Egypt from what has come to be called the *Papyus of Ani,* and see clearly that these writings have little, if anything, to do with Egypt. They are full of obscure imagery like the Ladder of Set and Pillars of Thoth that hint to an older theology, one extant long prior to the traditional Egyptian pantheon. There is a mystery these writings seek to explain that involves the secrets of resurrection and the Name of God – the divine key to the Arcanum known as Life Eternal.

When Abraham first laid eyes on the excavation at Giza and witnessed the pyramids rising out of the sands of the desert waste almost 4,000 years ago he knew he was looking at the earthly model of the City of God placed there by his Antediluvian Sethite forebears. The spiritual city where the eternal righteous will dwell ". . .lieth foursquare, and the length is as large as the breadth. . . the length and the breadth and the height of it are equal." (101) A perfect equilateral cube. The Great Pyramid is a shadow of this greater and future reality. The celestial city of the Greeks is the same as the Divine Tree of the Hebrews, both being images of the same archetype: an ideal cosmology as noted by John Mitchel in *The Dimensions of Paradise.* The gnostics too shared this concept. The *Pistis Sophia* text reads—"For God shall save their souls from all matters, and a city shall be prepared in the light, and all the souls saved, will dwell in the city, and inherit it. And the soul of them who receive mysteries will abide in that region . . ." The pyramid at Giza embodied terrestrial mysteries and its angle relates specifically to the earth. But the pyramidal city of God will be perfect, all its points equidistant.

In the New Testament book of Hebrews is a curious fragment that reads that Abraham did ". . .look for a city whose builder and maker was God." (102) Because we have no biblical references to such a historic quest by the patriarch we know that he did not look with earthly eyes. Abraham looked upon the monuments of Giza with spiritual sight that prophetically witnessed the coming of the City of God.

Rostau and the Resurrection

In Egypt of old all men feared the kingdom of Seker. He was a death god older than Osiris and his realm was filled with the blackest darkness beneath walls of sand. His shrine was pyramidal and the gate to his nether kingdom was called Rostau. (102) It was here that the souls of the dead drifted through subterranean chambers and halls and expansive galleries of rock alone, in utter darkness. However, the souls of the deserving can be assisted in this dreaded journey after death by the aid of the god Thoth. (104) With so many gods in Egypt, why Thoth? This can perhaps be best explained because it was Thoth who was associated to the Giza complex and the secret mysteries of death.

Rostau was more than a simple gateway, but a place of passage wherein lived the secret to resurrection. To remain in the kingdom of Seker was certain death. But through Rostau one could get out of Seker and enter into the Tuat, or the Other World. Rostau literally was the ". . .door of the corridors of the mountain," and it is evident by the writings of the Book of the Dead that *where* one chose to go in Rostau determined his fate. To the Egyptian, Seker was a darkened desert region, a waste that represented death itself and the only way out was to find the door to Rostau, which led into galleries and chambers of rock that in themselves had *choices* leading to different destinations within this massive gateway. Such is what we find embodied in the architecture of Giza. Once one enters the Great Pyramid he begins a steep descent into the monument. If one does not know *where* to look up (which would be a secret of the mysteries of Thoth*)*, then he will walk all the way down to an area *below* the pyramid into the bowels of earth, to an area with a well pit told by the ancients to descend into the abyss – a prison realm made by the Creator wherein ageless beings [fallen angels] and evil men reside until the Judgment. But if one does know where to seek the hidden door and entrance into the ascendant corridors of the pyramid, then he will pass through the Grand Gallery and ultimately find the Holy of Holies of the Great Pyramid. It is there that we will discover that the ceremonies of the Book of the Dead are symbolic of the mysteries of Tuat [Thoth] which are done in the Khert-Neter (the grave). (105)

In the area called the King's Chamber the disembodied spirit of the dead will learn the key to exiting Seker and entering the afterlife. The secret was also a part of the mysteries of Osiris, god of resurrection. Annually the erection of pillars throughout Egypt symbolized his resurrection long ago when the forces of darkness attempted to kill him. Because the name Osiris was originally found among Egyptian archives from distant antiquity the name supplanted the earlier title of the messianic hero that taught that all people can enter into the afterlife by following his example. In the Book of the Dead we read this amazing passage, "I have entered Rostau, and have seen the Hidden One who is therein. I was hidden, but I found the *boundary* [border]. I journeyed to Nerutef, and he who was therein covered me with a *garment*." (106)

This stunning passage reveals that the One God in Rostau is none other than Amen, the Hidden One, and that He alone was remembered by the people as Osiris, for Nerutef is the *tomb* of Osiris, god of resurrection. The secret herein is seen in that a god of resurrection does not need a tomb but for to exhibit that it does not have any power over Him or anyone believing in Him. Thus, Nerutef is the King's Chamber with its empty sarcophagus where the souls of the dead search for through the galleries of rock.

All of the elements of the arcanum are present here. The ability to "see" the Hidden God is rewarded with the ability to be clothed with a *garment* (new immortal body the tomb cannot contain). In the tomb of the Hidden God is the *boundary* between heaven and earth or what the prophet Isaiah called the *border to the Lord in the Land of Egypt.* In Rostau the wise in death will seek the tomb and look upon the empty sarcophagus in the King's Chamber and *believe* that He has arisen from death and has the power to offer all the life He now enjoys. This belief in the Hidden One is the key to resurrection and the receiving of the garment, for without it one cannot pass the border at the end of this world. Such an idea dates back to Sumerian beliefs. The Sumerian goddess Inana descended into the underworld by virtue of a pillar that she was not allowed to use after she adorned herself with a garment [PALA]. Intriguingly, the same word in Hebrew means "miracle." (107) The exact same story can be found in Babylonian legends concerning Ishtar, who had to pass through seven gates in her descent to the underworld. (108)

The Egyptian records claim that the Giza area was Rostau and that Osiris as god of resurrection was the god of Rostau. In fact, the Sphinx Stela of Thutmose IV refers to Giza as Rostau. (109) The connection this pillar of the Sethites has with the Egyptian belief in resurrection and the Christian belief in resurrection through faith in the Son of God is fascinating. The Greeks called the cross that Christ was crucified upon Stau-Ros, which is translated as Pillar of Wisdom. Obviously, as duly noted in occult lore, the inverted of these Greek syllables is the epithet *Rostau.* (110) Thus the Great Pyramid was the Wisdom Pillar.

If one follows the teachings of the Book of the Dead and looks closely "upon the hidden things in Rastau," (111) he may learn that his destination is not downward into the realms below earth, but upward [as the ascendant passages and airshafts (observation shafts) indicate]. Even as far back as the Egyptian *Book of Two Ways* (2050-1800 BC) it was known that there was a gate to the underworld in Egypt. The Book of the Dead affirms this, reading that, "Thou hast opened the gates to the sky, thou hast opened the doors to the celestial deep." (112) Even in the Pyramid Texts we read, "A stairway to the sky is set for me that I may ascend into the sky." Both the terrestrial deep (Abyss) below the earth and the celestial deep (realms of space and heavens) were accessible in Rostau.

Rostau served not only as a gateway between worlds but also as a point of no return. One could wander endlessly in Seker as a tormented disembodied spirit but once Rostau was entered this spirit either learned the secret of resurrection above or wandered aimlessly below to the Great Deep. Either choice was irreversible. The actual title Rostau in Egyptian derives from a group of archaic powerful beings that long ago rebelled against the Creator and became apostates (stau) whom Ra (the Creator typified by the sun) banished into the abyss. These rebels were imprisoned below the earth until the day when the souls of the damned will be annihilated. The Book of the Dead refers to them a few times as the Sons of Revolt that in primeval times caused a war in heaven and upon the earth itself as they followed Sebau, the serpent fiend. "The serpent fiend Sebau hath fallen headlong, his forelegs are bound in chains, and his hind legs hath Ra carried away from him. The Sons of Revolt shall never more rise up." (113) This Sebau is typified by the ancients as Draconis.

It is here again that the Egyptian texts align perfectly with the early Hebraic writings of the Book of Enoch. In the Enochian writings we find that God ordered the angel Raphael to:

> ". . .bind Azazel hand and foot, and cast
> him into the darkness: and make an *opening*
> *in the desert*, which is in Dudael, and cast
> him therein. And place upon him rough and
> jagged rocks, and cover him with darkness,
> and let him abide there forever. . . and on
> the day of great judgment he shall be cast
> into the fire. . ." (114)

This strange opening in the desert appears to be a special place reserved for disobedient angelic beings, and the office of imprisoning such rebellious entities further appears to be the special function of Raphael. In the Book of Tobit, an apocryphal text, Raphael chases a demon called Asmodeus from Persia where the demon was engaged in tormenting a girl and slaying her would-be lovers. On its own volition the demon flees straight to Egypt where he is caught by Raphael and there in Egypt Asmodeus is bound and chained. (115) Why would a demonic entity flee to Egypt? What protection might a spiritual being have there? Such a phenomenon concerning Egypt is not exclusive to Hebrew writings. The Greeks maintain traditions that long ago a great cataclysm occurred when flaming rocks were hurled to the ground from heaven that destroyed everything they crashed in to. When they began striking the earth, the gods ". . .fled in terror to Egypt." (116) Egypt marks the entrance between the three worlds of heaven, earth and the abyss. Such is also hinted at in a Roman ritual of exorcism. According to sources over a century ago a demonic being when exorcised from a tormented person is sent to keep company with Pharaoh and his hosts whom God ". . .in abyssum demersit." (117)

The evidence suggests that demonic beings that still have free access to earth from the deep cross over at will or during specific times. But the original Sons of Revolt that instigated the primordial rebellion are still bound. Other demons are bound as they perform transgressions upon the earth and are judged. Like Asmodeus. This Persian demon apparently attempted to descend back into the underworld to escape Raphael but was caught before he could pass through. Such an idea is conveyed also in the Gospels where the demons that identified themselves as Legion (many) begged Jesus not to bring judgment upon them, saying, "Hast thou come to torment us before the time?" They requested that Christ release them into the *deep*, and the body of water nearby served as a terrestrial symbol of the spiritual deep below the earth. Thus, the underworld, accessed at Giza, is a spiritual refuge for the evil beings that have had their judgment delayed for their participation in the dissemination of evil *knowledge* passed on to mankind.

Occult Arcana of Scripture

Antediluvian Theology

This research has served to reveal a belief system from mankind's earliest times known by the adherents of earth's most ancient and diverse theological and cultural backgrounds. This faith held that somewhere on this planet was a mountain made by God, a monument of divine origin erected over a deep well that held back the waters of chaos while the edifice itself commemorated the sacred place of the Creation. As Eden was of old protected by a Cherub, so too was this site watched over by a silent guardian. The monument was built upon a square foundation of living rock, inscribed on its four sides with writings by a civilization so connected to the Creator that their rebellion initiated a global cataclysm that buried this Golden Age culture – a catastrophe foretold within the myriads of inscriptions upon the building's surfaces.

This monument was the largest book on earth, containing the secrets of good and evil, life and death, the heavens and earth, and the dateless past to the unending future. It was an artificial mountain promised to come by God when he told Adam that He would build an altar on earth to commemorate his death, the earthly end of the first man made in the image of God. This colossal altar was also an enduring sign to all of humanity that death would reign for a season but in the end by the power of the mystery of God would the dead who were faithful be *reborn*.

It was this *testimony* in stone that Enoch "laid upon the earth" before the Deluge, which was built after his departure by the remaining Sethites at the exact location of his vanishing into the heavens. The prophets told that this testimony was to be located in Egypt, at the *border of the Lord*. Centuries after the flood men searched out this mountain, excavated it, and wrote entire libraries as they extracted knowledge from off of its surfaces, giving birth to the oldest surviving writings in the world today. But even if men had the means by which to ascend to the upper most courses of stones to read the highly apocalyptic and eschatological inscriptions, the end of all things would still remain unknown for the monument was never provided a capstone. The cornerstone is the ultimate secret – the revelation of the Name of God.

This mountain was the Great Pyramid, the edifice serving as a prophetic type of the Tree of Life and the Tree of Knowledge, a pillar of fire that alluded to earth's final incendiary rain in the last days; a terrestrial reminder that God dwelt in the Mountain. Its shape enigmatically conceals the Name of the Creator and it was likened to that of a ladder that no man could ascend save he that knew the name of the Ladder-the same being the Name of God. This ladder linked heaven to earth and the ascent to heaven was by this pillar, the hill of the Lord or Book of Life – all of these cited in Scripture and identified in the symbolism of the Pyramid. This pillar also had a descent, a gate that led downwards into the underworld domains, a dark passage where the dead were conducted down to the entrance to the hidden netherrealm beneath a hole in the desert in Egypt. It was a region of the Deep where languish certain archaic spiritual beings made mortal that had so long ago defied the ordinances of heaven and followed the Dragon to Eden in their campaign to pollute the seed of God.

The secret entrance into this mountain gate to heaven is God, who gives the redeemed a white *garment* once they pass the border. This garment is immortality; a body that defies death and the curse of aging degeneratively. Man's spiritual garment was taken when he succumbed to earthly knowledge, but with spiritual knowledge will this garment be restored. Meanwhile, we are wayfarers, sojourners, pilgrims with a single purpose – to bring as many others with us as we exit this world. When the number of white stones is reached will the Building of God be complete. Our destiny is to be prepared for the return of Eden, Eternal Earth, of which the garden of God in Genesis was but an eschatological shadow. An *image* of the future. To enter eternal Eden we must be adequately clothed.

The Great Pyramid ultimately identifies a belief in the future city of God, the New Jerusalem upon the holy mountain Zion. All of the former symbols are merely prophetic glimpses of Zion, the center of the navel [origin of life] of the world whereupon will be laid the Chief Cornerstone, the *true* Pyramid made of living rock cut not by human hands. This stone will descend once His building is complete, myriads of stones all perfect and without blemish, all agreeing within another in form and covered in a garment of white. Once we are unified in spirit will He descend to complete the Architecture of God.

The Arcanum in the Old Testament

The most important elements of this fascinating arcanum have been found profusely throughout the Old Testament writings. Much of the older books was taken from the surface of the Great Pyramid by Abraham when he visited

Pharaoh's court in Egypt and served as translator of the original Sumerian inscriptions. Though the books of Moses contains elements of the arcanum we will also see how the prophets too were all initiates into these mysteries.

In Genesis the Tree of Life was in the "midst of the garden." The tree is typified by the Great Pyramid that stands at the middle of the earth [Eden]. The Psalmist wrote, "For God is my king of old, working salvation in the *midst of the earth*." (1) Though many of the Psalms are definitely David's and his son Solomon's, there are others that contain glimpses into heavenly and earthly histories so remote that they must have originated from some alien parent source long forgotten, and of course, it is the effort of this study to show that this parent source was the Great Pyramid itself. Geographically the middle of the earth is the land of Goshen in the Nile Delta where Giza silently stands at its border. Even then in the 14th century BC this area was a refuge where the Israelites were saved from the judgments of God against Pharaoh so that, ". . .thou may knowest that I am the lord in the *midst of the earth*." (2)

This King of old mentioned by the Psalmist is the Stone of Israel in Genesis (3), Moses also calling Him the Rock (4) which he wrote was God's name. This is intriguing because the Hebrew word for name is the same as the word for *monument* [shem] (5), and the early Israelites inscribed the name of Jehovah within a radiating *triangle*. (6) Earlier in this book we learned that the number 10 was a prime triangular number, and in the tenth Sepharoth (10 divine utterances of God in the Creation) of Kabbalistic lore, God's name is Adonai Melech (Lord and King) with His enumeration being *malchuth*, which is interpreted as ". . .gate, temple of God; church." (7) These beliefs do not fade into obscurity with the end of the books of Moses but seem to grow progressively within the writings of the prophets.

The name of God was a closely guarded secret even in the days of the judges (8). The purpose of the Great Pyramid's ancient function was to be a testimony to the earth of the supremacy of the Son of the Living God, which amazingly, David's son Absalom copied. Such reveals the prevalence of the tradition's antiquity. "Now Absalom in his lifetime had taken and reared for himself a *pillar*; which is in the King's Dale: for he said, I have no son to keep my *name* in remembrance; and he called the pillar after his own name." (9) Here is a secret of the arcanum, that the Great Pyramid actually serves to bring into remembrance the name of the Son of God in its service as the pillar of the Creator. The pillar erected by the Sethites at the instructions of God architecturally conceals the Divine Name within its dimensions. According to the Book of Enoch the Son of Man was given His name before the creation of heaven and earth, and only *"through his name* [shem: monument]," shall salvation be obtained. (10) Absalom was the son of David and during this time God was called the Rock, also referred to as a *hightower* and *tower of salvation*. (11)

It was the Psalms of David and Solomon that appear to amplify this Arcanum with rich detail and extensions to the arcane symbols and motifs employed by the earlier writers of Scripture. In the Proverbs we read that ". . .the *name* of the Lord is a *strong tower*," (12) and in Psalms we see that "they that love His *name* shall dwell therein," (13) this "Mount Zion, which cannot be removed." (14) This holy mountain could not be removed because it stood on a "sure foundation." (15) The Psalms also read that ". . .His foundation is in the holy mountains. The Lord loveth the gates of Zion . . . glorious things are spoken of thee, O city of God. Selah." (16) This city is also called ". . .the mountain of his holiness, beautiful for situation, the joy of the whole earth, is mount Zion, on the sides of the north, the city of the Great King." (17) That Zion is the gate of God is clearly read in Psalm 118, ". . .this gate of the Lord, into which the righteous shall enter. I will praise thee; for thou hast heard me, and art become my salvation. The *stone* which the builders rejected is become the head of the corner." (18) No doubt this headstone identifies the Coming One who is represented by the cornerstone that is supposed to be atop the Great Pyramid.

Centuries later the prophet Isaiah wrote, "Behold, I lay in Zion for a foundation a stone, a tried stone, a precious cornerstone, a sure foundation; he that believeth shall not make haste. Judgment will I also lay in the line and righteousness to the plummet . . . for I have heard from the Lord of hosts a consumption [destruction by *fire*], even determined upon the whole earth." (19) The writings upon the pyramid were specifically designed to survive the flood some of which foretold of the future destruction of earth by fire. Interestingly, the line and plummet are architectural devices used by masons long ago for the accurate determination of measurements and true angles. This serves to infer that Zion was an architectural monument.

After expounding on the apocalyptic Day of the Lord, the prophet Joel wrote, "Whoever shall call upon the name of the Lord shall be delivered; for in mount Zion and Jerusalem shall be deliverance." (20) Though the name of God is hidden so are our spiritual names. Isaiah wrote, "I will give them an everlasting name, that shall not be cut off . . . even them that I bring to my holy mountain." (21) "And thou shalt be called by a *new name*, which the mouth of the Lord shall name." (22) "And I will give thee the treasures of darkness, and hidden riches of secret places, that thou may knowest that I, the Lord, which call thee by thy *name*, am the God of Israel." (23)

God covers Himself with "light as with a garment," (24) as our new divine names will be our glorified garments of light. Isaiah wrote that "He hath clothed me with garments of salvation, He hath covered me with a robe of righteousness." (25) This is what is promised to us through the prophet Zechariah when he wrote, "I have caused thine iniquity to pass from thee, and I will clothe thee with *change of raiment.*" (26) Those who do not receive this new garment of incorruptibility shall be as Adam and Eve, who, seeing that they were *naked,* hid from God. (27) As Amos wrote concerning the end times, "He that is courageous among the mighty shall flee away *naked* in that day." (28) Thus, the Sphinx guards a special area that in the future will be inaccessible to those who have not been given this new name in much the same way the Cherub guarded old Eden.

The locality of the Great Pyramid identifying the presence of the entrance to the underworld is also supported in the Old Testament writings. In a typological passage written by Ezekiel the prophet concerning Satan and his minions we read, "For they are all delivered unto death, to the nether parts of the earth, in the *midst of the children of men,* with them that go *down to the pit* . . . I *covered the deep* for him; and I restrained the floods thereof, and the great waters were stayed." (29) It is to be recalled that the pyramid at Giza was built over a well and that it was rumored among the ancients that this well was over a hollowed area that could very well be an extension of the well pit. This monument was the epitome of elder traditions of placing large stones over well mouths to hold down the chaos waters believed to have destroyed the primordial world both before Noah's day in a pre-Archaic Age and then again in Noah's lifetime. Ezekiel appears to have been given very old revelations from God concerning Lucifer, for it was this archangel's duty from the beginning of time to guard over the chaos and keep it back. Ezekiel also wrote that Lucifer was the ". . .anointed cherub that covereth . . .," (30) until he rebelled and became Red Dragon of Chaos, the personification of disorder. The Psalms writer declares that the wicked will be brought "down to the pit of destruction," (31) but Hosea best gives us the impression of one who stumbles in the darkness of the pyramid's descending passageway, and is lost: "For the ways of the Lord are right, and the just shall walk in them; but the transgressors shall *fall* therein." (32) In his proverbs King Solomon wrote, "The way of life is *above* to the wise, that he may depart from hell *beneath,*" and ". . .the way of righteousness is life, and in the pathway thereof there is *no death.*" (33)

The Lucifer mythos is very old. The earliest forms of the legends concerning this fallen angel tell that in the beginning, before the creation of mankind, there were five archangels that held offices directly beneath the Creator, the Spirit and the Word. These five divine beings administered all the affairs of the Godhead within the Creation. As appointed guardians over all material creation they were regarded as Watchers that were often represented in visions and archaic writings as wearing garments having many eyes. Lucifer's original office was that of guardianship over reptilian and amphibian life forms in the garden of God [Eden]. Michael was appointed guardian over those made in the image of God [mankind]. Other archangels were appointed over the beasts of the earth (carnivores and herbivores) and one for the fowls of the air. After Lucifer's fall those appointed to be under his dominion, such as the Great Lizards of the prehistoric world were lost in cataclysms and Satan (the Adversary) the fallen archangel was appointed over the Deep and became regent over the very chaos powers he was supposed to suppress. It was the fountains of the deep in subterranean reservoirs that broke forth flooding the pre-Archaic world before Adam and Eve.

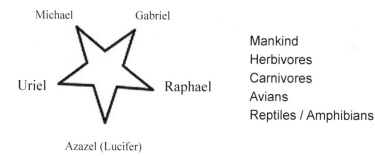

Michael	Gabriel
Uriel	Raphael

Azazel (Lucifer)

Mankind
Herbivores
Carnivores
Avians
Reptiles / Amphibians

The origin of the Pentagram does not derive from the appearance of a goat head, but the connection was definitely a good one made by the ancients in reference to the Scape Goat. The Israelites were instructed by God to lay the sins of the people upon a goat and send it out into the desert as penance for the nation. Satanists and occultists call this goat symbol the Baphomet. The symbols commemorated the fall of Lucifer, the ruin of the reptilian and amphibian animal kingdoms from their former glory, and ultimately symbolizes the fall of man. This is what Giza symbolizes to the world. The Sphinx typifies the Eternal Guardian over the Chaos powers of the Deep [Abyss] that Lucifer originally enjoyed as his own office. Now Satan is a fallen cherub that failed to cover the deep. The Sethites immortalized this story in stone at Giza, and with the Great Pyramid they unveiled the promise of the One that could not die Who would come and take over all of the angelic duties upon Himself in the future for the eternal security of mankind.

With Lucifer's fall there remained four archangelic beings over the material creation. This is evidenced in the visions of Ezekiel and John. In prophetic writings, especially as seen in the Revelation text, God's throne is surrounded by *four* beings covered in many eyes. These four have the faces of a lion (carnivores) lamb (herbivores), eagle (avian) and a human (image of God). The only creatures on earth (dry land) not represented in heaven are *amphibians* and *reptiles*, which are the forms evil angels have taken when anthropomorphically described be it in Hebraic prophetic texts to ancient Mesopotamian reliefs. In Genesis Lucifer is identified as a snake but by the end of human history in the Revelation record he is become a mighty Red Dragon with seven heads. The seven heads typify seven great demonic allies that will afflict earth with Lucifer in the End Days attempting to render the number of their human replacements incomplete. The alliance of seven powerful evil angels under Lucifer is a mimicry of the appointment of seven holy angels by God after the fall of Lucifer. After he became Satan the Godhead established another office of healing and power over malignant spiritual and demonic powers, appointing the archangel Raphael over this office. Two other archangels were appointed to make the seven complete, variously named Anael, Samuel, Cassiel and Zecharial. These guardianships over the prime four archangels concerned only land-dwelling creatures. The seas and oceans are the terrestrial abyss and have since the beginning typified the chaos.

These things were the focus of antediluvian theology embedded within the incredible secrets of the Giza complex – the fall of a divine being and his appearance on earth to thwart the destiny of mankind. But this Arcanum merely foreshadowed what was fulfilled in the New Testament. Like Lucifer, men lost their garments of light. But unlike him, we will be given new garments made of spiritual fires that will destroy this olden serpent.

Christian Renewal of the Ancient Arcana

Jesus is the central figure of Christianity, and rightly so, for He is the physical manifestation of the Arcanum, the hope of the Gnostics known by them as the Logos [Word]. There is a most profound analogy given by the Christ [Anointed One] that instantly invokes a visual image of the great Pyramid surviving the Flood, indeed, as it was intended to do: "whosoever cometh to me and heareth my sayings, and doeth them; I will show you to whom he is like: He is like a man which built a house, and digged deep, and laid the foundation on a rock; and when the flood arose, the stream beat vehemently upon that house, and could not shake it: for it was founded upon a *rock*." (34) This spiritual rock is elaborated on more when Jesus asked Peter whom he believed Him to be. Peter answered, "Thou art the Christ (Anointed One), the Son of the Living God." And Jesus answered this by saying, "Blessed art thou, Simon Barjona; for flesh and blood hath not revealed this unto you but, my Father which is in heaven. And I say also unto thee, that thou art Peter, and upon this *Rock* I will build my Church; and the gates of hell shall not prevail against it." (35) This rock is faith in Him and Jesus cleverly revealed one of the secrets of the arcanum by first calling this disciple by his first name, Simon Barjona (son of Jonah), and then *after* the apostle verbally acknowledged his faith Jesus called him Peter, a new name that signifies a *stone*. This name change affirmed for Simon that he was reckoned among those stones of the Church of the Living God that were set upon the true foundation beneath the Chief Cornerstone, which is evident by the Greek word for stone used by Jesus which was petros (as opposed to petra) which is diminutive and merely serves to describe a piece of a larger rock. (36) This amazing scenario occurred at an incredible site in the Holy Land. These famous and little understood words were uttered to the disciples at Caesari Philipii – at the foot of the triple-peaked Mount Hermon!

In reference to the Chief Cornerstone in one of His parables, Jesus said, "And whomsoever shall fall on this stone shall be *broken*; but on whomsoever it shall fall, it will grind him to powder." (37) To be broken, as in with a "broken and contrite spirit" is a state of humbleness and self-realization that one is unworthy of receiving an eternal inheritance while acknowledging the stone for the strength that is in it. Falling upon this stone (exercising faith in it) will keep one from being crushed by the Stone in judgment. Jesus spoke these things in parables, which are *images* of truth, a mode of conveying spiritual knowledge. True spiritual believers find no difficulty in comprehending the images conveyed within spiritual teachings. Those who understand shall know even greater things while the unreceptive remain blind to the hidden truths. Christ taught in this form, fulfilling an ancient prophecy that read, "I will open my mouth in parables; I will utter things which have been kept secret from the foundation of the world." (38) This example was followed by the apostles, and Paul too wrote, "But we speak the wisdom of God in a mystery, even the hidden wisdom." (39) By faith and insight we are able to comprehend His parables and dark sentences ". . .for the Spirit searcheth all things, yea, the deep things of God." (40)

By faith in the Stone ". . .ye are no more strangers and foreigners, but fellow citizens with the saints, and of the household of God; and are built upon the foundation of the apostles and prophets, Jesus Christ being the Chief

Cornerstone in whom all the building fitly framed together groweth unto a holy temple of the Lord; in whom ye also are builded together for a *habitation of God* through the Spirit." (41)   Peter too wrote in the imagery of a great building at which God sits at its apex:

> "You have tasted that the Lord is gracious.
> To whom coming, as unto a living stone,
> disallowed indeed of men, but chosen
> of God, and precious. Ye also, as lively
> stones, are built upon a spiritual house, an
> holy priesthood . . . wherefore also it is
> contained in the Scripture, Behold, I lay in
> Sion a Chief Cornerstone, elect, precious:
> and he that believeth on Him shall not be
> confounded. Unto you therefore which
> believe he is precious, but unto them
> which be disobedient, the stone which
> the builders disallowed, the same shall be
> made the head of the corner, and a stone of
> stumbling, and a rock of offense." (42)

As believers in Him we are a part of the temple of God (43), the pillar and ground of truth that is the Church of the Living God. (44) We are God's building, and as Christ is the image of the Invisible God, we as believers are images of God, unified by faith as stones built together in the image of "Mount Sion, the City of the Living God, the heavenly Jerusalem." (45) And as we ". . .have borne the image of the earthly, we shall bear the image of the heavenly," because our *names* are written in heaven. (46) Though we are often taught that passages like this are metaphorical or merely symbolic, it is evidenced by the Book of Enoch that at the Creation the stars of the sky were individually named before mankind was made, each star representing the ". . .names* of the righteous who dwell upon earth, and who believe in the *name of the lord* of spirits forever . . ." (47)

And such is the proof that the apostles were initiates of this arcanum and its mysteries. But these secrets long hoped for did not end with them. Even more enigmatic writings began surfacing that served to reveal that there were some among the believers who recognized that the arcanum was not a Christian invention nor a new revelation, but that it has roots extending back to the earliest times that men were upon the earth.

Christian Apocryphal Writings

The apocryphal writings were born out of a conviction best stated in 2 Esdras, "some things thou shalt publish, and some things thou shalt show secretly to the wise." (48) These early writers knew that a little learning was a dangerous thing, as says the old occult proverb. Early Christian sages identified with the Psalmist who wrote, "I understand more than the ancients, because I keep thy precepts," (49) while also conceding that ". . .it is the glory of God to conceal a thing," (50) rather than reveal their secrets to all because they were acutely aware that with knowledge and wisdom comes responsibility. As ". . .stewards of the mysteries of God," (51) these men guarded their holy secrets from the undeserving and profane because ". . .through knowledge shall the *just* be delivered." (52) Admonished to refrain from casting their pearls (wisdom) before swine (spiritually unclean), they relied on God to reveal "the deep and secret things," (53) to His chosen while the worldly people "were destroyed from lack of knowledge." (54) This wisdom is centered around Christ and His resurrection, who said, ". . .there is nothing covered, that will not be revealed, and hid, that will not be made known," (55) for in Christ "are hid all the treasures of wisdom and knowledge." (56)

The greatest treasure is ". . .the mystery which hath been hid from ages and from generations, but is now made manifest." (57) This mystery is His resurrection, an immortal inheritance that extends to all who have faith in Him. These sages concealed many of their observances and teachings in the Gnostic, Hermetic and also the Alchemical literature of early Christianity. The Philosopher's [lover of wisdom] Stone and the myth of the transmutation of base metals into pure gold by virtue of this stone is none other than the secret of resurrection by the power of the Stone ingeniously hidden so effectively to the ignorant as to have given rise to an entire pseudo-science that spawned countless vain treatises on alchemy from the first centuries of the Christian era until relatively modern times.

Diligent searchers of the Gnosis studied olden manuscripts of former religious and spiritual texts knowing that they were but a mere façade that concealed subsurface mysteries, esoteric secrets, mystical answers to eternal questions, spiritual precepts and knowledge so profound that it led the mind to the edges of divine wisdom. It was the general assumption that mythologies contained fragmented truths of religious ideals *originally* revealed. (58) Such a concept has been very difficult for modern Christianity to grasp.

To the Gnostic it was the act of unearthing the buried secrets of a thousand texts that revealed to them the Universal Mind in the language of the past, present and future. They regarded humanity as divine beings who have lost the knowledge of their own identity. They attempted to bridge the extreme differences among the ancient religious schools and mysteries by identifying all the universals within the various systems, exhibiting for all that behind the scenes of every major spiritual movement from times immemorial there is a common teaching embedded within them all – a universal gnosis.

Alexandria, Egypt was the center of Gnostic study, which is not surprising considering the vast amount of literature collected there. Undisputed authority of Gnosticism Manly P. Hall in his *Wisdom of the Knowing Ones* wrote that the Gnostics were philosophers who explored the dynamics of God's creation to comprehend the Universal Plan and will of the Planner. They diligently sought the universals in Christianity. Though the early church father Augustine wrote that ". . .the same thing which is called Christian religion, existed among the ancients," (59) the Church resented the Gnostic savants because these mystics pointed out to the early Christians the non-Christian elements and sources of their doctrines and beliefs (60), which earned them the undeserved title of Pagans. The Gnostics were deep thinkers and according to Manly P. Hall in *Mystics and Mysteries of Alexandria* many of the Gnostic astrological symbols derived directly from Sumerian precedents. (61) For these symbols of early Christianity to be copies of Sumerian pictographs lends credit to the claims of the Gnostics in that the elements of Christianity are truly arcane with roots into the ancient past. Prior to about the middle of the second century AD the Gnostics were not considered heretical. It was the later literalism of official Roman Christianity that led to the social disappearance of Gnosticism by the end of the sixth century AD. (62) However, records indicate that they remained a secretive sect well into the Dark Ages (63), and there is every possibility that Gnostic orders continue to exist today that are directly connected to their historic brethren.

One of the principle Gnostic figures was the person of Hermes. In an old text attributed to Hermes called the *Golden Tractate* we find:

> "All the sciences of the world, O son, are
> comprehended in this my hidden wisdom,"
> and that one seeking such must first be ". .
> .a patient guardian of the arcane secrets of
> philosophy." (64) These secrets of ancient
> wisdom came from the Stone– "Understand
> then, O son of wisdom, what the Stone
> declares. . . them that seek after me will

I make to know and understand, and to
possess divine things." (65)

According to Hermes the divine things are "given by our ancestors in
types and figures. Behold they are dead. I have opened the riddle, and the
book of knowledge is revealed, the hidden things I have uncovered, and have
brought together the scattered truths within. . ." (66) It is these scattered
truths concealed in types and figures that was invested in the prophets of old,
in dark sentences, so that those ". . .drowned in worldly godliness might not
discover." (67) It is for this reason that the eyes of men "see as through a glass
darkly," (68) or, only in part. Hermes was the central study of Gnosticism, a
fragmented memory of Enoch and the revelations received through the many
apocryphal texts attributed to him. The Gnostics knew that Enoch's writings
were highly symbolic and yet based off of actual history and prophetic visions
from the mind of God. They realized the world around them was an alien
world not their own, and that ". . .things are not what they seem." (69)

In *The Gnosis: Or Ancient Wisdom in the Christian Scriptures* by William
Kingsland we learn that exoteric doctrines concerning textual writings are for the
masses and are the surface texts themselves, while *esoteric* teachings are gleaned
by those who seek deeper into the writings of Scripture and find that the surface
text is but a covering of greater things. (70) A good analogy can be seen in that
originally the Great Pyramid was covered in beautiful white limestone casing
blocks faced completely over with tiny inscriptions that conveyed depthless
knowledge and secrets, however, even these archives of heaven and earth were
but a covering over the greater truths embodied in the structural designs of the
pyramid's chambers, corridors and actual brickwork. This is further taught in the
Zohar, a text of the Jewish Kabbala. We read, "The narratives of the doctrine are
its cloak. The simple only look on the garment, that is, upon the narrative of the
doctrines; more they know not. The instructed however, see not merely the
cloak but what the cloak covers." (71) The Gnostics believed very similarly
with the initiates of the Kabbala, believing that amongst the oldest writings in
the world was ". . .a body of teaching running through them all, back to the
most ancient times of which we have any literary records." (72).

Thomas Burgoyne in 1889 in his book *The Light of Egypt: Science of the
Soul and Stars* prefixed his peculiar book with an illustration of the Kabbalistic
version of the seven-pointed star. This illustration shows the seven spheres of
Creation, seven holy archangels, seven divine virtues, the seven colors of the
light spectrum and seven astrological symbols designating the ancient known
planetary and cosmic bodies in our solar system. Within the seven-pointed

star is an *eighth* sphere that exhibits the three holy attributes of the Godhead surrounding a *pyramid with an eye glyph* within it. Burgoyne wrote that this glyph represented the divine mind of the angelic creators. (73) It was believed by many that God created the universe through His angels. As revealed earlier in this book concerning the extreme antiquity of the seven-pointed star glyph, the Kabbalists were keepers to a sacred knowledge spanning millennia and incorporated within the design of the Great Pyramid. Interestingly, as if understanding this and also agreeing with the philosophy of the Gnostics, Thomas Burgoyne over a hundred and ten years ago wrote, ". . .As there may be many roads which ultimately lead us to the same mountain top, so there are many systems of occult training." (74) The occultist is a scientist of subtexts, a seeker of that which is hidden from the ordinary searcher.

The Kabbalic Star

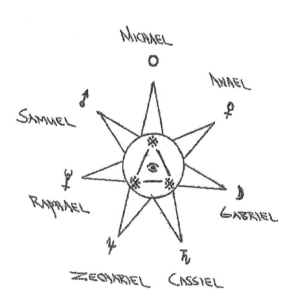

The Gnostics were Christians, but because of their teachings and discoveries they were persecuted. They were not alone. There are many Christian apocryphal writings from those times not considered Gnostic and contain the same elements and some even have more fragments of the arcanum knowledge. The apocryphal books were once very popular books that quickly fell into disrepute. The Romanized Church deleted them from the canon of Scripture and as a result most believers never came into contact with them. These fascinating works were then studied largely in secret by open-minded monks and bishops who passed them on to like-minded friends and members of their orders. The original meaning of apocryphal, or *apokruphos*, was that of a work that contained a secret knowledge too excellent for the masses. (75)

One of these apocryphal texts is the mysterious book called *The Shepherd of Hermas*, a title directly associating its contents with the wisdom literature of Hermes. Which is exactly how it reads. This work is extensive and was studied by no less than Irenaeus and other fathers of early Christianity. Origen and Eusebius thought it was divinely inspired and the writings were appreciated as well by Jerome and Athanasius. The book is made up of three large sections called Commandments, the Visions and the Similitudes and they are enigmatic, employing many of the symbols of the arcana already cited and explained throughout this book. In a vision an angel took Hermas to a special place and:

> "In the *middle of the plain* he showed me
> a huge *white rock*, which rose out of the
> plain, and the rock was higher than those
> [the seven] mountains, and was *square*, so
> that it seemed capable of supporting the
> whole world. It looked to me to be old,
> yet it had in it a *new gate*, which seemed
> to have been newly hewn out of it. Now
> the gate was bright beyond the sun itself;
> insomuch that I greatly admired at its
> light." (76)

Then did Hermas get shown the building of this white rock, for his vision involved a strange architectural project in the making. He watched in amazement as thousands of men assembled around six huge figures that instruct the men to build this tower *over a body of water* with bright square stones by placing them in a huge square. The stones used in the building project arose *out of the deep* (the primordial water source) and then each stone was carried *through* this gate before the builders could use it in their labors. Hermas wrote, "As for those stones which were drawn out of the deep, they put them all into the building: for they were polished, and their squares exactly answered one another, and so was one joined in such wise to another, that there was no space to be seen where they joined, insomuch that the whole tower appeared to be built as it were of *one stone*. (77)

After a while a seventh figure appeared who was much taller than the other six huge men that the others gathered around. This colossal figure ordered that all stones not carried through the gate to the building site be removed from the structure and replaced with others that passed through the gate. ". . .And when I diligently considered what a tower it was, I was extremely pleased: and he said unto me, bring hither some *lime and little shells*, that I may fill up the spaces of those stones that were taken out of the building, and put in again; for all things about the tower must be made even . . ." (78) The presence of joints and squares answering each other so that there ". . .was no space to be seen where they joined," as well as a cement of lime and little shells alludes to the construction of the Great Pyramid, which, when this was written, still appeared as one stone because the white casing blocks had not yet been removed. The fact that the ". . .tower must be made even . . .," is also a fact that the pyramid builders had lived with. If any stones were not plush the casing stones would not have fit perfectly on the monument. By perfectly aligning these stones the garment of white rock would easily cover the building underneath.

After the completion of the tower, the arcanum in the Hermas text is introduced in its fullest extent in these writings. Hermas asks the angel about these things and his inquiries do not remain unanswered.

"Hearken, said he, this rock, and this gate,
are the Son of God. I replied, Sir, How
can this be possible, seeing that the rock
is old, but the gate is new? Hear, said he,
O foolish man! and understand. The Son
of God is indeed more ancient than any
creature; insomuch that he was in counsel
with his Father at the creation of all things.
But the gate is therefore new, because He

appeared in the last days in the fullness
of time; that they shall attain salvation,
may enter into the Kingdom of God. You
have seen, those stones which were not
carried through the gate, were sent away
to their own places? I answered, Sir, I saw
it. Thus, he said, no man shall enter the
kingdom of God, but he who shall take
upon the *name* of the Son of God . . . And
he said unto me, Sawest thou those stones
that were cast away? They indeed bore
the name, but put not on their *garment*. I
said, Sir, what is their garment? And he
answered saying, Their very *names* are their
garment." (79)

After researching Hermas and many other apocryphal writings Gerald Massey in 1883 wrote in his The Natural Genesis that ". . .in Hermas, the Church takes the place of the pyramid and the rude stone monuments that were reared of old *above the water source*." (80) The Hermas text serves to explain why Christ enigmatically referred to Himself as the Way, the Truth, and the Life. The gospel accounts refer to Him as the Door and as many researchers of yesterday and today have discovered, the oldest representations of the Lord upon earth are of doors, gates and cave entrances into sacred mountains.

Another sage of early Christianity was named Ignatius, a man of profound learning whose many works have survived until today, writings once considered a part of the canon of Scripture to the Ante Nicene Fathers. In the *Epistle of Ignatius to the Philadelphians* we see a further connection between the pyramid imagery and the Lord. Ignatius wrote, "But to me Jesus Christ is instead of all the *uncorrupted monuments* in the world, together with those untouched monuments, his cross, his death, and resurrection, and the faith which is by him." (81) In Ignatius' time the casing blocks still clothed the Great Pyramid and it wasn't until centuries later that human hands corrupted the Gizean monuments. That there was a knowledge in those times of existing holy pre-flood relics, architectural fossils still standing seems to be alluded in Philo's writings as well; ". . .for although corruption had prevailed over all the men who lived on the earth from the excess of their iniquities, still there remain some *relics of antiquity* and that of which was from the *beginning*, and a slight seed of previous virtues; by which it is intimated nevertheless that the memory of the good deeds that have been done from the beginning is not wholly destroyed . . ." (82)

It can not be disputed that Ignatius was an initiate of this arcanum, for to the Ephesians he said they should be ". . .as becoming the stones of the temple of the Father, prepared for his building," and in his letter to Polycarp he began his message with ". . .having known that thy mind towards God, is fixed as it were upon an immovable rock." (83) His familiarity with the gospel of John where Christ said, "I am the door; by me if any man enter in, he shall be saved," (84) and the writings of Hermas is clearly seen in his epistles where he wrote that ". . .He is the door to the Father; by which Abraham, Isaac, and Jacob, and all the prophets enter in; as well as the apostles, and the Church, and all these things tend to the unity which is in God. Howbeit, the gospel has somewhat in it far above other dispensations; namely, the appearance of our Savior . . ." (85) Tragically, when Ignatius was bishop of Antioch in Syria about 110 AD he was cited to Rome during the reign of Emperor Trajan and fed to wild beasts in the Coliseum.

One other early Christian writer who had some knowledge of the arcanum was Barnabas, who wrote that when believers lived in ". . .the high den of the strong rock," God will "go before them, and *make plain the mountain*, and will break the gates of brass, and will snap in sunder the bars of iron; and will give thee dark, and hidden and invisible treasures . . ." (86) The phrase make plain the mountain refers to the future dissemination of secret information and hidden knowledge promised to all believers, no doubt referring also to the true significance of the Great Pyramid. Earlier in this work we learned that treasures from the antediluvian world were buried by the Sethites underneath the Giza plateau in halls and chambers cut out of the rock that were to be discovered at a predetermined time. The gates of brass and bars of iron is figurative for hell and the power of the underworld over men, a power that the pyramid symbolically subjugates by its placement above the entrance to the netherworld.

Secrets of the Genesis Narrative

The most fundamental aspect of the arcanum is that the writings of the Scriptures, principally Genesis, are layered in rich symbolism that serve to conceal deeper mysteries than the surface narratives convey. The Genesis account of Adam and Eve begins with these symbols: a garden, two trees, one of life and the other of knowledge and a serpent that deceived them. The garden is a prophetic type of how eternal earth will be, the restoration of Edenic paradise. This arcanum has unveiled a tremendous amount of evidence that the tree of life and of knowledge were not literal trees, but architectural monuments with inscriptions upon them written by God. Such would not have been the only time God has written actual writings for man. The Ten Commandments were written with a finger of God, and so was MENE MENE TEKEL UPHARSIN, the enigmatic message written to the Babylonian king who lost his empire in the days of Daniel the prophet. The finger of God also wrote in the sand when Jesus Himself was brought a woman caught in adultery, the Lord saying, "He that is without sin cast the first stone." Writing in the sand must have struck a powerful fear into the hearts of these Pharisees who sought to trap Jesus, for a man was before them claiming to be God who was also writing in the sand during a conversation involving *judgment*. These men of learning knew well the inference being made by Christ, for the Scriptures clearly read that ". . .the wicked are written *in the earth*." (87) It is this author's belief that Jesus was writing the *names* of the Pharisees who brought the woman in the sand.

Another such writing of God in the beginning concerns the tree of life and tree of knowledge. Trees were particularly venerated long ago because they were seen as a source of nourishment, shelter, shade and building materials. For this reason was this symbol employed to describe two monuments in Eden accessible to man that were covered in the writings of the Creator. One was the Book of Life made accessible to Adam and Eve and the other was the forbidden Book of Knowledge of Good and Evil. This is consistent with the Sumerian belief that the tree of life was merely an *image* of the truth. The name for the Sumerian protector of the Tree of Life, NIN.GISH.ZI.DA is also translated as Lord of the *Artifact* of Life. (88) These trees in Eden were actually *containers of knowledge*.

Just as the trees were symbolic types of deeper truths, so too is the serpent figurative for something else. The serpent that literally spoke with Eve was not a true snake. The writings of the Book of Enoch tell us that before the Flood evil spiritual beings against the commandments of God taught mankind forbidden knowledge not meant for human comprehension, such as hybridization and metallurgical sciences, herbalism, astrology, warfare, feminine cosmetics and how ". . .to kill an embryo in the womb." (89) Abortion. Evidence of such forbidden information is also found in Enoch in the form of an astounding metallurgical secret: that *lead* is not naturally produced from the earth. (90) How did this become known in antiquity? Lead is radioactive waste, a byproduct of radioactive decay of heavier isotopes such as uranium and plutonium to less radioactive elements. In the beginning, which was *perfect*, lead would not have existed. Lead deposits and trace elements are evidence of a series of prehistoric catastrophic events and ancient man's awareness of it was by supernatural means.

This knowledge were delivered unto men by demonic beings bent on frustrating the plans of God in replacing them with a glorified humanity. Such ancestral memories earned these beings the name of *demon*, which is from an old root meaning "to know." The serpent in Genesis is from a Hebrew word *nahash*, itself derivative of NHSH, which means *to decipher, find out*. (91) The Christian Gnostics believed that the serpent meant "instructor." (92) The Egyptian hieroglyph of the serpent (cobra) is the determinative for "special keeper of concealed secrets," (93) and the serpent sign called the *tet* of Egypt signifies "speech; to tell." (94) Philo wrote that the serpent was actually a "dragon uttering the voice of a man." (95) In Greek drakon means "the seeing one," and is a word for serpent. Another word for serpent was ophis, from optesthai (to see), a root from which our English *optics* derives. Python is yet another Greek word for snake, literally meaning "the knowing one." (96)

The serpent was the arch deceiver who convinced Eve to listen to him as he taught her knowledge gained from the surfaces of the Book of Knowledge of Good and Evil. Mankind was then living in a perpetual state of perfection and harmony with the Creator, and the Adversary, typified as the snake in Genesis, knew that he had to cause mankind to fall in order for him to become the mighty red dragon we find in the Revelation. His evolution from serpent to seven-headed red dragon is a popular myth embedded in the lore of virtually every culture on earth, a destiny encoded in the symbols of Scriptures that typify him. No other being was more qualified than the former archangel once called Lucifer, or the Day Star to teach Eve the difference between good and evil. In the *Gospel of Nicodemus* we read a glimpse of these elder traditions: "O Prince Satan, thou keeper of the infernal regions, all thy advantages which thou didst acquire by the *forbidden tree*." (97)

In order to gain spiritual dominion over the earth, Satan had to reduce mankind to earthly beings bereft of their own divine essences. When Adam and Eve ate of the tree of knowledge at the tempting of the serpent they were stripped of their "garments of light." (98) This is why God forbade Adam to touch the tree of knowledge, so long as the good and the evil are linked together." (99) In the Quran we find that Iblis (Satan) refused to bow down to mankind, a passage in reference to an *Accursed Tree*. This divine and cursed tree was the tree of Zaqqum, which is the *food* for the sinner, a tree that springs in the heart of hell. (100) Because Lucifer had already taken forbidden knowledge and lost his first estate, he sought to make mankind suffer his fate as well, a belief also reflected in the Quran: "Lo! Those of old and those of later time will all be brought together at an appointed time on a day known only to Allah. Then Lo! You, the erring, the deniers, you surely will eat of the tree of Zaqqum." (101) The fallen spiritual beings lost their garments of light and sought desperately to keep the men of the earth from acquiring their lost positions among the divine government of God. They knew that if they could divert worship away from the Creator they could keep as many souls from Him as possible in order to delay their own judgment. These entities according to the Quran were made of smokeless fire and called the jinn. They were led by Iblis, who orchestrated a rebellion against Allah. Once ousted from heaven these beings were found guilty of having men worship them on earth. (102)

Evidence that the fruit eaten by Eve and shared with Adam was not actually a fruit is found in the *Book of Adam and Eve I* (103) which claims that in the garden of Eden ". . .eating and drinking" was unknown to Adam and Eve. Evidently nutritional sustenance was not required until they lost their garments of light. This fruit was no more literal than when Christ said, "You will know them by their fruit," which was a reference to Proverbs 11:30, "The fruit of the righteous is a tree of life; and he that winneth souls is wise." This is what the Adversary did. He deceitfully won their souls (albeit temporarily) by the dissemination of evil knowledge, securing himself terrestrial kingship over Eden (also temporary). In the Egyptian *Book of the Dead* a hieroglyphic text reads, "he hath *eaten* the knowledge of every god," (104) which was a prerequisite to obtaining safe passage through the underworld on one's way to the Afterlife. This is similar to Nepalese Tantric writings, which claim that heavenly beings were created before mankind and later visited earth, *tasting its food* and remained trapped here for eating it. (105) This is a complete reversal of what happened to mankind. Humans tasted divine knowledge they were not permitted to indulge in and lost their glorified bodies – this being after heavenly angels tasted earthly food and were cursed to remain here for defiling their bodies, as found in the Nepalese writings.

Amazingly, the eating of knowledge to obtain salvation is found in the esoteric writings of the Book of Enoch, which reads, "And on that day were two monsters parted, a female monster named Leviathan, to dwell in the abysses of the ocean over the fountains of the waters. But the male is named Behemoth, who occupied with this breast a waste wilderness named Duidain, on the *east of the garden* where the elect and righteous dwell, where my grandfather *was taken up*, the seventh from Adam." (106) This passage was a part of the fragmented Book of Noah and was written from the perspective of Lamech, father of Noah. The seventh from Adam of course is Enoch, taken up into heaven at Achuzan, the antediluvian site now called Giza where Methuselah and other Sethites erected the pyramids and Sphinx as per the divine instructions given to Enoch in heaven. The records of the ancient Hebrews reveals that another monument [pillar] was erected before the deluge, as has already been detailed in this work, that was destined to be buried beneath the sea by the flood and remain there. But the Giza complex was to survive this cataclysm and endure the millennia to be a continual reminder to man of earth's future fiery deluge. The author of this part of the Enochian fragments asked an angel what these two beasts represented, but the angel said, "Thou son of man, herein thou dost seek to know what is *hidden*." (107) Amen?

To the archaic mind the wilderness deserts and oceans represented places on earth that signified death, regions roamed by the creatures of death such as scorpions and crustaceans. Oceanic waters were believed to be residual left over from a prehistoric flood that ruined the Old World. Deserts were viewed in much the same way, a place where earth itself was still dead. Nothing is fruitful in a desert, it was popularly believed, because God visited destruction upon it in a prior epoch. Thus the sea and desert became places where evil was wont to reside. "May the curse depart to the desert," was a popular expression in Babylonian verse. (108) The name Duidain is also Dendain, from the Hebrew Din-Dayyan, or, Judgment of the Judge. (109) Deserts and oceans are symbols of *judgment*.

Though in distant antiquity the identities of Leviathon and Behemoth were shrouded in mystery, symbols identifying themselves as *food*, by the meticulous assembling of the varied elements of the arcanum as seen throughout this work we understand that Leviathon and Behemoth together are metaphors for the Tree of Life and Tree of Knowledge, and by extension, the Giza pyramids [behemoth] and their guardian Sphinx [leviathan] that rests over the Deep. There is another similar interpretation well favored by this author. Leviathon could also be a reference to the other pillar of the Sethites that was specifically designed to be destroyed with the flood. It now lies beneath the ocean somewhere on earth. This would identify the two types of land surfaces in the world representing judgment. Behemoth identifies the dry land whereas Leviathon the ocean.

In Genesis God gave to mankind the beasts of the earth as *food* (110), which terrestrially, leviathan (great serpent) and behemoth (huge beast) are beasts of the earth that probably walked the earth and swam the seas in prehistoric times when the Great Lizards reigned under original Draconian Earth. Poetically, as the Adversary feeds upon the souls of humanity in his effort to delay judgment so too has God given over Satan's earliest minions to be resources of mankind in the form of fossil fuels, coals, bitumens and natural gases all formed from the decomposition of billions of prehistoric life forms.

Concerning these two beasts, Enoch wrote, "And these things I saw toward the Garden of the Righteous. And the angel of peace who was with me said, "These two monsters, prepared *conformably* to the greatness of God, shall feed . . ." (111) Apparently, though the Enochian text is broken it contained a reference to *feeding the righteous*. This is derived from Jewish writings claiming that Behemoth and Leviathon were created to be *food* for the righteous in Messianic times. (112) Since Leviathon and Behemoth are made *conformably* to the greatness of God just as man is but an earthly *image* of God, these two beasts may be images of God in beast form prepared for consumption by mankind at an appointed time. The Psalms also refer to Leviathon as being *meat* to the people inhabiting the wilderness. (113) In the beginning of man the learning of forbidden knowledge corrupted Adam and Eve, and the very beings (animals) that they were appointed to exercise dominion over and guard became their sustenance in the exact same way that the Adversary delayed his own demise by feeding on the spirits of humanity.

It is this revelation that is unveiled in the arcanum and it is the Great Pyramid that foreshadows the time when mankind will be freed from the curse after divine fires purge the spirits of the holy, when terrestrial fires consume the earth and when eternal fires fuel His judgment. There is nothing more fitting than to end this text with an emphatic Amen! However, there is one other curious word integral to the arcanum also found abundantly and with equal mystery throughout the Scriptures yet to receive worthy attention. This word is *Selah*, and like Amen it was an expression of hope referring to the Coming One, a phonetic expression meaning Fire of the everlasting. (114) But both will have to wait, for this work is not finished.

Archive Six

The Lost Scriptures of Giza

It has long been recognized that Abraham was the patriarch of the three great international, trans-cultural religions of Judaism, Christianity and Islam. We have reviewed definitive evidence that Egypt's priesthoods were touched by the patriarch, and that these revelations became the fundamental beliefs of India as well. In our quest to piece back together the lost scriptures of Giza and their messages to humanity we would do well to explore more of these fragments.

A Jewish tradition reinforces this thesis linking Abraham to Egypt and India along with the Great Pyramids. This tradition holds that Abraham received the mystic knowledge from Hermes himself according to the Alexandrian text called the *Kybalion*. Herein we read–

> From the land of the Ganges [India] many
> advanced occultists wandered to the land of
> Egypt and sat at the feet of the Master . . .
> from other lands also came the learned
> ones, all of whom regarded Hermes as the
> Master of Masters and his influence was so
> great that in spite of the many wanderings
> from the path on the parts of the centuries
> of teachings in these different lands,
> there may still be found a certain basic
> resemblance and correspondence which
> underlies the many and quite divergent
> theories entertained and taught by the
> occultists of these different lands today. (1)

The Hermes traditions reflect both Enoch before the Flood and then Abraham after it. According to Jamblichus, Hermes composed 20,000 books and the Egyptian historian-priest Manetho wrote it to be 36,000 books. (2) No man has ever written so many books. This confusion was born long ago from the knowledge that the interpreter (Abraham) of Hermes' (Enoch's) writings had access to a truly vast collection of writings dating from the times before the Great Flood. This Hermes was often associated to the Thoth of the early Egyptian traditions and wall-texts, a memory of Enoch the Scribe. Writing over twenty-two centuries ago at Alexandria, Egypt, Manetho asserted that before the cataclysm [Flood] in Egypt the god Thoth inscribed books upon the Siriadic Columns [Great Pyramids]. After the Flood, at a later period, the *Second Thoth* came to Egypt and translated these writings in the vulgar tongues of men, the original texts having been composed in a sacred language. (3)

In a single tradition we find that a vast corpus of knowledge on the past and future was once intact, inscribed upon pillars, surviving a global disaster that wiped out the civilization that preserved this knowledge, were rediscovered, interpreted and taught to men who collected what they deemed pertinent when they returned to their own countries. So enormous was this knowledge that the nations of men preserved it in *fragments* and nowhere on earth was it preserved in its entirety. Even in the American southwest on the opposite side of the earth this memory still lives among the last of the Hopi. They hold that at the end of the world will come the Great Purification, a purging of wickedness from earth and restoration of peace. But prior to this great purification will come a terrible global disaster and the *ancient knowledge will be restored.* This ancient knowledge according to them were from sacred stone tablets fashioned by the Great Spirit in the beginning that contain all the teachings, instructions, prophecies and warnings about the end of the world. Long ago these tablets had become separated but one day they will be reassembled and put back together before the Great Purification begins. (4) Earlier in this book a Hopi depiction of the Great Pyramid with secret entrance in form of

a step-pyramid with casing blocks was depicted. The Way Home was *through* a deity that served as a door into the pyramid, a belief very popular among the Phoenicians and Carthagenians who fashioned amulets of a god holding its arms up like *two pillars* in the shape of a pyramid. (5)

Carthage as a Phoenician civilization was densely populated with the descendants of Israel. The Hopi representation is made more profound because a step-pyramid hieroglyph in Egyptian means "to ascend." (6)

In the Arabic traditions of Abraham we again find Abraham linked to these motifs. He is said to have possessed a tablet of symbols by which he used to know the past, the present and the future, similar to the Sumerian Tablet of Destinies. (7) No doubt onlookers were astonished watching Abraham at the base of the Great Pyramid as he studied the small writings upon the white limestone casing blocks while consulting the tablet covered in sigils and symbols by which he used to *translate* the "scared language." As shown earlier in this work, Abraham was taught the pre-flood language by those very men who survived the Flood.

That Abraham ventured into the Great Pyramid and discovered something in the King's Chamber is alluded to in an Arabic tradition that maintains that he opened a very ancient coffer and found therein the truly old books of his ancestors Adam, Enoch and Seth. (8) This of course would refer to the Granite Sarcophagus in the Kings Chamber that once had a sliding granite lid. This is the mysterious Box of the Lord enigmatically referred to in the Egyptian writings, like this– "Lord of the earth in a Box is thy Name; all the gods to the utmost are humiliated at the words of the *Lord of the Chest.*" (9) It was from inside this "chest" in the Great Pyramid that the *Word* of the god emerged. This exact same concept was later replicated by the Israelites when they preserved a copy of the Torah, the Books of the Law of God and the Tables of Stone inside the holy Ark of the Covenant, or Box of the Lord.

Abraham is particularly venerated in Islam. In the holy city of Mecca rests the Kaaba, Islam's holiest shrine, forbidden to all westerners. At the center of the mosque is a 50' cube covered in silk embroidered with Quranic verses in golden thread—a shrine said to have been built by Abraham, though there are no biblical or non-Arabic traditions of Abraham ever travelling into Arabia. Inside is a stone said to have fallen from heaven, in fact, a meteorite. The square is linked to the Great Pyramid's square base which was covered in casing blocks [a garment] covered in writings – and some of the pre-Islamic Arabian verses embroidered upon the silk garment may indeed have their origin with writings once adorning the Great Pyramid.

The Hopi were not alone in the Americas to recognize such a unique history. A fascinating discovery has surfaced in Ecuador. An ancient metal plate of unknown antiquity and origin of exquisite detail has been found that clearly depicts a perfect picture of the *Great Pyramid* guarded by sphinx-like creatures, each block of the structure individually detailed with even a layer of casing blocks and a topstone with a smiling face! The *Chief Cornerstone* symbolizing the Savior. Above the topstone is a sunburst like an eye with rays emanating like the Great Seal of the United States. But the most compelling confirmation that this metal plate indeed depicts the Great Pyramid in Egypt is found in that the lowest course of blocks is *covered in inscriptions* in an unknown script of strange symbols. (10) A photo of this discovery and amazing plate can be viewed in Vol. 9 No. 1 and 2 of *Legendary Times* magazine on pages 46-47 in an article by Cornelia von Daniken entitled Secrets of the Lost Tayos Gold Library. This magazine can be obtained very cheaply through Book Tree of San Diego.

The Chief Cornerstone has arisen from the tomb symbolized by the Empty Sarcophagus to soon take His position upon the Monument of Man, of which the Great Pyramid is the great symbol. He is the Son of the Living God and He is found in the very oldest beliefs of Egypt. One of God's early titles in Egypt was IU, which was recognized at the old cult center of Annu, a Father-Son priesthood venerating Ptah and his divine son IU. One of His titles was Atum-Iu, the Father-Son. (11) Iu was equivalent to the Hebrew Yah, the eastern Yu and the later Egyptian Christian [Coptic] and Gnostic Yao/Iao as in the Books of Jao. When the Danites departed from Canaan in the 14th century BC and became the Danaan settlers of the pre-Greek Peloponnesus and coasts of Asia Minor they were called by the local populations as Io, for peoples in antiquity were identified by the names of the gods they served. Thus, the ancient *Ionians* were the descendants of Israelites and it was these people who built the seven cities wherein were later located the seven churches of Christianity found in Revelation 1-3 like Ephesus, Thyratira, Smyrna, Corinth, Thessalonica, etc.

We must not overlook the geographical importance of the religious cult center of Annu. The city of Annu was later known as On where many of the Israelites dwelt in Lower Egypt. It was later called Memphis and Heliopolis and according to Diodorus over two thousand years ago it was claimed to be the oldest city in Egypt. (12) This city of Annu was the closest city to the Great Pyramid complex, only a few miles away, and remarkably, the original meaning of Annu was *pillar*, being the Stone that marked the Foundation. Further linking this site to the Great Pyramid is that the Heliopolitan priesthood associated the god Set [Sethites, builders of the pyramids] with the city of Annu (13) and the priests claimed that the oldest monuments in Egypt were built by an earlier race. (14) Considering that Annu was the oldest city in Egypt this Heliopolitan belief is very telling. It was here at biblical On that Abraham visited and taught and his revelations were immortalized in hieroglyphics and it was this particular priesthood that venerated the Hidden one . . . *Amen*, who was the Father and Son into One. (15) Egyptologists largely concentrate on the Osirian Cult and on Isis when expounding upon things Egyptian but scholars and archeologists have long noted that the worship of Osiris and Isis came *late* in the history of Egypt and there is a very biblical and historical reason for this. In 1447 BC the country of Egypt was virtually destroyed in a series of catastrophes and the Israelites departed the land in the Exodus. The surviving people of Egypt, devastated, blamed the God of the Israelites for their misfortune and they immediately scoured the temples and monuments throughout Egypt and scraped off all known references and depictions of the Virgin giving birth to the Son and the cartouches of the Father-Son. The importance of Set to the Israelites was known and this prompted the Egyptians to demonize Set and his name and depictions were also destroyed as well as that of Iu. Archeologists have found much evidence of this wholesale ruination of the older gods and faiths. Fortunately, because the Egyptians did not climb to the top of temples, obelisks and other structures many references survived and archeologists have also found many depictions of these older gods and faiths in tombs from earlier periods. The Osirian and Isis cults only took hold of the population of Egypt *after* the Israelites were gone.

Amen was the Hidden One, the invisible Lord of the Chest, He who promised redemption and resurrection, concepts taught by Abraham when he was in Egypt from 1837-1825 BC. So fervently did the Egyptians believe in a resurrection that they mummified their dead in elaborate rituals and preserved the individual internal organs in jars and provided victuals for the dead. They took the belief to the extreme believing that to be resurrected there had to be some of the body remaining intact. It was Abraham's teachings at this time that became the fundamentals of Brahmanism in India and Zoroastrianism in Elam/Persia. It is to those lands we now traverse.

At approximately 470 BC Xanthos of Lydia wrote that Zoroaster's ministry was 600 years before the Trojan War. (16) Like many historic chroniclers, Xanthos used the anciently well-known Trojan War date as a chronological reference, our BC-AD system nonexistent then. The Trojan War was an international Mediterranean conflict lasting ten years beginning in 1239 BC and ending in 1229 BC with the Fall of Troy that coincided that year with a series of natural disasters. Xanthos' 600 years is on the mark for Zoroaster was none other than Abraham who's ministry at Giza and Annu in Egypt was from 1837-1825 BC. Xanthos could not have been more precise. In *The Fountainhead of Religion* (1927) Ganga Prasad relates that Zoroaster was a contemporary of Abraham around 1900 BC (he being 47 years old in 1900 BC and that Zoroaster was from Arran, but biblically, Abraham was from *Harran* [Haran]. (17) Mohammedan scholars long ago linked Abraham to Zoroaster and in the Vernacular Persian Dictionary we find that Zardushta [Zoroaster] *was* the Abraham of scripture. (18)

The earliest relics of the Zoroastrian writings are the Gathas, dating back to at least the 14th century BC. (19) The Gathas are devoid of the fantastic and are merely *fragments of a larger literature.* (20) Pliny believed that Zoroaster's original writings numbered 2,000,000 verses (21), but this is merely an indirect memory of the immensely extensive texts upon the Great Pyramid's lower casing blocks. The name *Gathas* may have been preserved because Abraham when in Egypt was known to have priorly lived in the land of the Philistines, Gath being a major city. The Gathas were regarded as especially sacred, having remained untouched by editors and are included in the Zend Avesta, the holiest writings of Persia. Remarkably, the finest writings are the *oldest* and it is a known fact that the Avestan language of early Iran's religious texts is closest to the Sanskrit of the Vedic writings of India. (22)

Scholars believe that the Zend Avesta is older than the Old Testament writings and that the Vedas are *older* than the Avestan texts which were supposedly revealed to mankind in the beginning of creation and many historians believe that there are no books in the library of humanity older than the Vedas. (23) Professor Max Muller wrote that ". . .there exists no literary relic that carries us back to a more primitive state in the history of man than the Veda," (24), and Ganga Prasad wrote that ". . .their ultimate origin is still lost in geological antiquity," noting also that the language and religion of the Vedas and Zend Avesta had a common source, both seeming to have derived from a now extinct *parent source.* (25) At the very least the Brahmans calculated that their religious books dated thousands of years into the remote past. (26) This "parent source" was upon the Great Pyramid's lower casing blocks on the four faces of the monument, which leads us to an intriguing fact. India is not known for pyramids, and yet, in the Hindu *Purana* we find mention of ancient pyramids in earth's infancy. (27) Perhaps the Puranas, which were old sources of knowledge, are actually a compound of two very ancient words (Pur-ana), which alludes to their origin: *Pyr-Annu.* And the Four Faces of Brahma would be the four sides of the Great Pyramid near Annu from which the Puranas derived.

Scholars note that Zoroaster's eschatology was extraordinarily advanced, and taught of the *Day of the Lord and the coming of the Savior* [Saoshyant] to bring bodily resurrection to all men. (28) It was Abraham that laid the foundation to the religion and faith that would arise almost two thousand years later known as *Christianity*. The elements of the Christian faith were born in Egypt, taught by Abraham to the sages of many nations who took these teachings back to their homelands and constructed entire religions based off of these revelations. It was at Egypt that these teachings were disseminated and it was at Egypt over 17 centuries later that this faith was *put back together* by scholars at Alexandria by the Gnostics.

The Gnostic beliefs and writings apparently stem from multiple sources, an amalgamation of fragments taken from old Persian, Babylonian, Egyptian and Greek beliefs. The links to ancient Judaism are unmistakable, and by extension this means that Gnosticism has roots in early *Israelite* institutions. The Israelites en masse were deported into Assyria, Babylonia, Media, Persia and northern India. Then Judah was deported into Babylonia and Persia. Through Asia Minor, Cyprus and Phoenicia the early Greeks absorbed wave after wave of Israelite migrations and Egypt from 450-30 BC again filled up with the descendants of Judah called the Jews. At Alexandria in Egypt travelers from all over the Mediterranean, Greekdom, the Middle East and India visited and brought their treasured writings to the famous university and Library of Alexandria from 300 BC to 30 AD where scholars and the intellectual elite *put back together* the fragments of the elder faith dispersed among the peoples of the earth from back when Abraham taught these things at Annu and Giza in the 19th century BC. As the Alexandrian scholars collected more and more parchments, scrolls, stelae, wooden tablets and stone plates from the East, the Aegean, southern Egypt and the Mediterranean cultures they began seeing the stunning correspondences between all ancient religions. And the greatest eschatological belief of all between all peoples was that of the coming Savior who was to be born among men who was going to teach the Truth. The movement began, known as the Way, which was later popularized as Christianity and it was the Gnostics that made up the *original* body of believers. Gnosticism had a great cultural center at Samaria and a canon of very old writings, a copy of the Torah older than that possessed by the Jews at Jerusalem and they possessed numerous writings allegedly written by many patriarchs, prophets and even Enoch himself. Christianity is its purest form was Gnosticism. As the early Christian communities recognized Jesus as the Savior embodied within the flesh of a man, it was His *message* of resurrection and forgiveness that fulfilled the Old Testament prophecies of the coming of a New Covenant. As the Gnostics and their various Greek, Egyptian, Jewish and Samaritan sects were the first to accept the tenets of Christianity we clearly see that it was a faith adopted by those who had descended directly from the early Israelite peoples, that Christianity is the *revival of ancient Israelite faith*. Since 931 BC when the ten tribes broke away from the Kingdom of Judah to form the Two Kingdoms, these people have been enemies. The Israelites and the Judahites fought a number of wars against each other and this continued through early Christianity as the descendants of Israel, now Christians, were hunted and brutally dealt with by secular authorities at the instigation of Jews who are partially descended from both Judah and Edom. The history of Christianity is a history of European peoples constantly struggling against foreign invaders like the Moors and then the Turks who all received aid from local Jewish communities. Europeans retaliated over and again in deporting Jews out of their kingdoms and states. Even today there is much hostility between Christian Europeans, descended from the Ten Tribes of Israel and the Jews. The animosity is ancestral, racial and since the inception of the Christian faith is has become religious.

Universal Language in Antiquity

Long ago there was a single global civilization, a universal code of law, a religious system and canon, recognized branches of science and even one race of people. All of this was unified by a single *language* and mathematical system. Every bit of this was destroyed and only fragments have been preserved in obscure monumental iconography, religious statuary, old teachings believed to be mythic, the rituals of cults and priestly sects, the biblical records and other remarkably detailed writings from long ago and the legends and lore of seemingly primitive peoples who remember phenomena and institutions far more advanced than they are capable of understanding.

All too often we read that writing was invented by the Sumerians prior to 3000 BC but this conclusive assertion is basely solely on the fact that no other writings found exhibit evidence of earlier antiquity. While this appears as sound logic the Sumerians themselves claimed that they were the descendants of those intellectual masters who survived the Deluge. Their tablet records affirm that highly advanced writings and mathematics existed prior to this cataclysm. Writing was thus not an invention but a *preservation*, a fact clearly evident in that Sumerian exhibits no signs of development. This is because its earliest formative periods were buried deeply by the Flood and the earlier culture that later became Sumer was *not* located where the post-diluvian settlers occupied. The end of Sumer was not geographically in the same place as the beginning of this people. Their original lands of origin could have been anywhere on this planet, even a locale presently a mile under the ocean.

Three of the oldest accounts known to scholars [but relegated to myth] concerning a primordial universal language are strikingly similar in construction:

"Once upon a time, the whole Universe,
the people in unison, to Enlil in one tongue
gave praise." (29) —Sumerian text of
Enmerkar and the Lord of Aratta

"And the whole earth was of one language,
and of one speech." —*Genesis 11:1*

"And all the earth was of one tongue and
words of union." —*Book of Jasher 7:46*

As does Genesis and Jasher convey, so too does the Enmerkar text reveal that there was a rift in man's ability to communicate, a fact recorded by the Babylonian historian Berossus who wrote, "The gods introduced a diversity of tongues among men who until that time had all spoken the *same language*." (30) This has been confirmed by the archeologist G. Smith who over a hundred years ago found a Babylonian tablet that reads ". . .the building of this illustrious tower offended the gods. In the night they threw down what they had made. They scattered them abroad, and made strange their speech." (31)

In the Jubilees account we find that Abraham learned ". . .the language which has been revealed, for it had ceased from all the mouths of the children of men." (32) It was by learning this elder language that he was able to translate the inscriptions upon the casing blocks of the Great Pyramid. Even across the planet we discover in the Mayan *Popul Vuh* that in the olden days all the earth spoke one language (33) and many Native Americans believed that their ancestors spoke a "Beloved Speech." (34) Even the Egyptian historian Manetho wrote that there once existed a universal "sacred language," (35) which leads us to the Greek accounts, this Aegean culture having so many uncanny connections to Egypt.

According to Pliny, Aristides claimed that an Egyptian named Menes invented the alphabet. (36) Menes means *moon*, a Greek reference to the wedge-shaped characters of cuneiform writing that was invented by the Sumerians and Menes was merely the beginning of Egyptian Dynastic history, the name Menes being the same as Anam, a famous Babylonian king from Sumer who left the Persian Gulf area to rule over Egypt as shown in *Lost Scriptures*. Anam was ruling when Abram, learned in all the mysteries of Thoth visited Egypt and translated the writings for Pharaoh's Court found on the Great Pyramid after it was excavated from the diluvial deposits. Thoth is an Egyptian memory of Enoch, builder of the Great Pyramid by design [Sethites constructing it], who is called Palamedes in Greek. Palamedes, Thoh and Enoch are the same person, inventor of the alphabet *before* the cataclysm whose Greek name means *ancient intelligence*. (37)

The famous *Sybylline Oracles* (38) reads that on an early date on Earth ". . .the tongues of men were diversified by various sounds, and the whole earth of humans was filled with fragmenting kingdoms," (39) and the Greek historian Hestaeus studied olden traditions learning that the survivors of a Flood settled Senaar [Shinar] in Babylonia but were driven away later by a diversity of tongues. (40) Even Plato asserted as much. In his *Symposium* he wrote ". . .there was a time, I say, when we were one, but now because of the wickedness of mankind God has dispersed us . . . and if we are not obedient to the gods, there is danger that we shall be split up again." (41)

It is truly a credit to the ancient Greeks that the New Testament books were composed in this script. The Hebrews claim that their language is of divine origin, and its association to numerical values of interest to this thesis cannot be doubted. The Greek alphabet shares this characteristic with the Hebrew. The Greek is a highly symbolic alphabet based off of an older one constructed with letters that were originally *symbols* of great and universal antiquity. This was probably hidden to the average literate Greek but was definitely known to mystic sages who comprehended their geometrical and gematrical values.

The fourth letter of the Greek alphabet was Delta △, the number for the *earth* that intriguingly, was linked to the idea of a door or gate. The eighth letter is H, which is but an abbreviated form of the Ladder of Heaven [pillar/ pyramid icon], an appropriate symbol for the number representing the *new beginning* of something. In Greek the number 10 is depicted as a *pillar* | and the number 70 is a circle O. The number 80 is a glyph so old that it continues to baffle historians ⊓ , this being the principle design of thousands of dolmans found all   around the world. Even upon South Pacific atolls and tiny islands bare of other monuments, these rock portals are found everywhere. There happens to be five of them forming the inner sanctuary of Stonehenge. The number 700 [circle times the pillar] is the enigmatic trident , or upper half of the Tree of Life Ψ . The Ω is 800, the Omega symbol that represents the End which the sign   for the constellation Leo evolved from. The number 900 [100 times judgment] happens to retain its antediluvian significance for 900 is ʓ , the Sickle of Judgment used by the Gardener when His harvest [mankind] has bore fruit.

In *Lost Scriptures* we find a tremendous amount of evidence linking the Great Pyramid's structure to the concept of a gigantic stone tree linking heaven and earth because it was a gigantic pillar between the two providing a hidden gate to humanity geometrically concealing the name of God in living stone. This same concept is discovered within the meaning of the word *name* in Semitic languages, *shem*, which also maintains a variant interpretation as *monument*, a word preserved in the Egyptian root *sem* which signifies a ". . .representation on the ground of likeness," (42) better understood as a *symbol*. And this is exactly the purpose of symbols, to convey knowledge by visual forms attached to significant meanings of ten with ideas very different than the geometry conveys.

The universal symbol of the tree is probably the most widely recognized image in the entire ancient and modern world, the triangle being the second, and by far. The mystic association of the pyramid being a symbol of the divine tree is alluded to in the Alexandrian writings of the Book of Adam and Eve where we read, "For we know thy marvelous works, O God, that they are great, and that by thy power thou canst bring one thing out of another, without one's wish. For thy power can make *rocks to become trees and trees* to become rocks." (43) This is evidence that the sages of Alexandria knew more about the background scenes of the Genesis story of Eden than is taught even today. The Babylonians, Chaldeans and other Euphratean cultures regarded the cedar tree as the "revealer of the oracles of heaven and earth," (44) and trees are a part of the kingship iconography in Sumerian and Akkadian.

The tree was a symbol for that which endures, that which *unifies heaven and earth*, which is why we find that humanity in the Zodiacal symbolism is identified with the exact same symbol as that used to depict the weapon of the gods against the Adversary and Chaos:

Man is the Thunderbolt, the Vajra of India and the Divine Battleaxe, the Labrys of the Creator against those gods that rebelled against Him. The high branches of the tree in heaven and the low roots in the ground in the underworld were linked together by the trunk of this organic pillar just as humanity unified heaven and earth by the fusion of a divine spirit empowered by God within a frail shell of human flesh made out earthen clay.

Trees were fitting examples of eternal life. They are the oldest living organisms on the planet. There stand trees today in the United States that were already 2000 years old when Christ walked the Earth 2000 years ago. These 4000 year-old living fossils are huge, called Sequoia Gigantea in the western states known as the famous Redwoods which are only a few centuries older than the ancient Bristlecone Pines. These incredible forests began growing shortly after the Deluge in 2239 BC and they show no signs of dying. These dateless organic pillars of the earth do not die by natural causes, termites do not affect them and they are as strong and dense as they were thousands of years ago. Similar trees of great antiquity have been found on uninhabited South Pacific islands and the biblical texts and Sumerian writings tell of the legendary Cedars of Lebanon that were also renowned for their immense size and age before they were lost to construction projects throughout the Middle East as far as Egypt. The longevity of trees and their productions useful to mankind is why the Scriptures read that ". . .the tree of the field is a man's life." Had not the Flood brought ruin to the Old World's ecological systems and civilization, changing the topography, soil distribution and climates then these forests of primordial trees would not be between 4,300 and 2,300 years old, but much older.

The tree was a symbol of *knowledge*, an idea conveyed in Genesis in the Tree of Knowledge and at Giza where the Great Pyramid was anciently covered in millions of minute inscriptions long ago. All knowledge known today is written upon trees: each book a branch of human experience spread throughout forests of libraries where all men visit to attain understanding. Every time we read words on paper, placards, poster, billboards, we learn from *trees*. The advancements of our technological micro-industrialized civilization have not altered this archaic fundamental truth. The link between trees and learning was known in the days of Aristotle, who wrote that knowledge was divided into *branches*. (45)

Even older than the Greek alphabet is the Chinese pictographic writing, a mode of literal communication where symbols convey entire thoughts and ideas. Truly do these characters need qualified attention to detect symbolic associations with our thesis. The word "tempter" in Chinese is made up of a unique combination of characters that means independently *devil, cover* and *tree*. (46) These three ideas are definitely biblical, for the Tempter, or Lucifer, was the "...cherub that *covereth*," who fell and was replaced by another – who is symbolized at Giza as the Sphinx guardian that covers the entrance of the Deep. He was the devil who used knowledge, obtained from a tree in Eden, to tempt Eve. What is absolutely fascinating here is that the early Chinese symbol for *tree*, from its origin to its later stylized modifications, embodied the same concept as that particularly ancient symbol for *man*. (47)

Ancient Arcana of the Revelation

The Book of the Revelation is commonly attributed to John the Apostle, however, many scholars are in agreement that he did not author it because the literary style of this apocalyptic text is very different from his gospel and letters. Others believe that there are definitive clues that show that John indeed wrote this book. It is the author's opinion that John did record the events of the vision of the Revelation and that he was inspired to write the account in a specific way. He was a witness to supernatural events, and thus affected by the supernatural he was divinely inspired to record his vision in a certain way. Much of what he visually and audibly perceived he truly did not understand.

It is further the author's belief that John was not the first to see and experience the Revelation apocalypse. There is a tremendous amount of evidence from a wide variety of sources that Enoch witnessed the vision long before the flood *as we have it today* over three thousand years before John did. Incidentally, Enoch's version was designed to be time-released after the passage of millennia. This is ascertained from the opening statement of the Book of Enoch:

> "From them [angels] I heard all things, and
> I understood what I saw; that which will
> not take place in this generation, but in *a*
> *generation which will succeed at a distant*
> *period*, on account of the elect." (48)

The return to popularity of this prophetic text is a direct result to its contents having been recorded in antiquity for our time period in history. It is amazing to realize that the information in Enoch would never have been taken seriously (as history notices) until relatively modern times because the data it reveals requires us to have accommodating information on a variety of other topics and belief systems that only a century ago we did not have access to. Simply put, the Enochian text is an archaic time capsule only recently brought to light of incredible glimpses into the future of societal and spiritual conditions on earth prior to and during the last days of Draconian rulership of earth.

Incredibly, this is exactly what the Book of Enoch says about itself. The text predicts that correct translations of itself would be dispersed throughout the world: "Now will I point out a mystery: Many sinners shall turn and transgress against the Word of Uprightness. They shall speak evil things: they shall utter falsehood; *execute great undertakings*; and compose books in their own words. But when they shall write all my words correctly in their own languages, they shall neither change or diminish them; but shall write all correctly, all which from the first I have uttered concerning them." (49)

Powerful evidence that Enoch was a witness of the Revelation vision before John can be seen easily by comparing both accounts of the Book of Enoch and the Revelation. Both men were taken up into heaven in vision where they saw seven spirits of God (50) before His throne, and heard the voice of God promise that the saved shall partake in the tree of life (51), saw the redeemed clothed in white garments (52), looked upon a city, a temple residence with new pillars prepared for the elect (53). Both were made aware that the righteous would dine with God forever and ever (54) and that they would have thrones allotted to them (55); they witnessed four beings around God's throne that eternally praise the Creator with *four voices* (56), and both men even recorded entire phrases in virtually identical manners despite the language rifts and separation of centuries and possibly millennia, such as when John in Revelation wrote that the lord ". . .hast created all things," but in Enoch He "hast made all things." (57) Also, both looked at a sea of angels before God, John describing their number as ". . .ten thousand times ten thousand, and thousands and thousands," while Enoch wrote ". . .myriads and myriads who were before Him." (58)

John saw an altar of souls belonging to the righteous who were unjustly slain who cried out for vengeance as their prayers ascended unto heaven to God, pleas that Enoch also witnessed that came from the blood of the righteous. (59) These men watched as the cataclysmic events upon the earth unfold and men on earth attempted to hide their faces from God upon His throne. (60) They viewed beautiful fountains of living waters that would be given to the righteous in the New Earth (61) and also watched as a star fell from the sky to earth in the apocalypse. (62) John wrote that during the last days men would worship ". . .devils, and idols of gold, silver, and brass, and stone, and of wood . . .," and Enoch wrote that ". . .they shall worship stones, and engrave gold, silver, and wood images. They shall worship impure spirits . . ." (63) John recorded that the False Prophet ". . .deceiveth them that dwell on the earth," Enoch wrote that ". . .they [evil spirits] became ministers of Satan, and *seduced those that dwell upon the earth*." (64) Both writers claimed that the wicked shall burn in the presence of the righteous (65) and that in the apocalypse blood will flow up to the breasts and bridles of horses. (66) While John heard angels declare that the Creator is Lord of lords and King of kings, Enoch heard them say that he is ". . .Lord of lords, God of gods, King of kings." (67)

Both men experienced a future celebration of all the redeemed, angels and mankind, praising God after the old earth and heavens passed away (68) and they watch as a powerful angel appeared and opened the Abyss and cast the Evil One into the blackness (69), and they heard that his judgment shall be burning forever and ever. (70) They watched as the books in heaven were opened, also the book of life, on Judgment Day (71), and those not found therein were judged and cast into the lake of fire according to John, but Enoch calls it ". . .the flaming abyss." (72) Both men wrote that they personally watched the old heavens and earth pass away and be replaced with new ones. (73)

The Revelation text is not a mere mysterious writing, but in Greek it is a literary masterpiece parallel to the top 1% of the greatest literature ever produced in that language. It just may be the greatest Greek grammatical text ever produced. There are many more similarities with it and the Enochian text and there is every possibility that the Book of Enoch was a literary masterpiece in its original language also, however, its value is greatly undermined due to the passage of so much time and its carrying over through Ethiopic, Greek, Aramaic, Hebrew and quite likely very long ago, Sumerian. The present Enoch was penned around the second century BC but it was apparently copied from an older Greek manuscript that was in itself a copy of an even older version most likely in Aramaic. (74)

The discovery of the Dead Sea scrolls conclusively shows that the Enochian writings antedate Christianity. The hundred or so passages in the New Testament books that find their precedents in the Enochian writings (75) would tend to lend credence to the argument that John just copied the Book of Enoch and created the Revelation record; however, this argument has never been made by scholarship due to the uniqueness of the Revelation text. Despite any academic arguments against such a possibility, the greatest proof that the Revelation was a vision seen by John that was even priorly seen by Enoch is found not in the phraseology and ideas conveyed by John, but in the usage of *dozens* of symbols and motifs that are alien to Greek and Hebrew iconography, but are prevalent everywhere in *Sumerian* historic and religious tablet writings and artwork. Many of the basic tenets of the arcanum of the Great Pyramid are found abundantly in the Revelation, however, these concepts were so cleverly concealed by the days of John the Apostle as to have been rendered *extinct* and would have meant little or nothing to early Christianity, aside from a few sages mentioned earlier in this book. But even they could not have understood these glyphic representations and explicit apocalyptic imagery as the Sumerians would have. But with the latter century's worth of tablet and relief translations of Sumerian and Akkadian the Revelation is now understood with almost perfect clarity.

It is time for scholarship to take on probably the most penetrating of all arcane mysteries and answer for us today this question: Why are the oldest writings in the world so similar? This is not a light statement. It has for too long been ignored that the same symbols, same plot lines, same pantheons, and same histories are found in the earliest texts known to man, their disparities a natural consequence of the fragmentation of civilization in the mists of the distant past. The evidence that there existed long ago a single parent culture, a parent theology, universal language and archive of writings is profound. In vain do modern experts and scholars attempt to explain this anomaly by claiming that the similarities between the writings and cultures of different nations was due to borrowing, but this is a shallow attempt to circumvent the evidence. There are stunning similarities between the oldest writings that simply cannot be explained by borrowing, especially because some of these cultures were so far removed from another that borrowing just did not occur. Aside from racial and cultural materials introduced at later dates, the earliest texts basically tell the same stories. This is consistent not only with their histories, but even the elder prophecies align perfectly. The Hermetical literature, Gnostic and Kabbalistic traditions mirror older beliefs and writings and in themselves offered little new that more ancient writings did not already convey. The Apocryphal and Pseudopigraphical books largely born at Alexandria from older copies of unknown books are little different from the oldest writings. The Quran of Arabia too contains elements that were not Arabian. The Greek masters like Plato, Socrates, Aristotle, Anaxamander, and others introduced scientific and philosophical ideals in Grecian and Alexandrian culture and learning that were but mere reflections of earlier discoveries and concepts. The amazing scientific clarity of Ovid's *Metamorphosis* writings on the Creation is but a copy of the creation texts of *Atrahasic Epic*, Babylonian seven tablets of the *Enuma Elish* record, Hesiod's *Theogany*, the Mayan *Popul Vuh*, Egyptian Book of the Dead, Gnostic *Pistis Sophia* and the Genesis record. The Scandinavian *Elder Edda*, German *Volsungasaga*, the Four Ancient Books of Ireland, and even elements of the *Beowulf* epic are but renditions of the archaic Sanskrit Vedic scriptures of the *Mahabarata*, the *Bhagavad-gita* and Puranic writings of India. There are even parallels between the Gnostic Nag Hammadi texts and the Dead Sea scrolls that span back millennia before these writings were penned. The Celtic writings that have survived are stunningly similar to the famous *Odyssey* and *Iliad* of Homer and Virgil's *Aeneid*. The Revelation book in our Bibles was spread out throughout the world. The apocalypse was a belief powerfully impressed upon the ancients. The Viking *Ragnarok* prophesies tell the Revelation with the perspective of a mariner and essentially mirror the apocalyptic imagery of the first cataclysm involving giants and end of the Draconian system as well as end-time motifs and symbolism. Likewise the Aztecs were very familiar with the Revelation record. At the city of Tenochtitlan was excavated the famous Stone of the Fifth Sun, erroneously called by many the Calendar Stone. This 24-ton relic displays catastrophic symbols and the unfolding of the end of the present world. Incredibly, the epicenter of the artifact shows a god with a sword coming out of his mouth the same way Revelation describes Christ at His Second Coming.

The most obvious denominator between all of these writings is the fact that all of them, no matter their origin, seem to be abbreviated versions of much larger writings. They appear in all respects to be condensed texts. Such is the case with the Hebraic writings of Jubilees, the *Book of Jasher* and even the *Book of Enoch*. The Enochian writings abruptly change topics from time to time and vary in writing styles as if over the centuries the portions deemed of lesser importance were edited out or rearranged to shorten the impossibly long text. Originally, Enoch was probably a massive stone tablet library. Scholars have already identified separated texts within the Enochian book, writings once called the Book of the Watchers, Book of Giants, Book of Noah and parts of the *Secrets of Enoch* may have been a part of this work. The Book of Giants, or at least a lengthier version was found among the Dead Sea scrolls.

Enoch wrote 366 books according to his own account. (76) Such a vast amount of literary material would fill a small library assuming they were average-sized works. But the evidence dispersed throughout this book suggests that these writings were extensive. The Book of Jubilees claims that ". . .there is nothing in heaven or on earth, or in the light or in the darkness, or in sheol or in the depth (abyss), or in the place of darkness (which is not judged); and all their judgments are ordained and written and engraved." (77) It is also the Jubilees text that claims that Enoch learned all the secrets of the angels and of creation, of heaven and earth and he ". . .wrote down everything." (78) To recount all the previously mentioned evidence that the Great Pyramid was built at Enoch's instruction is not necessary, but we must take into consideration that the possibility exists that the writings upon this monument long ago were indeed the Enochian inscriptions spoken of in the Testaments of the Patriarchs writings among other sources and that they were engraved upon four faces of the Great Pyramid before the Flood. We know that the pyramid was constructed using a measuring factor of *seven* and that this mystical number related specifically to the earth and that the seven-pointed star is how the ancient architects measured the elusive 52° angle. In taking all of this into consideration even the astute critic should find it worthy of attention that 366 Enochian books divided by seven equals the pyramid angle of 52°. Coincidence or Providence? The peculiar number 366 also comes up in Christopher's Dunn's research in his fascinating book *Giza Power Plant: Technologies of Ancient Egypt*. He wrote that by dividing the base of the pyramid by the ancient Egyptian cubit (25 inches) you arrive at 366. (79) Either this is yet another cunningly deceptive coincidence in a long chain of *thousands* of coincidental links all secured together as displayed in this work or the prophet Enoch five thousand years ago deliberately wrote 366 books and mentioned it in his writings so as to *in a future generation* reveal to mankind his brethren that the Great Pyramid *is* the sign and witness of the Creator's divine plan for mankind.

The eschatological glimpses and apocalyptic writings of the Revelation are popularly regarded as prophecies of doom concerning the end of the world, and to those of this present world it virtually is. But to the spiritual initiates of this arcanum the Revelation is the key to these arcane mysteries of the Creator, the colophonic end of the Arcanum that was first introduced in the narratives of Genesis. The Book of Genesis is the Alpha text and Revelation the Omega, these being the beginning and the end of the revelations of God. Though thousands of years apart and written in different languages, these two works unveil interlocking secrets that are meant only for believers in Him.

Second and first millennium BC tablet writings of religious importance contained colophons, which are statements at the *end* of a tablet that either reiterate or compliment the text's first statement or beginning thought. Often colophons restated the beginning of these documents by employing the same phraseology and symbols. Because of this, historians and translators have been able to identify when as ancient text ends and another starts. The Revelation of Jesus Christ is the perfect colophonic text that makes Genesis complete. Both books maintain an interwoven pattern of symbols and motifs that exhibit the depth, longevity and importance of the Arcanum: the hidden wisdom and knowledge of life eternal.

It is before John witnesses the events of the tribulation and beyond that Christ utters a series of astonishing prophesies that are enigmatic and ignored by most Christians who are unaware that the language and symbols employed by Jesus span back to the beginning of the world, statements that apply to every initiate of this arcanum. Jesus says, "To him that overcometh will I give to eat of the *tree of life*, which is in the *midst of the paradise* of God," and

"...I will give to eat of the hidden manna, and I will give him a *white stone*, and in the stone a *new name* written, which no man knoweth saving he that receiveth it." (80) The hidden manna is spiritual knowledge and wisdom of Him, the true Tree of life (our eternal sustenance). Manna is in reference to the angelic food given to the Israelites in the wilderness, a strange substance that kept these people alive and healthy for decades in a land that was barren and devoid of resources.

It is with the promise of the white stone that the arcanum is seen with greater clarity. The old mystery schools and priesthoods of various cultures attempted to preserve and replicate this mystery though its original meaning and spiritual significance had long since been lost in much the same way that ancient architects tried in vain to replicate the magnificence of the Great Pyramid without the slightest clue as to the monument's original purpose. The Christian apocryphal writings come closer to unveiling the esoteric secret in identifying white stones as people that make up the building blocks to the temple of God. To be awarded a white stone signifies that our Maker has seen us fit, holy and acceptable building materials as members of His body. Thus, in the later apocryphal writings the Church was likened to that of a pyramid form, its blocks none other than the chosen, the elect and the redeemed that arose from the clutches of hell beneath and away from the Adversary who originally seduced them out of their garments of light. Hundreds of years before Christ's appearance on earth initiates into the mysteries of Babylonia, Thracia, other parts of the Aegean, Crete, Rome, Egypt and other civilizations were led down dark corridors full of representations of hellish creatures, they were sprinkled with water (symbolizing the baptism of rebirth), and once the new initiate emerged he was given a *new name*. And this name was engraved upon a white stone. (81) In ancient Egypt the white stone was awarded to those who passed the tests of the judges of Amenta (hidden underworld). (82) Pausanius claimed that white stones were symbols of the gods as found in *Lost Language of Symbolism II*.

The white stone in Revelation is further emblematic of a new garment. Jesus said, "Thou hast a few names even in Sardis which have not defiled their garments; and they shall walk with me in *white*; for they are worthy. He that overcometh the same shall be clothed in *white raiment*: and I will not blot his name from the book of life, but I will confess his name before my Father, and before His angels . . ." (83) As the largest and oldest book (container of knowledge) in the world, the Great Pyramid represents the unending majesty of God's Word in stone. This monumental relic itself was covered in a white garment of limestone casing blocks that effectually covered the millions of bricks beneath them so perfectly that originally the entire structure appeared as one body of rock. The blocks beneath were covered perfectly by the white stones above them. The theory of some researchers and mathematicians that the casing stones numbered 144,000 is made all the more profound by the passage in the Book of the Revelation where in vision John witnessed 144,000 people upon Mount Sion with the Lamb of God with ". . .His father's *name* written in their foreheads." (84) These are the elect having died as martyrs for Him on earth.

The connection to Mount Sion as the city of God is further made in the Revelation. Jesus says, "He that overcometh will I make a *pillar* in the *temple of my God*; and I will write upon him the *name* of my God, and the name of the *city* of my God, which is New Jerusalem, which cometh down out of heaven from my God: And I will write upon him my *new name*." (85) The pillar in the temple promise is a spiritual guarantee that He will make us into *repositories of divine knowledge*, for such was the archaic function of the pillar with its inscriptions. Further, as a creation of God we will support our Maker just as pillars support those things that are above them. Sion was the beginning of the symbolism prophetically foreshadowing the reality of the future city of God (86) of which the pyramid serves as an architectural type that concealed the name of God. Toward the end of the Revelation text John watches as Christ descends to heaven from earth . . ." And he had a *new name* written, that no man knew but he himself . . . and his name is called the Word of God." (87)

One might naturally ask why a city will be necessary in the future on a perfect Eternal Earth. This author is absolutely convinced that the end of earth's present age is actually the beginning of the government of the Everlasting. As resurrected and glorified repositories of divine knowledge and wisdom we will be emissaries sent all over the Universe to proclaim the Word of God. We are but a speck in the vast cosmos. Our mansions and home will always be within the great City of the Living God on Eternal Earth, but as servants of the Most High we will visit other worlds and teach those civilizations the mysteries and goodness of God. As the Redeemed we will have an eternal testimony that other intelligent beings will find astounding, for in the worlds of the future sin and death will not be known. The initiates of the Arcanum of Jesus the Christ will be the interstellar priests of the Word charged with bringing the creation closer to the Creator, who will speak and teach with the authority of those who survived the Chaos and overcame the deceits of the Dragon. The redeemed will be a unified body of eternal replacements who will fill in the positions of the third of the heavenly positions lost at the

Draconian Rebellion. But unlike those two-thirds that never left their divine estates, the redeemed will have the testimony of having lived as mortals, died, and resurrected by the power of the Godhead. These survivors will each have a unique story, having lived before the Great Flood or shortly afterwards. Others walked among the civilizations of Mesopotamia or in deepest Africa. From the lost cultures of America to ancient India, among the Scandinavian Vikings and northern Celts, from out of the Aegean cities of the Greeks and even the suburbs of Egypt, and from the tropical jungles of a thousand islands there has always been a remnant that truly knew Him for the salvation He is. Spiritual rebirth belongs to those that seek it and not to any particular culture or religion. The elect of Zion will be from all time periods and walks of life. From old bannisters in England to peasant in Israel who actually touched Jesus, Roman of yore to American school teacher, Soviet physicist to Vietnamese shrimper, kings and prisoners, the uneducated and sage—all the redeemed will have testimonies differing from one another relative to their lifetimes and circumstances. But all of them will proclaim the glory of God in saving them from whatever their circumstances were. One of the Elect will visit a distant solar system and spread the Word of God, followed by another at a different time who will do the same, but from an entirely different perspective.

Such are the secrets encoded and surrounding the arcanum of the Great Pyramid of Giza, the Word of God in stone surrounded by civilizations that had absolutely nothing to do with its creation and design. As the pretended sages of humanity over the millennia have thought to contrive different methods by which to obtain eternal life, so also have the engineers and regents of historical eras committed the ultimate blasphemy in their vain attempts to replicate the architecture of God. But through it all He has remained hidden to those who refused to see but has manifested Himself to all who have earnestly sought Him. This ultimate signature of the occult arcana and its spiritual wisdom is revealed clearly in the Revelation text in the *only* passage in the entire Bible where God is called by this name:

> "These things saith the Amen, the faithful
> and true witness, the beginning of the
> creation of God." (88)

Apocalypse of Matthias the Scribe

I.

1. I was at study in my chamber till even time, and in the book of the inscriptions of Enoch, I read, For the books are many, and in them you will learn all the Lord's works, all that has been from the beginning of creation and will be till the end of time.

2. Overwhelmed with reverence and in deep thought, I prayed unto the Lord. With my heart did I give praise to Him.

3. I meditated upon the bricks of the wall and studied how one brick differed from another in form. In the Spirit I began to muse over the works of men.

4. But a presence disturbed me.

5. Fear seized me and I closed my eyes in prayer, and felt the force of motion within my being.

6. Then did I still, and opened my eyes as warmth overspread my body. Before me stood a handsome and exceedingly tall man.

7. And I looked around and perceived that I stood upon the sands of a desert by a riverbank at the middle of the earth. It was twilight, but dusk or dawn I did not know.

8. Elect of He of heaven, spoke the man to me, and I perceived him to be one of the holy ones of God, take your pen and write the things you see and hear. And in my hands were a pen of strange aspect and a prism. I then knew by reason of my studies that I was to write upon its four faces. And I held the prism in my right hand.

9. Come and see all that you shall write, said the messenger to me, and you shall write them from right to left, from bottom to top and over all four faces of the

prism. But fear not, O scribe, the One that has set you to task shall put His words in your heart.

10. This instruction I heard. I looked at the prism, and in dismay I cried to the messenger, But Sir! I cannot finish this task for its top is missing!

11. And to the tall man did I lift it up, but he admonished me, O faithless man! Think you that He cannot complete the end, which was written from the beginning?

12. Confused and ashamed, I bowed before this man for in him did I perceive great wisdom. But his words comforted me. Who are you, Sir? And where is this desert place you have brought me, this place of judgment?

13. And the messenger of the Lord advanced toward me in the space of seven steps. I am a holy one of heaven, said he, the numberer of secrets am I called, for my name is Palmoni. And I have brought you back to the beginning, to a place of testimony, for by virtue of your wisdom and searching in what is written are you chosen to see what lies hereafter. You stand in the place where judgment began.

14. While I thought upon his words he led me away from the riverbank in the east, and I came to stand before a giant beast in the sand with human face. I wondered at its beauty, and I could see in its face vast knowledge and purity of spirit. Also I wondered when the Lord had made such a thing.

15. There are hid greater things than I, for men have seen but few of His works, said the beast to me.

16. What are you, I asked, and why are you hidden from the sight of men? But the beast was silent as it gazed east.

17. The holy one said, He is keeper to the path of life, and of knowledge. In him are heaven and earth tightly fitted together. And he is the guardian cherub of the pillar of knowledge when the earth is wrapped in darkness. By judgment is he made strong.

18. And I, Matthias, wrote this testimony I heard and saw, though I understood not the words of the angel Palmoni.

II.

1. I finished my writing as the sky grew brighter with approach of morning. The beast gazed east, and startled, I beheld a certain number of stars that from heaven fell. And a star fell to the west.

2. Disturbed and of a shaken spirit, I asked, What does this mean? That stars should fall upon the face of the desert before the day is born?

3. With low voice, in the manner of one who mourns, the messenger said, The time comes when their iniquity shall be remembered, and judgment no longer delayed. The fiery revolving sword comes in haste, and their sonship has been appointed to the images of God.

4. And these things I wrote.

5. Then did a foul wind of sulfurous aspect assail my senses from the west. A shadow in the form of a man appeared, having markings in the likeness of many eyes.

6. The air became cold and burned upon my skin. Great fear such as I have not known seized me, and I cried. The hairs of my skin stood on end, my throat thirsted and my bowels troubled me for pain. O Lord! What is this evil you bring upon me?

7. And again did the holy one admonish me, O faithless and miserable man! Fear not this empty vessel, for he is one of the stars of heaven that observes in hell. He is called and chosen to bear witness to the words that you shall write, for the prism is appointed to his master, the lord of the Deep.

8. At these words I gasped, and I trembled for fear of the prism in my grasp. I fell to my knees in the sand and cried, Woe am I that the Lord makes me to write a testimony for hell!

9. But the tall man picked me up and his touch strengthened my limbs. Warmth did return to my skin and breath into my throat. And I was not fearful any more. Lean not upon your own understanding, O servant of the Most High, but look–

10. And I looked, and beyond the cherub that guarded I beheld a great mountain with perfect sides. I counted

three sides of the mountain, but in my heart I knew it had four faces. And the mountain was one of its own light.

11. I approached this holy mountain, and a voice like the sound of many waters said, Remove your shoes, O scribe, the ground beneath this sand is sanctified by the eternal Name of the Maker. It was the cherub that spoke.

12. Again I felt the wind. Fear seized me and I removed my shoes.

13. I neared the mountain as darkness lifted and the light of the morning sun marked the time from evening to morning. The messenger followed, but the one of shadow did not pass the cherub.

14. What is the name of the Lord, sir? Can you tell me? I asked the messenger.

15. No. And nor can I tell you the number of His name, for you have yet to know your own.

16. But my name is Matthias, Sir.

17. Yes, said he, all born on earth are given earthly names. But the name of the Lord is hidden under a breath. Everything with breath has uttered the name of the Maker, which name is found also in the form before you.

18. At these words did I wonder greatly as I looked at the mountain. And these things did I write upon the prism.

III.

1. And I beheld, and lo, the light of the sun was cast upon the great mountain, and a desire to ascend it like a stair into the heavens entered my heart. I was amazed to see the whiteness and beauty of this mountain.

2. Its foundation did appear to be above the earth, for the morning mists covered the face of the ground.

3. Be this the work of human hands? I asked, but again did the messenger admonish me.

4. No. This mountain is the witness of the Maker, and the work of His hands, a testimony to all creation of that which was, which is, and what shall be. Now go! Examine the pillar of God.

5. I obeyed him and approached the mountain. I marveled that it looked like one smooth stone. But as I drew closer I examined its brickwork of fine craftsmanship and smooth white blocks large and without blemish. Stones of equal size and beauty.

6. Their height one upon another reached to the top of this holy mountain. And I perceived that it was without a cornerstone. The stones were cut perfectly and tightly fitted together.

7. And I remembered the cherub.

8. As I turned, the tall man said to me, Darkness has given way to the light. The fiery revolving sword now guards the way of knowledge and the cherub sleeps till summoned.

9. And I looked, and lo, the cherub was a great stone in the sand and the one of shadow still maintained his place.

10. As the sun moved in great haste across the sky, I wrote the things that I heard and saw.

IV.

1. After I committed those things to writing did I gaze back at the stones of the mountain. And I wondered at the number of them. How many stones do this mountain make? I asked.

2. Only the Maker knows the number of them in His work, replied Palmoni.

3. But are you not the numberer of secrets, who alone could answer my question?

4. Yes, I am he, but the number you seek is hid in the stars that fell, said he. For all that are called, chosen and faithful will be given a white stone like unto these, with a new name. But as it is written, the wicked are written in the earth.

5. I marveled at these words, and asked, Why sir, do you speak to me in dark sayings difficult to know?

6. And he said unto me, Because, O man, the fear of the Lord has given you wisdom beyond your years. And it is written, The parables of knowledge are in the treasures

of wisdom. And you, servant of the Spirit, are counted as one of the remnant on earth that in all truth understand the things you see.

7. Then did I continue my search of the mountain, and lo, I perceived the appearance of words of an unknown kind upon the face of the stones.

8. There were thousands upon thousands and countless many stones. And on them all were written words of mystery.

9. As I watched, my vision became altered and in the Spirit I beheld the formation of newer words. I was perplexed, for this writing I knew was one of songs uttered not by human tongues.

10. Words became merged with other words and symbols. Though their meanings were not made known to me, by wisdom of the Spirit did I know that these were songs of power.

11. In amazement did I watch as newer words became visible to me, and by observation I learned that newer signs emerged as words became visible beside other words, some in lines from right to left and others from bottom to top.

12. And this work of God was in the likeness of the prism in my hands for shape.

13. My awe continued when my eyes saw that each stone's writings also formed larger writings of this same song-speech, stone to stone.

14. My soul filled with wonder as more lines of words and glyphs did my eyes distinguish. Is there no end to the writing upon these stones? I asked as I watched as words of smallest size formed those of even greater, and lines of symbols branched out like limbs on the tree planted by a river.

15. And the messenger answered, The end lies in the beginning, and eternal is the Word, O scribe. The winds ceased, for the wind blew steadily till that time, the desert fell silent and the sun stood in its place above the mountain as the music of many leaves as they praise God in their movements filled my ears. I was about to inquire of this music, but the Spirit hindered me.

16. The sun stood above the mountain and cast shadows into the writings, a thousand thousands of shadows upon the face of the mountain like the countless leaves of a great tree when it stands beneath the midday sun.

17. The mists departed, and I looked, and the roots of the mountain were buried in the foundation of the earth like the deep roots of a mighty tree upon the ground.

18. And the shadows deepened upon the face of the mountain like boughs supporting many branches and leaves, lines and shadows of words also became visible where but stone had been before.

19. Once more, I fell to my knees. Rent between awe and horror at the sight of this living rock did I cry, O Lord! My eyes have gazed on that which is eternal! On wisdom concealed from men, on knowledge and wise design hidden from the sons of men! And I was faint from wonder, for before me stood a tree of magnificent size and unsearchable knowledge!

20. Yes, O scribe, with eyes do you see, said the messenger while he picked me up, good and evil do these words contain. But the good has been fulfilled. And as the way of life is hidden since Eden because of evil, to evil you are to write, for the way of knowledge has not been given them. And you shall write down all the words of the hours of darkness that the watcher might prepare his lord in the Deep.

21. For it was he who first took the fruit from the pillar of God and led his brethren into sedition and exile.

22. But how can I, a vessel of earth, discern the script of angels? I asked.

23. And he looked upon me and said, These be words of power and vision, and I have been chosen to read to you things no others are appointed to know. For the revelations of God are hidden in numbers. Listen and see O scribe, these things that you shall write.

24. At hearing this I prepared my pen, and the prism I held in my right hand. And the one of shadow watched me.

V.

1. Then did the numberer of secrets look into the living rock of the stones of the tree and read the words of mystery.

2. I heard his voice, but understood not this speech. The words were words of a beautiful and mournful music. I stilled, and the eyes of my spirit saw a vision.

3. I looked, and lo, sheep were grazing in a field made small by the presence of a mighty forest, and the trees cast forth long shadows. All the sheep faced the east.

4. Then did a lion with wings like an eagle come out of the wood, and around its neck was a collar of gold. The lion watched the sheep as the wings took flight and became an eagle that flew to the west.

5. And the lion walked away.

6. Then came a bear out of the wood with a collar of silver about its neck. Many sheep did it chase into the field. And the bear walked away.

7. I watched, and lo, a leopard with a coat like many eyes came out of the wood. It chased many sheep into the field, and upon its neck were four collars of brass. And the leopard walked away.

8. Then the eagle, being made powerful, hunted in the wood, and it gathered the collar of gold of the lion, the silver collar of the bear, and the four collars of brass from the leopard. And he bound them with a chain of iron.

9. And power was given to the eagle to watch the sheep, as I watched the spirit of Babel enter its heart. And certain dragons in the east hated the eagle, for they hungered for the sheep.

10. The sheep prospered under the shadow of the eagle's wings. And in the east did the dragons think an evil thought.

11. The eagle, at the time appointed, took gold, silver, brass and iron and did make an image with seven faces with many eyes that did watch over the peoples of the earth. And the faces watched the dragons. And the number of the names of the dragons was nine, and nine was the number of their end. And they sang a song of

fury and of hate that brought terror to the sheep of the
field, and hurt them. But the eagle and the image of its
design were without harm.

12. And a shepherd having the likeness of an image of
God, and with the number of man, did visit the sheep.
And he healed them. With peace did he subdue the
dragons for a time upon the earth.

13. With light he made the sheep to see, and also great
knowledge was given them. But the light was not good,
and a crown was given unto him.

14. And a third part of the dragons made war against
the one in the likeness of an image of God, but he smote
them mightily by the power of the trees of the forest and
made the earth red with their blood.

15. He then made the pasture of the sheep to be greater
in wideness. The sheep gave him a scepter of silver
and beneath the shadow of the trees did the sheep find
pasture.

16. Then a curse from heaven smote the earth. The
world hungered as a horseman that comes from a long
journey.

17. But the sheep fed upon the green grass of the
pasture.

18. The nations gathered and were fed by the likeness
of the image of God, and the nations hungered, and
gave him a seat of brass to rule over them from the land
between the rivers.

19. And the heavens angered because of this blasphemy,
and the names of blasphemy given unto the shepherd by
the sheep.

20. The arrows of God fell upon the nations, there was
pestilence, death and the powers of the Deep increased
upon the circle of the earth. And the images of God
were pale with fear and with sickness. And they fell
prey to the beasts of the earth.

21. But the likeness of the image of God prospered,
and a rod of iron was given unto him. And with it did
he hunt many who loved the sheep, for in him they saw
no shepherd. These are they whose names are written
in heaven, and they are called and elect. And an altar of
vengeance was prepared for them, for they were smitten

to keep them from the evil to come.

22. And I beheld, and lo, certain stars from heaven to earth fell, the sun and the moon darkened and the foundations of the earth roared as a woman that gives birth at a late hour. And the stars were stars of ruin. And as I looked up, the chief ones of the earth grew terrified, and the Deep waited.

23. As I watched, the prism in my right hand became like unto a son of an image of God, and to my astonishment, it spoke:

24. Hear the Word, O eagle! You have become an abomination, and have fallen from your former state, says the Ancient of Days that appointed you. And because you have performed a godless work in the spirit of Babel, judgment from heaven shall fall upon you! For the trees of the forest have plotted against their Maker, and in the shelter of their boughs have you sought counsel.

25. And the earth shall see your end, and be terrified, for the great nation of many tongues and peoples in the sea shall be no more! And your transgression shall be written in the earth, for by oppression and deceit have you bewitched and subdued the kingdoms of the world beneath the rod of iron.

26. And the form of the son of the image of God disappeared, and the prism within my grasp did I hold. As I wondered at this, I beheld, and lo, a star from heaven fell in the west, and the eagle burst before me into flames and was no more.

27. And the world was terrified, and many cities of the nations fell in that same hour. The earth did groan and shake mightily by the power of the star of ruin.

28. And the dragons made a covenant against the one in the likeness of an image of God, and against his seat that was made strong by the image with seven faces.

29. Then were the ancient ones below the earth awakened.

30. The messenger ceased his singing, and the visions departed my eyes.

31. I looked, and in the hands of Palmoni were seven tablets of a stone of dark aspect. They were covered on

both sides with the script of angels. Take up these tables of stone, O scribe, and bury them in the earth before the keeper of knowledge, for their seals are broken. And knowledge has been increased upon the Deep.

32. I obeyed, and took the seven tablets and placed them in a hold that I made in the sand before the feet of the stone cherub, and buried them according to the word of the messenger. Then did I write all those things that I heard and saw.

33. And the one of shadow watched me.

VI.

1. Again did the angel read from the stones of the tree, and a song of mystery brought vision to my eyes.

2. I beheld as stars fell to the earth and wrought a great destruction upon the habitations of the images of God.

3. A bright star appeared and divided the light from the darkness. From evening till morning for the space of seven days did it descend upon the earth, growing in its brilliance.

4. The foundations of the earth were angered and the rocks of the ground split as in the day the son of the image of God was crucified. And the star struck the earth with great fury and tumult; the sea and the waves did roar so that dry land was troubled. The earth cast forth her fury in pillars of smoke, and the sea and the sky did burn.

5. The will of the Maker was then wrought upon the earth with force and the day and the night were quickened so that the space between the evening and the morning was shortened.

6. This miracle was done to save the remnant of the elect from being overcome by the likeness of the image of God.

7. And the confinement of the stars was made complete.

8. And a star descended, a root in the earth of a tree was he, who had power to open the gate of the Deep. The place of the lost released them who were of old cut off and had their boughs removed.

9. And a voice from heaven commanded the destroying angel and his angels, and said, You shall come up! for darkness was over the face of the Deep till that time. And four mighty ones did serve the prince.

10. The dragons of the east did behold the end of the eagle, and wondered with great terror. And they thought an evil thought.

11. Then did they remember the third part of their seed that was subdued by the shepherd of the sheep, and with great fury to destroy did they devour the seat of the likeness of the image of God. And his seat was on the Euphrates River.

12. And at the bidding of the trees did the dragons turn and advance against the pasture of the sheep, and think to devour them.

13. But the likeness of the image of God was their chosen shepherd, and great fire from heaven did fall and consume them to death in the vale of Hamongog. The sheep were without harm, for such was the will of the trees.

14. And into the hands of the likeness of the image of God did the sheep place their souls. But he was not good, for he was in likeness only to His image, and in His image was he not made.

15. And some of the sheep knew by virtue of their wisdom that the likeness of the image of God was not a shepherd. And he was smitten and did die.

16. But in death did the likeness of the image of God live by power of the destroying angel. And this was done in accordance with the mystery of God.

17. To the elect did the likeness of the image of God become the seed of a mighty dragon, for they were not blind, and in him they saw no shepherd. And the sheep understood the design of the trees and their shadows of seeing.

18. And a third part of the earth was without form, and void, and wrapped in darkness. Then did the Maker look back to the day of the beginning, for it was the will of God that a third part of everything He had created and made in the beginning time be destroyed.

19. Then did the image of gold, silver, brass and iron

with seven faces become a mighty red dragon with many heads. And the heads were of a lion, a bear, the four heads of a leopard and the head of an old serpent that brought forth the seed.

20. And I watched, and lo, the dragon became a tall tree of the forest. And the trees were stars of knowing. These trees were from of old, and they did lift up their voices in terrible words in songs of fury.

21. And the stars shined their light into the four corners of the earth, but the elect they could not find. And the trees were full of wrath for human blood they sought.

22. The seed of the dragon made his seat in the pasture, and did curse the earth with great abomination from his seat. The image of God on earth was brought to desolation, and blasphemy stole the souls of the blind by the light of the likeness of the image of God.

23. And the number of his name was made known to the elect, and they marveled, for in the name of the son of the image of God did he come. And the blasphemy of the Spirit was committed upon the earth.

24. Then did the holy one cease his singing and the vision departed my sight. I looked, and lo, the numberer of secrets gave unto the watcher a vessel of drinking made of a dark sand like glass. The vessel was full of blood that did spill onto the sand.

25. And I heard the cries of many who were unjustly slain from the blood on the sand. Drink, said the holy one, of the abominations of the stars. And the watcher did drink.

26. At that time I looked to the heavens, and the stars were in the sky, for the sun had descended the west gate while I was in vision, and the moon was at its station in the night. And I looked at the giant statue of stone, but it was not stone, for the cherub had awakened.

27. I looked at the stones of the tree, and lo, the face of the white mountain was like still water and no tree in it could I perceive any more. And I wondered.

28. Hear, O watcher, the word of He that rode upon a cherub in the heavens that were of old, said the keeper of knowledge as the moon ascended, The third part of the breach of heaven is now healed, and your sonship given

over to the images of God by the power of the Word, that the Godhead may again be One!

29. And after this did the numberer of secrets command the one of shadow to pick up four and then three black and heavy stones hewn not by mortal hands from the sand, and the writing on them was like the script of the angels of death.

30. And the angel of the west became fearful, but obeyed. I listened, and to my wonder did the writings make noises like storm clouds in the west.

31. What be these dark and heavy stones and why does the one of shadow fear them? asked I.

32. These are the seven thunders of the evening withheld from the beginning, testimony and judgment not given unto you to know. For it is written, that they shall not be tormented before the time, said the tall man. And he commanded the watcher to bury them in the sand. And he obeyed.

33. Then did I write these things. And I, Iasoneus Matthias, surnamed Mercurias, do declare by the Spirit that I wrote all that which was placed into my heart upon the prism. And as the moon neared the end of its testimony, I waited. I stood before the holy one as the watcher watched me.

VII.

1. When the darkness was advanced and the night old, the tall man, an angel of the Almighty sent to me in vision, banished the one of shadow, saying, Go, O watcher of the Deep, take this testimony inscribed by the hand of man, and prepare the songs of blasphemy and darkness.

2. Reap a harvest of blasphemy and judgment, and make ready the powers of darkness.

3. Take this testimony, O watcher, and plant it in the Deep where hide the dominions of blasphemy. Prepare your master, for the hour comes when his horns are broken and boughs hewn asunder.

4. And in the prison of judgment will he make his kingdom for a day of time beneath the sand.

5. And the one of shadow took the testimony from my hand. I watched, and the watcher descended into the earth to the west.

6. Astonished, I looked at the angel and he said, Be not troubled, for not all is given unto you to know.

7. But you are blessed, O man, for you believe on the son of the image of God, and are rewarded with sight.

8. And the angels of light shall go before you, but the blind will have their inheritance with the angels of darkness, for in blasphemy do they lead the blind to ruin.

9. And I thought back to all I had seen, and asked the angel, What means this testimony of revelations I have witnessed? Who is the one of shadow? And the images of God? What are these strange angels, the curses that smite the earth, the sheep, and the trees that deceived them?

10. How is it that a lion has wings? What of this blasphemy against the image of God upon the earth, and why did they fall prey to it? Is this great nation of many tongues and people in the west sea?

11. Where now is the son of the image of God, and when will these things come to pass?

12. And he looked down upon me, and said, The Eternal has made His testimony to be hidden on earth by wisdom of the son of the image of God.

13. By numbers is wisdom measured.

14. And one is the number of the Mighty; two is of perfect union, binding together, and of guardians and things guarded;

15. Three be a pure number, of unity in spirit and allegiance; four is of things on earth and of worldly dominion;

16. Five has the power to divide and yet be whole;

17. Six be the number of man and the images of God, the sum of creative powers and divine forethought;

18. Seven is of things divine and of perfection;

19. And eight is of the beginning, for when seven pass does divine appointment begin anew;

20. But in nine lies judgment for iniquity, and nine is the number of those that have fallen short of the path, an evil sum;

21. And ten is the holy sum, the number of a thing built by the Creator, the number of completion and wholeness;

22. But in ten and one is disorder and emptiness, the number of them that are blind and lost, the sowers of chaos;

23. And ten and two is holy, twice the number of man, for it is the sum of those in service to Jah, and is the number of testimony as signs in the heavens;

24. But ten and three be of rebellion against Him, and of disillusionment, a sum of evil;

25. And greater secrets numbers conceal than these. But let him with wisdom understand these words, for these be words unveiled in numbers.

26. A score was hidden in paradise, the ancient number of knowledge;

27. A score and four is the sum of those in service to the Arbiter of this world;

28. Two score be trial and testing, and take heed to this mystery! In two score ten times a thousand thousands be the number of the stars of knowing that kept not their first estate.

29. When this number is made complete shall all things come to pass.

30. And many more be the secrets of creation, not given unto the blind, O servant of the living rock.

31. I heard the words of the heavenly servant, and of a shaken spirit I asked the messenger, Am I not reckoned among them that shall live to know these things?

32. Then before me did he change into a brilliant form of colors I had not known, and said to me, The powers of life rest in death, for nothing is made alive till it dies, O Iasoneus.

33. Then did I find myself in my chamber with the book of the seer's engravings open before me. And it was dawn outside my window.

34. The spirit of memory was with me and I did write a record of all the words of the one called Palmoni, who visited me.

I.M.

Complete Bibliography

The Book of Enoch: trans. Richard Lawrence, LL.D (Artisan Pub.)

The Book of Enoch: trans. R.H. Charles (1912) (The Book Tree)

The Book of Jasher: trans. Albinus Alcuin (800 AD) (M.M. Noah & A.S. Gould, N.Y. 1840; reprint 2000 AD The Book Tree)

The Book of Jasher (Artisan Pub.)

The Book of Jubilees: trans. Rev. George H. Schodde (Artisan)

The Old Testament Pseudepigrapha: J. H. Charlesworth (Doubleday & Co.)

The Lost Books of the Bible: (Crown Publishing, INC. & Gramercy Books)

The Lost Books of the Bible and the Forgotten Books of Eden: (World Bible Publishing)

Antiquities of the Jews: Flavius Josephus, trans. 1736 AD William Whiston (Hendrickson Pub. 1987)

Old and New Testaments (King James Version)

Apocrypha

Encyclopedia American: (Grolier)

Dictionary of Deities and Demons of the Bible: edited Karel Van der Toorn, Bob Becking & Peter W. Vander Horst (Brill: William B. Eerdman's Pub.)

Smith's Bible Dictionary: (Barbour)

Strong's Exhaustive Concordance: (World Publishing)

The Holman Bible Dictionary: edited Trent C. Butler, PH. D. (Holman Bible Publishers)

Atrahasis: trans. Albert T. Clay (1922) (The Book Tree)

The Vedas: trans. Ralph T.B. Griffith (1892) (The Book Tree)

Enuma Elish: Seven Tablets of Creation: L.W. King (The Book Tree) orig. published 1902 by Luzac & Co.

Babylonian Influence on the Bible and Popular Beliefs (1897): A Smythe Palmer (The Book Tree)

Pistis Sophia: A Gnostic Gospel: trans. 1921 by G.R.S. Mead (reprint by The Book Tree)

The Wisdom of the Knowing Ones: Manly P. Hall (Philosophical Research Soc.)

The Way of Hermes: trans. by Clement Salaman, Dorine Van Oyen, William D. Wharton, Jean Pierre Mahe (Inner Traditions)

Mystics and Mysteries of Alexandria: Manly P. Hall (Philosophical Research Society)

Alchemy Rediscovered and Restored: A Cockran (1999) (The Book Tree)

Ancient Symbol Worship (1875): Hodder M. Westropp & C. Staniland Wake (The Book Tree)

Nature Worship (1929): Anon.; Intro by Ted St. Rain (The Book Tree)

The Lost Language of Symbolism (1912): Harold Bayley (The Book Tree)

The Gnosis: Or Ancient Wisdom of the Christian Scriptures: William Kingsland (London, George Allen & Unwin Ltd., reprint by The Book Tree)

Ancient Pagan and Modern Christian Symbolism (1869): Thomas Inman (Peter Eckler Pub., reprint by The Book Tree)

The Secret Books of the Egyptian Gnostics: Jean Doresse (MJF Books)

The Hiram Key: Christopher Knight & Robert Lomas (Fairwinds Press)

A Dictionary of Freemasonry: Robert Macoy (Gramercy)

The Divine Pymander: trans. John D. Chambers (The Book Tree)

Bloodline of the Holy Grail: The Hidden Lineage Revealed: Laurence Gardener (Element)

The Complete Pyramids: Mark Lehner (Thames & Hudson)

The Great Pyramid: Prophecy in Stone: Noah Hutchings (Hearthstone)

The Natural Genesis (1883): Gerald Massey, Vols. I & II (reprint Black Classic Press)

Ancient Egypt Light of the World (1907): Gerald Massey, Vols. I & 2 (reprint Black Classic Press)

The Origin and Significance of the Great Pyramid: C. Staniland Wake (1882) (Reeves & Turner, London)

The Magnificent Numbers of the Great Pyramid and Stonehenge: Bonnie Gaunt (Gaunt)

Beginnings: The Sacred Design: Bonnie Gaunt (Adventures Unlimited Press)

The Murder of Tutankhamen: Bob Briar (G.P. Putnam's Sons, NY)

The Giza Power Plant: Technologies of Ancient Egypt: Christopher Dunn (Bear & Co.)

Gods of Eden: Egypt's Lost Legacy and the Genesis of Civilization: Andrew Collins (Bear & Co.)

The Light of Egypt: The Science of the Soul and Stars, Vol. I (1889): Thomas Burgoyne (Astro Philosophical Pub. 1903)

Nile Valley Contributions to Civilization: Anthony T. Browder (Institute of Karmic Guidance)

The Egyptian Book of the Dead: trans. E.A. Wallis Budge (Gramercy Books)

Sun Lore of All Ages: (The Book Tree)

Stellar Theology and Masonic Astronomy (1882): Robert Hewitt Brown (D. Appleton & Co., NY, reprint The Book Tree)

The Glory of the Stars: E. Raymond Capt (Artisan)

The Story of Astrology: Manly P. Hall (Philosophical Research Society)

The Book of the Ancient and Accepted Rite of Scottish Freemasonry: Charles T. McClenachan, Revised and Enlarged Edition (Macoy Pub. & Masonic Supply Company)

The Secret Language of the Stars and Planets: A Visual Key to the Heavens: Geoffrey Cornelius and Paul Devereaux (Chronicle Books)

Atlantis: Mother of Empires: (1939) Robert B. Stacey-Judd (Adventures Unlimited Press, 1999)

The Shadow of Atlantis: (1940) Alex Braghine (Adventures Unlimited 1997)

From Atlantis to the Sphinx: Colin Wilson (From Internaitonal Pub. Corp.)

The Genesis Race: Will Hart (Bear & Co.)

Fallen Angels and the Origins of Evil: Elizabeth Clare Prophet (Summit University Press)

The Chronology of Genesis: A Complete History of the Nephilim: Neil Zimmerer (Adventures Unlimited)

From the Ashes of Angels: Forbidden Legacy of a Fallen Race: Andred Collins (Bear & Co.)

Our Cosmic Ancestors: Maurice Chatelain (Temple Golden Publications)

The Magus: A Complete System of Occult Philosophy, Vols. I & II: Charles Barrett (The Book Tree)

Mars Mystery: Graham Handcock (Crown Pub.)

Cloak of the Illuminati: William Henry (Scala Dei)

The Gods of Eden: William Bramley (Avon)

The Cosmic Code: Zechariah Sitchin (Avon)

The Wars of Gods and Men: Zechariah Sitchin (Avon)

When Time Began: Zechariah Sitchin (Avon)

The Stairway to Heaven: Zechariah Sitchin (Avon)

The Lost Realms: Zechariah Sitchin (Avon)

The Lost Book of Enki: Zechariah Sitchin (Bear & Co.)

The 12th Planet: Zechariah Sitchin (Avon)

Ancient Mysteries: Peter James & Nick Thorpe (Ballantine)

Ancient Man: Handbook of Puzzling Artifacts: William R. Corliss (Source-Book Project)

Mathematical Mysteries: Calvin C. Clawson (Plenum Press)

The Encyclopedia of Wicca and Witchcraft: Raven Grimassi (Llewelln)

The Meaning of the Glorious Quran: trans. Arafat K. El-Ashi (Amana Pub.)

The Greek Myths: Robert Graves (Penguin)

The White Goddess: Robert Graves (Noonday Press)

Temple of Wotan: Ron McVan (14 Word Press)

Book of the Hopi: Frank Waters (Penguin)

Lost Cities of North & Central America: David Hatcher Childress (Adventures Unlimited)

Lost Cities and Ancient Mysteries of South America: David Hatcher Childress (Adventures Unlimited)

The Popul Vuh (1908): Lewis Spence (The Book Tree)

The Civilization of Ancient Mexico (1912): Lewis Spence (The Book Tree)

New Evidence of Christ in Ancient America: Blaine M. Yorgason, Bruce W. Warren & Harold Brown (Stratford Books)

God is Red: Vine Deloria, Jr. (Delta Books)

The Complete Works of Philo: Philo

Poleshift: John White (A.R.E. Press)

Symbols and Legends of Freemasonry: J. Finlay Finlayson (The Book Tree)

The Land of Osiris: Stephen S. Mehler (Adventures Unlimited Press)

Ancient Structures: William Corliss (Sourcebook Project)

The Earliest Civilizations: Margaret Oliphant (Facts-On-File)

Atlantis: The Antediluvian World: Ignatius Donnelly & Egarton Sykes (Kessinger, reprinted Book Tree)

The Riddle of the Pacific: John M. Brown, 1924 (Adventures Unlimited)

Secret Cities of Old South America: Harold T. Wilkins, 1952 (Adventures Unlimited)

The Histories: Cornelius Tacitus, translated Alfred Church & William Brodribb (Penguin)

Civilization or Barbarism? Cheikh Anta Diop (Lawrence Hill Books)

The Histories: Herodotus, translated Aubrey de Selincourt/revised John Marincola (Penguin)

Tracing Our Ancestors: Frederick Haberman (Covenant)

The Secret in the Bible: Tony Bushby (Joshua Books)

The Discoverers: A History of Man's Search to Know His World and Himself: Daniel Boorstin, 1983 (Vintage)

Origin and Evolution of Freemasonry: Albert Churchward, 1920 (reprint Book Tree)

Rule by Secrecy: Jim Marrs (Perennial)

The Herder Dictionary of Symbols: English translation Boris Matthews (Chiron)

The Fountainhead of Religion: Ganga Prasad 1927 (reprint Book Tree)

Zoroastrianism: John W. Waterhouse, 1934 (reprint Book Tree)

Galactic Alignment: John Major Jenkins (Bear & Co.)

The Dimensions of Paradise: John Michell (Adventures Unlimited)

Tales of the Prophets: Great Books of the Islamic World: Muhammed ibn abd Allah al-Kisai, trans. W.M. Thackston, Jr. (Great Books of the Islamic World)

Natural History: Pliny the Elder, translated John F. Healy (Penguin)

Archive-by-Archive Bibliography

Archive One
The Pillar of Enoch

Memories of Enoch
1. Encyclopedia Americana: Vol. 26, p. 6
2. When Time Began, p. 86
3. From the Ashes of Angels: Forbidden Legacy of a Fallen Race, p. 223
4. When Time Began, p. 135
5. Book of Sirach 49:14
6. Book of Jubilees 4:17-26
7. Book of Jasher: preface of Alcuin trans., p. iv
8. Ibid.
9. Smith's Bible Dictionary: 144
10. Book of Jasher: preface of Alcuin trans. p. vi
11. Ancient Symbol Worship, p. 39 footnote
12. The Natural Genesis Vol. II, p. 120
13. Book of Jasher 3:2, 9:12
14. Book of Adam & Eve II 8:10-13
15. Ibid at 8:17
16. Book of Enoch 21-22:1-2; 25-27, R.H. Charles translation
17. Book of Adam & Eve I 24:4
18. Book of Jasher 3:17
19. Ibid 3:16
20. Forgotten Books of Eden, p. 81
21. Fallen Angels and the Origins of Evil, p. 410, 9
22. Secrets of Enoch
23. Book of Jasher 3:24
24. Secrets of Enoch 48:6
25. Hebrews 10:1
26. Exodus 25:9, Numbers 8:4
27. 1 Chronicles 28:11-13
28. Antiquities of the Jews: Book I ch. 2:3 69-71
29. Isaiah 19:19-20
30. 2 Corinthians 13:1
31. Strong's Exhaustive Concordance Heb/Lex. #1496
32. Ibid #1468

Mystery of Zion
33. Wycliffe Bible Dictionary, p. 782
34. Deuteronomy 3:9, 4:48

35. Ancient Symbol Worship, p. 49
36. Ibid p. 50-51
37. Jubilees 4:17-26
38. Ibid, 8:10, 15-17

Coptic Traditions of the Pyramids

39. Origin and Significance of the Great Pyramid, p. 103-104
40. Ibid, 104-106
41. Ibid, 104-108
42. Ibid, 104-108
43. Ibid, p. 109
44. Ibid, p. 106, 110
45. The Natural Genesis Vol. II, p. 226
46. Ancient Egypt Light of the World, p. 266
47. Origin and Significance of the Great Pyramid, p. 18
48. Ibid, p. 117
49. Ibid, p. 116

Graeco-Egyptian Fragments

50. Divine Pymander, p. viii
51. Ibid, p. viii
52. Ibid, p. xviii
53. Secret Books of the Egyptian Gnostics, p. 190, citing Scott in Hermetica, Vol. III, p. 139
54. Origin and Significance of the Great Pyramid, p. 95
55. Ibid, p. 112
56. Ibid, p. 119
57. The Temple of Wotan, p. 77
58. The Way of Hermes, p. 9
59. Ibid, p. 30-31
60. Ancient Egypt Light of the World Vol. I, p. 303
61. Ibid, Vol. I, p. 266
62. Gods of Eden: Brambley, p. 62
63. The Natural Genesis Vol. II, p. 205

Masonic Records of Enoch

64. A Dictionary of Freemasonry, p. 478
65. Book of the Ancient and Accepted Rite of Scottish Freemasonry
66. The Hiram Key: Anno Mundi MDCCCX
67. Book of Jubilees 8:2-3
68. The Hiram Key, p. 336
69. Laurence Gardner, citing Second Messiah, p. 282-286, Lomas & Knight
70. The White Goddess, p. 278
71. Origin and Significance of the Great Pyramid, p. 41
72. Ibid, p. 57-58

Archive Two
Symbols of the Godhead Upon the Earth

Arcane Images of the Divine Pillar

001. Jeremiah 32:20
002. Atlantis: Mother of Empires, p. 207
003. Sun Lore of All Ages
004. Ancient Pagan and Modern Christian Symbolism, p. 63
005. Holman Bible Dictionary, p. 1113; Wycliffe Bible Dictionary, p. 1345
006. Holman Bible Dictionary, p. 1113
007. The Natural Genesis Vol. II, p. 191
008. Genesis 29:2-3
009. Job 38:30
010. The Natural Genesis Vol. II, p. 191
011. The 12th Planet, p. 189
012. Proverbs 22:28
013. Ancient Symbol Worship, p. 82
014. The Lost Book of Enki, p. 5
015. The Magus Vol. II, p. 169, citing Biographia Antiqua
016. Origin and Significance of the Great Pyramid, p. 112
017. Babylonian Influence on the Bible and Popular Beliefs, p. 23
018. Wycliffe Bible Dictionary, p. 1345
019. Ancient Pagan and Modern Christian Symbolism, p. 132
020. Sun Lore of All Ages, p. 235
021. Origin and Significance of the Great Pyramid, p. 57
022. Ancient Pagan and Modern Christian Symbolism, p. 133, 132;
Encyclopedia of Wicca, p. 132
023. Divine Pymander, p. 150, note 4
024. 1 Kings 7:21, 2 Chronicles 3:17
025. Stellar Theology and Masonic Astronomy, p. 161
026. Dictionary of Freemasonry, p. 73
027. Ancient Symbol Worship, p. 64
028. The Magus Vol. II, p. 64
029. Lost Language of Symbolism, p. 162
030. Nature Worship, p. 83
031. The Magus Vol. II, p. 64
032. Divine Pymander, p. 100-101
033. Sun Lore of All Ages, p. 142
034. Divine Pymander, p. 5, citing Plato: Timaeus 37
035. Secret Language of the Stars and Planets, p. 137
036. The Magus Vol. I, p. 11
037. Malachi 4:2
038. Ancient Egypt Light of the World Vol. I
039. The Magus Vol. I, p. 89
040. Book of Jasher 31:52

041. Ibid, 23:42-43
042. Genesis 31:45
043. Genesis 35:14
044. Genesis 28:12-13
045. Ancient Symbol Worship, p. 82
046. Joshua 24:24-27; 2 Kings 23:3

Pillar . . . Or Divine Mountain?

47. Stairway to Heaven, p. 136-137
48. Wars of Gods and Men, p. 177, citing Ake Sjoberg & F. Bergmann in Collection of Sumerian Temple Hymns
49. Cloak of the Illuminati, p. 113-114
50. From the Ashes of Angels: Forbidden Legacy of a Fallen Race, p. 191
51. The Temple of Wotan, p. 240, 99-101
52. Ibid, p. 36, 245
53. Ibid, p. 246-47
54. Babylonian Influence on the Bible and Popular Beliefs, p. 104
55. Wisdom of the Knowing Ones, p. 67-69
56. Ancient Egypt Light of the World Vol. I, p. 349
57. The Natural Genesis Vol. I, p. 345
58. Lost Cities of North and Central America, p. 255
59. Popul Vuh, p. 104
60. Ibid, p. 49
61. The Natural Genesis Vol. I, p. 344-46
62. From the Ashes of Angels: Forbidden Legacy of a Fallen Race, p. 144
63. Ibid, p. 145, 148
64. Ibid, p. 146
65. Ibid, p. 149
66. Ibid, p. 317-318
67. The Story of Astrology, p. 61
68. The Natural Genesis Vol. II, p. 51-52
69. Book of Jubilees 8:15-17
70. Ibid, 36:9
71. Secret Books of the Egyptian Gnostics, p. 254
72. The Natural Genesis Vol. I, p. 430
73. Secret Books of the Egyptian Gnostics, p. 73
74. Temple of Wotan, p. 67
75. Pistis Sophia: Preface xvii: intro: XXVI
76. Ibid, p. 2-9
77. Book of the Secrets of Enoch 20:3
78. Mathematical Mysteries, p. 24
79. The Natural Genesis Vol. II, p. 316; Vol. I, p. 224
80. The Shadow of Atlantis: p. 234
81. The Glory of the Stars, p. 93
82. The Complete Works of Philo: Questions & Answers On Genesis II, p. 824

83. Lost Language of Symbolism, p. 162
84. Ancient Pagan and Modern Christian Symbolism, p. 127
85. Cloak of the Illuminati, p. 113
86. The Natural Genesis Vol. I 539
87. Enuma Elish: Seven Tablets of Creation Vol. II p. 208-10
88. Discourse to the Greeks: Josephus: 3
89. Psalm 24:3-10

Mysterious Relation to the Number Seven

90. The Natural Genesis Vol. II, p. 225; Vol. I., p. 424
91. The Story of Astrology, p. 82
92. The Secret Language of the Stars and Planets, p. 142
93. Epistle of Barnabas 13:9
94. Beginnings: The Sacred Design: 171
95. Temple of Wota, p. 231
96. Lost Language of Symbolism, p. 133
97. Ibid, p. 140
98. Ancient Pagan and Modern Christian Symbolism, p. 81
99. Lost Language of Symbolism, p. 32
100. Beginnings: The Sacred Design, p. 148
101. The Shadow of Atlantis, p. 232

Archive Three
The Great Pyramid of Enoch

Writing on the Wall

1. Magnificent Numbers of the Great Pyramid and Stonehenge, p. 4
2. The Complete Pyramids, p. 39
3. Magnificent Numbers of the Great Pyramid and Stonehenge, p. 3
4. Gods of Eden: Brambley, p. 59
5. Wisdom of the Knowing Ones, p. 105
6. Gods of Eden: Collins, p. 18
7. Wisdom of the Knowing Ones, p. 91
8. Origin and Significance of the Great Pyramid, p. 111, 103
9. Ibid, p. 119
10. Ibid, p. 119

Beneath the Casing Stones

11. Nile Valley Contributions to Civilization, p. 104
12. The Great Pyramid: Prophecy in Stone
13. The Complete Pyramids, p. 34
14. The Magnificent Numbers of the Great Pyramid and Stonehenge, p. 12
15. The Genesis Race, p. 79

16. The Magnificent Numbers of the Great Pyramid and Stonehenge, p. 4
17. Beginnings: The Sacred Design, p. 148

Enormity of the Great Pyramid

18. God is Red, p. 125
19. Nile Valley Contributions to Civilization, p. 110
20. Ibid, p. 120
21. God is Red, p. 125-26
22. Gods of Eden: Brambley, p. 58
23. Stellar Theology and Masonic Astronomy, p. 175

Relics From the Age of Replication

24. The Murder of Tutankhamen, p. 62
25. Gods of Eden: Brambley, p. 172
26. Lost Cities and Ancient Mysteries of South America, p. 137
27. New Evidences of Christ in Ancient America, p. 167
28. Aztecs: Reign of Blood and Splender, p. 41
29. Ibid, p. 120
30. Secret Language of the Stars and Planets, p. 151
31. The Lost Realms, p. 49
32. Aztecs: Reign of Blood and Splender, p. 61
33. Revelation 19:15
34. Aztecs: Reign of Blood and Splender, p. 11
35. Ancient Man: Handbook to Puzzling Artifacts, p. 765
36. Nature Worship, p. 57
37. Ibid, p. 53-54

Secret Door to Giza

38. Origin and Significance of the Great Pyramid, p. 107
39. Ancient Egypt Light of the World Vol. I, p. 227
40. Ibid, p. 227
41. Book of the Hopi, p. 65
42. Ibid, p. 65

Mysteries of the Ascendant Corridors

43. Our Cosmic Ancestors, p. 72
44. Nile Valley Contributions to Civilization, p. 110
45. The Natural Genesis Vol. II, p. 225
46. Origin and Significance of the Great Pyramid, p. 56
47. The Natural Genesis Vol. I, p. 351
48. Babylonian Influence on the Bible and Popular Beliefs, p. 30
49. Ancient Egypt Light of the World Vol. I, p. 394
50. From the Ashes of Angels: Forbidden Legacy of a Fallen Race, p. 27
51. The Natural Genesis Vol. I, p. 360

52. Bloodline of the Holy Grail: The Hidden Lineage of Jesus Revealed, p. 183
53. Enuma Elish: Seven Tablets of Creation Vol. I lxiii-lxix
54. Job 26.13
55. Ancient Egypt Light of the World Vol. I, p. 7
56. The Natural Genesis Vol. II, p. 386
57. Book of Enoch 64:1-3
58. Obsolete
59. Obsolete
60. Obsolete
61. Lost Language of Symbolism, p. 116
62. Wisdom of the Knowing Ones, p. 139
63. Lost Language of Symbolism, p. 115
64. Ibid, p. 219
65. The Story of Astrology, p. 56
66. Ibid, p. 54-55
67. Lost Language of Symbolism, p. 282
68. Ibid, p. 316
69. Wisdom of the Knowing Ones, p. 139
70. Lost Language of Symbolism, p. 116
71. Psalm 8; Hebrews 2; 1 Corinthians 6:3
72. Genesis 1:14
73. Book of Enoch 35:2-3
74. Babylonian Influence on the Bible and Popular Beliefs, p. 13
75. Ibid, p. 14
76. Pistis Sophia, p. 26

The Hidden One

77. Beginnings; The Sacred Design, p. 143
78. Mars Mystery, p. 110
79. Gods of Eden: Collins, p. 134
80. Ibid, p. 136
81. 1 Corinthians 13:12

Archive Four
Secrets of God in Egypt

What the Scholars Have Buried in Siriad

1. The White Goddess
2. The Murder of Tutankhamen, p. 34
3. Encyclopedia Americana Vol. 4, p. 246
4. From Atlantis to the Sphinx, p. 81
5. Murder of Tutankhamen, p. 19

6. Testament of Simeon 3:14
7. From Atlantis to the Sphinx, p. 54
8. Magnificent Numbers of the Great Pyramid and Stonehenge, p. 67

Guardian of the Deep

9. Ancient Mysteries, p. 213
10. Ancient Man: Handbook of Puzzling Artifacts, p. 752
11. Dictionary of Deities and Demons of the Bible, p. 190
12. Sun Lore of All Ages, p. 272
13. The Natural Genesis Vol. I, p. 396
14. Nile Valley Contributions to Civilization, p. 113
15. Atlantis: Mother of Empires, p. 222
16. The Glory of the Stars, p. 31
17. Encyclopedia of Wicca, p. 384
18. Book of the Dead, p. 392-93
19. Nile Valley Contributions to Civilization, p. 71
20. Ancient Egypt Light of the World Vol. I, p. 338
21. Ibid, p. 337
22. Babylonian Influence on the Bible and Popular Beliefs, p. 41
23. Ancient Egypt Light of the World Vol. I, p. 336
24. Ancient Mysteries, p. 184
25. Lost Language of Symbolism, p. 75
26. Nature Worship, p. 23
27. Ancient Mysteries, p. 221
28. Wars of Gods and Men, p. 59
29. Ancient Egypt Light of the World Vol. I, p. 337, 30, 345
30. Book of the Dead, p. 150
31. Ancient Egypt Light of the World Vol. I, p. 446
32. From Atlantis to the Sphinx, p. 39
33. Ibid, p. 51
34. Origin and Significance of the Great Pyramid, p. 35
35. From Atlantis to the Sphinx, p. 39-40

Testimony of Thoth

36. Book of the Dead, p. 23, 343
37. Mystics and Mysteries of Alexandria, p. 17
38. Ancient Symbol Worship, p. 50
39. Ibid, p. 81
40. The Way of Hermes, p. 80
41. Ibid, p. 80
42. Lost Language of Symbolism, p. 270; Chronology of Genesis: A Complete History of the Nephilim, p. 76 referring to numbers 8 and 52.
43. Book of the Dead xii-xiii
44. Book of Jasher 14:2

45. Book of the Dead xiii
46. Ibid, p. 7
47. Ibid, p. 442
48. Ancient Symbol Worship, p. 54-60
49. Fallen Angels and the Origins of Evil, p. 69
50. Ibid, p. 64
51. Book of the Dead, p. 82
52. Ibid, p. 82-83
53. Ibid, p. 113
54. Ancient Symbol Worship, p. 57
55. Ibid, p. 60
56. The Natural Genesis Vol. II, p. 31
57. Ancient Symbol Worship, p. 59
58. Ibid, p. 59
59. Ibid, p. 56-57
60. Book of the Dead, p. 181
61. Lost Language of Symbolism, p. 161
62. Book of the Dead, p. 302
63. The Natural Genesis Vol. II, p. 28
64. Judges 13:18
65. Book of the Dead, p. 109
66. Ibid, p. 111, 113
67. Nile Valley Contributions, p. 268
68. Stellar Theology and Masonic Astronomy, p. 26-27
69. The Natural Genesis Vol. I., p. 338
70. Atlantis: Mother of Empires, p. 269
71. Wycliffe Bible Dictionary, p. 58
72. Lost Language of Symbolism, p. 13
73. From the Ashes of Angels: Forbidden Legacy of a Fallen Race, p. 188
74. Strong's Concordance Heb/Aram. Lexicon #543
75. Book of the Dead, p. 165
76. Revelation 3:14
77. Colossians 1:15
78. Wars of God and Men, p. 150
79. Origins and Significance of the Great Pyramid, p. 94
80. Ibid, p. 57
81. Book of Jubilees 21:8
82. Testament of Simeon 2:13
83. Quran, surah 87:19-20
84. Secret Books of the Egyptian Gnostics, p. 185
85. The Hiram Key, p. 336
86. Ibid, p. MDCCCX of Annus Mundi
87. Mystics and Mysteries of Alexandria, p. 20
88. Book of Jasher 14:2
89. Divine Pymander, p. 154-55, citing Contra Julianum lib. v. 176b

90. Book of the Dead, p. 10
91. Origin and Significance of the Great Pyramid, p. 22, 61, 62
92. Gods of Eden: Collins, p. 173
93. Ibid, p. 173-75
94. Atrahasis, p. 82-84
95. Mystics and Mysteries of Alexandria, p. 123
96. The Vedas, p. 4, 13, 15-16, 151
97. Ibid, p. 6
98. Ibid, p. 53, 15
99. Our Cosmic Ancestors, p. 55
100. Book of the Secrets of Enoch 35:1-3
101. Revelation 21:16
102. Hebrews 11:10

Rostau and the Resurrection

103. Book of the Dead, p. 145
104. Ibid, p. 145
105. Ibid, p. 661
106. Ibid, p. 570
107. Cloak of the Illuminati, p. 114
108. Lost Language of Symbolism, p. 176
109. Gods of Eden: Collins, p. 153
110. Cloak of the Illuminati, p. 104-105
111. Book of the Dead, p. 359
112. Ibid, p. 90
113. Ibid, p. 343-344
114. Book of Enoch, p. 9:4-6
115. Book of Tobit 8:3
116. Greek Myths, p. 134
117. Babylonian Influence on the Bible and Popular Beliefs, p. 68

Archive Five
Occult Arcana of Scripture

Antediluvian Theology/The Arcanum in the Old Testament

1. Psalm 74:12
2. Exodus 8:22
3. Genesis 49:24
4. Ibid 32:3-4, 18
5. Cloak of the Illuminati, p. 135
6. Ancient Symbol Worship, p. 76
7. The Magus Vol. II, p. 38
8. Judges 13:18

9. 2 Samuel 18:18
10. Book of Enoch 48:23, 50:3
11. 2 Samuel 22:3, 32, 51; 1 Samuel 2:2
12. Proverbs 18:10
13. Psalm 69:35-36
14. Ibid 125:1
15. Isaiah 28:16-17
16. Psalm 87:1-3
17. Ibid 48:1-2
18. Ibid 118:17-23
19. Isaiah 28:16-17, 21
20. Joel 2:32
21. Isaiah 56:5, 7
22. Ibid 62:2
23. Ibid 45:3
24. Psalm 10:42
25. Isaiah 61:10
26. Zechariah 3:4
27. Genesis 2:25, 3:7
28. Amos 2:16
29. Ezekiel 31:14-15
30. Ezekiel 28:14
31. Psalm 55:22-23
32. Hosea 14:9
33. Proverbs 15:24, 12:28

Christian Renewal of the Ancient Arcana

34. Luke 6:47-48
35. Matthew 16:16-18
36. Wycliffe Bible Dictionary, p. 1477
37. Matthew 21:44
38. Matthew 13:35
39. 1 Corinthians 2:7
40. 1 Corinthians 2:10
41. Ephesians 2:19-21
42. 1 Peter 2:3-8
43. 1 Corinthians 2:16-17
44. 1 Timothy 3:15
45. 1 Corinthians 3:9-10, Colossians 1:15, Hebrews 12:22
46. 1 Corinthians 15:49, Luke 10:20
47. Book of Enoch 43:1-2

Christian Apocryphal Writings

48. 2 Esdras 15:16
49. Psalm 119:100

50. Proverbs 25:2
51. 1 Corinthians 4:1
52. Proverbs 11:9
53. Daniel 2:22
54. Hosea 4:6
55. Matthew 10:26
56. Colossians 2:3
57. Ibid, 1:26
58. Lost Language of Symbolism, p. 7
59. Pistis Sophia: Forward: Paul Tice
60. Wisdom of the Knowing Ones, p. 41-50, 29
61. Mystics and Mysteries of Alexandria, p. 123
62. Lost Language of Symbolism, p. 7
63. Wisdom of the Knowing Ones, p. 72
64. Alchemy Rediscovered and Restored, p. 138
65. Ibid, p. 141
66. Ibid, p. 145
67. Ibid, p. 157
68. 1 Corinthians 13:12
69. The Gnosis: Ancient Wisdom of the Christian Scriptures, p. 18
70. Ibid, p. 26
71. Ibid, p. 82
72. Ibid, p. 81
73. The Light of Egypt: Science of the Soul and Stars, p. 12
74. Ibid, p. 159
75. The Gnosis: Ancient Wisdom of the Christian Scriptures, p. 73
76. Shepherd of Hermas: Book III Similitude IX:13-14
77. Ibid, Book I, Visions III: 24-25
79. Ibid, Book III, Similitudes IX:86
79. Ibid, Book III, Similitudes IX:108-113, 123
80. The Natural Genesis Vol. II, p. 192
81. Epistle of Ignatius to the Philadelphians 2:21
82. Philo: Questions & Answers On Genesis II v. 827
83. Epistle of Ignatius to the Ephesians 2:10; Epistle to Polycarp 1:2
84. John 10:9
85. Epistle of Ignatius to the Philadelphians 2:23-24
86. Gospel of Barnabas 10:5-9

Secrets of the Genesis Narrative

87. Jeremiah 17:13
88. The Cosmic Code, p. 44
89. Book of Enoch 68:17-18
90. Ibid 64:7
91. Gods of Eden, p. 55
92. Secret Books of the Egyptian Gnostics, p. 168

93. Cloak of the Illuminati, p. 113
94. The Natural Genesis Vol. II, p. 157
95. Babylonian Influence on the Bible and Popular Beliefs, p. 97
96. Ibid, p. 107
97. Gospel of Nicodemus 18:9
98. Book of Adam and Eve I 51:5-7
99. Secret Books of the Egyptian Gnostics, p. 293
100. Quran, surah 17:60-61, 44:43-44, 37:64
101. Ibid 56:49-52
102. Ibid 7:11-12, 18:50, 15:26-27, 55:14-17, 51:56
103. Book of Adam and Eve I 25:2
104. Book of the Dead, p. 67
105. The Natural Genesis Vol. II, p. 147
106. Book of Enoch 60:7-11
107. Ibid 60:2-3
108. Babylonian Influence on the Bible and Popular Beliefs, p. 74
109. Ibid, p. 79
110. Genesis 9:2-3
111. Book of Enoch 60:23-24
112. Ibid 60:7 (notes
113. Ibid 74:14
114. Lost Language of Symbolism, p. 299

Archive Six
The Lost Scriptures of Giza

1. Kybalion, p. 17, 8
2. The Secret Teachings of All Ages, p. 93
3. The Antediluvian World, p. 80
4. Poleshift, p. 3
5. Symbols, Sex and the Stars, p. 201
6. The Discoverers, p. 84
7. Rule of Secrecy, p. 356
8. Tales of the Patriarchs, p. 76
9. Symbols of Legends of Masonry, p. 30
10. Cornelia Von Daniken, Secrets of the Lost Tayos Gold Library, Legendary Times, Vol. 9, No. 1 and No. 2, p. 46-47
11. Origin and Evolution of Freemasonry, p. 167
12. Origin and Evolution of Freemasonry, p. 126
13. Origin and Evolution of Freemasonry, p. 126
14. Gods of Eden: Collins, p. 152
15. Origin and Evolution of Freemasonry, p. 167
16. Zoroastrianism, p. 14
17. The Fountainhead of Religion, pgs. xxiv, 45-46

18. The Fountainhead of Religion, p. 49
19. Zoroastrianism, pgs. 44, 13
20. Zoroastrianism, p. 23
21. Zoroastrianism, p. 44
22. Zoroastrianism, pgs. 47-48, 50
23. The Fountainhead of Religion, pgs. xiv-xxv
24. The Fountainhead of Religion, pgs. xxv-xxvi
25. The Fountainhead of Religion, pgs. xxv-xxvi, 222, 157
26. The Great Secret, pg. 12
27. The Antediluvian World, pg. 273
28. Zoroastrianism, pgs. 94-95
29. Discoveries Vol. 44, Ron Wyatt (Wyatt Archeological Research)
30. The Wars of Gods and Men, p. 198
31. Daniel the Prophet, p. 18
32. Jubilees 12:27
33. The Natural Genesis Vol. II, p. 223
34. Out of the Flame, pgs. 97-98
35. Ancient Symbol Worship, p. 16
36. The Greek Myths, p. 183
37. The Greek Myths, pgs. 182-183
38. Sibylline Oracles 3:106-107
39. Dictionary of Deities and Demons of the Bible, p. 874
40. The Chaldean Genesis: G. Smith cited in The 12th Planet, p. 150
41. Dialogues of Plato, p. 192
42. Origin and Evolution of Freemasonry, p. 78
43. Book of Adam and Eve I 63:15
44. Symbols, Sex and the Stars, p. 211
45. Philosophy of Aristotle, Psychology Book II:5
46. Evolution Cruncher, p. 643
47. Earliest Civilizations, p. 71

Ancient Arcana of the Revelation

48. Book of Enoch 1:2
49. Ibid 104:7-9
50. Rev. 1:4/Enoch 89:32
51. Rev. 2:7/Enoch 24:9
52. Rev. 3:5/Enoch 89:41
53. Rev. 3:12/Enoch 89:39
54. Rev. 3:20/Enoch 61:17
55. Rev. 3:21/Enoch 105:26
56. Rev. 4:6-8/Enoch 40:2-6
57. Rev. 4:11/Enoch 9:4
58. Rev. 5:11/Enoch 14:24
59. Rev. 6:10/Enoch 47:1-2

60. Rev. 6:16/Enoch 61:4-9
61. Rev. 7:17/Enoch 48:1
62. Rev. 9:1/Enoch 85:1
63. Rev. 9:20/Enoch 97:8
64. Rev. 13:14/Enoch 53:6
65. Rev. 14:10/Enoch 48:8-9
66. Rev. 14:20/Enoch 98:3
67. Rev. 17:14/Enoch 9:3
68. Rev. 19:1/Enoch 39:7
69. Rev. 20:1/Enoch 21:5-6
70. Rev. 20:10/Enoch 10:6-15
71. Rev. 20:13/Enoch 89:29-31
72. Rev. 20:15/Enoch 89:33
73. Rev. 21:1/Enoch 92:17
74. Fallen Angels and the Origins of Evil, p. 17
75. Ibid, p. 18
76. Book of the Secrets of Enoch 68:3
77. Book of Jubilees 5:14
78. Ibid, 4:21
79. Giza Power Plant, p. 131
80. Revelation 2:7, 2:17
81. Stellar Theology and Masonic Astronomy, p. 17-18
82. Ancient Egypt Light of the World, p. 696
83. Revelation 3:4-5
84. Ibid 14:1
85. Ibid 3:12
86. Ibid 21:10
87. Ibid 19:13-13
88. Ibid 3:14

About the Author

Jason M. Breshears is a researcher of occult antiquities. Four of his previously published works are nonfiction with extensive bibliographies concerning fascinating information on ancient civilizations, cataclysms and the modern establishment's attempts to suppress these discoveries from the public today. These works are published by Book Tree in San Diego. Much of the data Breshears discloses is totally original research not found in any other books published today. His current bibliography shows 1157 nonfiction books that he has read and data-mined during a 19-year period. His other published books include:

Nostradamus and the Planets of Apocalypse. The prophecies of Nostradamus are considered to be the most amazing and accurate ever foretold—if one knows how to read them. The code for understanding them and when they will occur has been revealed in this book. It also maps out the entire historical chronology of planetary cataclysms starting in 4309 BC, covering the cyclical return of Nibiru, the planet Phoenix, and more. 116 pgs, 6 x 9, $14.95

Anunnaki Homeworld: Orbital History and 2046 AD Return of Planet Nibiru. The author uses scientific cycles, mathematical formulas, advanced geometry and historical records to predict the cataclysmic return of the most legendary rogue planet in the solar system. He provides us with an exact year, and does so confidently, due to his extensive research. Includes extensive historical records, chronologically presented, to identifying the cyclical patterns involved. 164 pgs, 8.5 x 11, $19.95

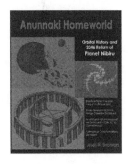

When the Sun Darkens: Orbital History and 2040 AD Return of Planet Phoenix. By using foundational scientific evidence and various prophecies, the return of the legendary Phoenix, an outer rogue planet that often brings destruction, is predicted. We have, in this book, the most extensive and accurate rendering of the cycle of the Phoenix. Some of us, according to the author, will live to see its return. 128 pgs, 6 x 9, $14.95

TO ORDER CALL 1-800-700-TREE (8733) 24 hrs., all major cards accepted. Buy any two of the avail. titles, get 10% off and free shipping.

Made in the USA
Columbia, SC
08 January 2024

30090260R00122